POLICE BATTALIONS OF THE THIRD REICH

POLICE BATTALIONS OF THE THIRD REICH

Stephen Campbell

Schiffer Military History
Atglen, PA

Dedication
To Marilyn and Elizabeth.
To Misha Pilsudski, who never actually lived; yet through my daughter's voice he was brought to life.

Book design by Robert Biondi.

Library of Congress Catalog Number: 2007932744.

Printed in China.
ISBN: 978-0-7643-2771-1

Published by Schiffer Publishing Ltd.
4880 Lower Valley Road
Atglen, PA 19310
Phone: (610) 593-1777
FAX: (610) 593-2002
E-mail: Info@schifferbooks.com.
Visit our web site at: www.schifferbooks.com
Please write for a free catalog.
This book may be purchased from the publisher.
Please include $3.95 postage.
Try your bookstore first.

In Europe, Schiffer books are distributed by:
Bushwood Books
6 Marksbury Ave.
Kew Gardens, Surrey TW9 4JF
England
Phone: 44 (0)20 8392-8585
FAX: 44 (0)20 8392-9876
E-mail: info@bushwoodbooks.co.uk
www.bushwoodbooks.co.uk
Free postage in the UK. Europe: air mail at cost.
Try your bookstore first.

CONTENTS

INTRODUCTION

Historians of the German Police invariably divide the police battalion's wartime existence into three periods. The first when they operated as independent battalions, the second is after the 1942 merger of the battalions into regiments, and finally in February 1943 when they became SS police regiments. I have chosen to follow a battalion throughout its entire lifespan in this book as it was rare for a regiment to operate with all of its battalions attached. Just as infrequently would a battalion find itself at full strength as squads and companies were constantly being detached for temporary duty with the SS and the SD.

I have converted the German Police ranks to their equivalent in the U.S. military. The SS ranks I have left as is. German police, especially officers, often held both a Police rank and a SS rank. I have used the English translations of German terms or words whenever possible except when the German word or term has entered the English vocabulary.

I would like to thank H.L. deZeng IV for his guidance and suggestions. I would never have known where to begin without his help. His kind words were far more valuable to me then I think he will ever realize. Of more importance to the reader is his allowing me to use his notes on the activities of the German Police in the Slovenia region of Europe.

The Axis History Forum was of great assistance. Many were the members who either helped me by answering questions or by their knowledgable posts on the subject of the German police and SS.

In this book I have attempted to detail as much of the history as possible of the German Police Battalions sent from the Reich to the occupied countries, primarily those of the east. I have in some instances omitted details of units that deserve more attention. In many cases this was done to keep this book to a manageable length.

One primary source for the material in this book was: Georg Tessin, Hans Adolf Neufeldt, and Jurgen Huck, Zur *Geschichte der Ordnungspolizei 1936 to 1945*, Koblenz: Bundesarchiv, 1956. Also of enormous help was Stefan Klemps book, *"Nicht ermittelt" Polizeibataillone und die Nachkriegsjustiz Ein Handbuch*, Klartext, Verlag, Essen 2005. I also made use of the U.S. Holocaust Museum's excellent library. I would like to thank the staff there for their patience and help. I would especially like to thank Michelean Amir who truly has "the patience of a saint." I have included in the bibliography a number of books and websites that explain, perhaps far better than this book, the horror that Hitler let loose upon the innocent of the world.

For those who may have corrections, suggestions or comments please feel to email me at stevcampbell@hotmail.com.

CHAPTER ONE

THE GERMAN POLICE

The German Police Battalions existed prior to the rise of National Socialism. In the years following World War I the ranks were filled with veterans who espoused various versions of right wing nationalism. Regardless of the version they believed in, they all shared one core belief; that Germany had not lost the war, rather it had been "stabbed in the back" and betrayed at home. Who were these people that cost Germany its victory? The blame may have differed depending on the group's nationalistic worldview but the Jews were always a popular choice.

The Reichstag fire on February 27, 1933, was an event created by and used for the benefit of the Nazi party. As a result the Nazi party went from the largest minority party (32%) to the only political party in a very short time. Hitler acted quickly using the powers granted him through the Enabling Act to destroy any organized resistance and begin consolidating control over the bureaucracy. In order to appease the one institution he could not dissolve, the Army, he purged the SA in 1934 and shot its leader.

The period of 1933-1936 was a period of consolidation and expansion of Nazi party control over the state bureaucracy. For the police, that meant purging the ranks of those who were deemed politically incorrect or members of the SA. Germany during this period did not have a national police force. Each of the sixteen states maintained their own police force and no states police were allowed to cross another states boundary in pursuit of a felon. Totalitarian governments are called police states but who actually runs the national police apparatus is a matter of party politics and in Germany in 1936 the winner was Heinrich Himmler, *Reichsführer* of the SS and Police.

In 1936 the uniformed German Police became a national agency under Himmler's command rather than the fragmented state based model. A universal police uniform patterned on the uniform of the German army was introduced in green rather than field grey. This reorganization created the Order Police (*Orpo* or *Ordnungspolizei*) which had two main branches, the *Schutzpolizei* (*Schupo*) and the *Gendarmerie*. The *Schupo* policed the cities and urban areas; The *Gendarmerie* was responsible for the rural areas and the small villages with fewer than 2000 inhabitants.

The *Orpo* was run by a General of the Police whose headquarters were in Berlin and who reported directly to Himmler. For most of its existence the head of the *Orpo* was Kurt Daluege a dedicated Nazi since the 1920s. He was quietly replaced while technically still holding his position in 1943 because of poor health, possibly the result of heavy drinking and was replaced by Alfred Wünnenberg. Kurt Daluege was tried and hung for war crimes in Prague on October 24, 1946.

The Reich was divided into police districts, *Befehlshaber der Ordnungspolizei* (BdO) run by a senior police general. Each BdO would a have a number of *Kommandeur der Ordnungspolizei* (KdO) representing a large city or rural area. This same system was replicated in the conquered territories. While a BdO may be the supreme police officer for his region, in reality he answered to the Higher SS Police *Führer* (HSSPF) who maintained a parallel organizational structure. The HSSPF was created by Himmler in 1937 and after that the police were subordinate to the party and an auxiliary of the SS. The police did not become publicly a part of the SS until February 1943. The HSSPF was the true ranking police officer and could and did call on the police formations to perform political policing. Political policing in this context meant the use of the police to achieve Nazi party goals for his area of operation. These goals usually entailed the subjugation or cleansing of an occupied areas populace.

A German enlisted police recruit's level of training between the two world wars was very similar to what an enlistee in a light infantry unit would receive. His training would include the use of rifles, grenades, and automatic weapons such as the machine pistol, and heavy machine gun. Prior to 1936 the state police often had field mortar platoons and armored car companies as part of their table of organization.

German police officers were not the equal of Army or Waffen-SS officers when it came to combat tactics and leadership. Their background as police officers is what qualified them for command positions. This was not a problem when their troops were performing transport duty, ghetto watch, or providing security for mass executions. It did become a liability later in the war when they had to fight trained soldiers. Unfortunately for them they were often only called upon as a last resort. This often meant that they were called on to engage Russian armor and were crushed as a result.

A police battalion was formed using men from a specific geographical area. An example is the city of Hamburg that provided the manpower for a number of the 100 series police battalions because it had a large population base to draw on. Another battalion might raise its troops from a couple of smaller cities or an area inside an administrative region. These men were then organized in battalions whose battalion number reflected the area they were raised in. Germany was divided into a number of these regions and they were called a *Wehrkreis*. Hamburg Police battalions for example were raised in *Wehrkreis* X (10). It was the same administrative system used by the regular army.

The police battalions were created by recalling reservists and using active duty NCOs and officers as cadre. Occasionally active duty police would be asked to volunteer for duty with a battalion. The battalion would then be sent to refresher training in weapons, tactics, and attend political indoctrination classes. The length of their training was usually six months in the early years of the war. The battalion would then be shipped to a final assembly point where it would await its movement orders, or after the invasion of Russia it would be transported to the city it was to be stationed in or operating from. Some of the police battalions from Hamburg began their journey to Poland in 1939 in Hamburg city buses.[1]

These battalions were intended for rear area security and antipartisan duties and their equipment and training reflected this. Generally the heaviest armament they possessed was the crew served heavy machine gun. The German version used by police battalions was the Maxim machinegun that was widely used in World War I. It fired a 7.92mm round from a cloth belt that held 250 rounds. This weapon continued to be in use by the police for much of the war. Some battalions had antitank platoons except the weapons they were issued were no match for the Soviet tank. In 1936 many of the younger and better-trained police had been transferred to the army along with any quality equipment as cadre for the expansion of the army. This left the police with a high proportion of older men.

The following is what the 4th company of the III/Police Regiment 5 (Police Battalion 66) was issued in December 1942:[2]

4 MG Model 08 and 4000 rounds per weapon
9 MG Model 26 and 3000 rounds per weapon
9 Machine Pistols and 650 rounds per man
83 Carbines, 1898 Model and 150 rounds per man
137 Pistols, 1908 Model 7.65 MM and 50 rounds per man
135 Bayonets
2 Hand grenades per man

14 Binoculars 6 x 30
14 March compasses
8 flare pistols with 10 flares in white, red, and green
13 Wire cutters
13 Claw hatchets
17 Folding stools
48 shovels (short)
13 bicycles
137 gasmasks
137 flash lights
75 cleaning kits
1 field kitchen

The Model 1908 Heavy Machine Gun (Maxim)
Caliber: 7.92mm (.311 inch), same as the German infantry rifle
Muzzle velocity: 2,821 feet per second
Sighting range: 2,200 yards
Optical 2.5x telescopic sight. Extreme range: (at 32 degrees) 4,400 yards

Rate of fire: 400 to 500 rounds per minute
Length, (excluding muzzle attachment): 43 inches
Barrel length: 28.35 inches
Weight (filled with water): 48.75 pounds
Water capacity: 7 pints. Mount Model 1908 Schlitten (sled)
Weight of mount: 75 pounds
Weight of gun and mount: 140 pounds
Minimum height (sledge prone on ground): 11 inches
Manufactured at Spandau Arsenal
Brass cartridge case

Ammunition came in standard ball, armor piercing, and armor piercing tracer (1 of every 10 rounds)
Weight of filled belt: 16 pounds
Crew: normally 5 men per gun

Did the police see themselves as members of the SS, regardless if they were not officially members before 1943? The officers were members of the NSDAP and SS in significant numbers, especially among those who had started the war as junior officers. I believe many of the enlisted men also saw themselves as members of the SS especially after the invasion of the USSR. I base this assumption on the number of *feldposts* (letters home) from members of the police battalions that were marked as SS *feldposts* two years before they were officially an SS organization

The battalions were motorized to a level not found in most of the regular army battalions but it was often with vehicles seized from Czechoslovakia or Austria. Like every statement you can make about the German military during the war there were exceptions as they were still fielding a number of battalions with bicycle mounted companies early on in the war. They did reach Himmler's goal of complete mobility far faster then regular army units some of whom never were completely motorized.

A battalion had the following basic composition: the commanding officer, usually a major and his adjutant who was a lieutenant; his staff, which consisted of two officers and twelve enlisted men; a supply officer, usually a captain, was in charge of the NSKK (support) company. He had four officers and ninety-two men under him. A communications officer, usually a lieutenant, was in charge of the signals staff of eighteen enlisted men. There would be a medical officer who had six enlisted assistants.

The battalion commander had three or four line companies available for duty in the field commanded by captains or a senior lieutenant. Each company at full strength had approximately a hundred men. A company consisted of two or three platoons that were commanded by lieutenant or senior NCO. Each platoon contained two squads commanded by a junior lieutenant or NCO.

The battalion upon arriving at the city that it had been assigned to would occupy its quarters. Police companies were quartered occasionally in unusual barracks. I have found seminaries, castles, parsonages, and schools listed. It was not uncommon for a battalion at this point to be split up. The battalion staff would be quartered in the city, and each company would be detached and sent to a nearby town. Companies and platoon size elements were constantly sent to provide security for or participate in SD and SS operations.

In the final two years of the war the battalion would find itself taking part in large multiple police regiment antipartisan operations. In February 1943 the police were transferred to the SS which was official recognition of the unofficial reality. The police regiments operating in Army Group North and Center in the final year of the war found themselves constantly fighting in ad hoc battle groups and they would take a severe mauling as did the German army. Rarely though were they asked to stand and die like the regular army units. The police regiments in the south for the most part continued participating in even larger partisan operations and gradually withdrew into Italy or to cities along the Adriatic coast.

German police officers riding in Kassel Germany 1941.

German police parade through the Brandenburg Gate. Author's copy.

Right: The Model 1908 Heavy Machine Gun, Caliber 7.92mm.

Below: German police in a Tatra T27 truck.

Bottom: Pre-1936 German police on parade.

Above: 1940 German brothers. The one in the police uniform has the SS Runes denoting membership in the SS.

Left: German police Oberwachtmeister with the SS Runes indicating he is a member.

Opposite
Top: Orpo Officers School at Furstenfeldbruck where they are participating in a training exercise with the SS.

Bottom: Orpo Officers School at Furstenfeldbruck.

Above: Orpo Officers School at Furstenfeldbruck participating in a training exercise with the SS.

Left: Checking papers.

Below: Practicing urban patrolling in Altona, a suburb of Hamburg 1931.

Opposite: Marching from the barracks.

Above: Field Exercises with the Maxim 1931.

Below: Weapons drawn.

Right: Celebrating the New Year in 1931.

CHAPTER TWO

INTO POLAND

Germany invaded Poland on September 1, 1939 executing the Wehrmacht's Operational Plan "Case White" with 1.8 million troops. With them came twenty-one police battalions and 1,279 gendarmes. On September 17, 1939 the Soviet Army invaded from the east as Stalin and Hitler had previously agreed upon. The Polish army fought gallantly but it was spread thinly and had almost no modern armor. There was little to no air support as the air force had been caught by surprise and destroyed on the ground by the Luftwaffe's surprise attacks. On September 27, 1939 Warsaw surrendered. The Soviet and German armies met at Brest Litovsk and divided Poland amongst themselves as outlined in the Molotov-Ribbentrop agreement.[1] Poland as an independent nation ceased to exist and World War II had begun.

As part of the preparation for this invasion on August 25th 1939 *SS-Gruppenführer* Reinhard Heydrich upon receiving direct orders from Hitler authorized Operation Tannenburg.[2] The long term goal of this operation was to erase in the minds of the surviving Poles the idea of Poland as a nation and people. To accomplish this the first phase required killing or shipping to concentration camps anyone who was capable of organizing a resistance to the Nazi occupation or who could help preserve the concept of Polish uniqueness an identity. The targeted groups were members of the aristocracy, clergy, intelligentsia, and any communist who had been foolish enough to remain behind.

The men assigned to this operation were organized into *Einsatzgruppen* (Operation Groups). There were six *Einsatzgruppen* created for Operation Tannenburg and a special operations group, the z.b.V. (Special Operations Group). The actual organization of the *Einsatzgruppen* was left to Dr. Werner Best, a lawyer and a *SS-Brigadeführer*. Dr. Best when selecting personnel for the *Einsatzgruppen* stated he was looking for SS officers who would "ruthlessly and harshly work to achieve National Socialist aims."[3] Originally it was thought that 2,000 men would be enough to staff the five *Einsatzgruppen* that would be needed. This number was expanded to seven by early September 1939. Of the 4,250 personnel assigned to the *Einsatzgruppen* 2,250 of these were *Schutzpolizei*. The *Schutzpolizei* (*Schupo*) were the men that made up the police battalions.

The *Einsatzgruppen* went into Poland prepared. A master list containing names of people who fit the categories above had been compiled before the invasion by the SD and SIPO. The list, known as the "Special Persons List", had 61,000 names of Jews and Christians on it. German sympathizers inside Poland had helped provide many of these names to the SD who had begun compiling the list in 1936. These sympathizers would continue to assist the Germans after they arrived and profit from the arrangement until 1945. After the war in an ironic reverse of what the Third Reich had planned they would be expelled from Poland. The Jews were not yet the primary target although Heydrich had given orders to concentrate them in ghettoes near transportation hubs.[4]

The formation of *Einsatzgruppen* to follow the army into a country that had just been annexed by the Reich was not a new idea although prior to the invasion of Poland little information exists about them. The Sudentland, Austria, and Czechoslovakia all had *Einsatzgruppen* active within their borders immediately after they became a part of the Reich. French MacLean's book *The Field Men: The SS Officers Who Led the Einsatzkommandos: the Nazi Mobile Killing Units* lists

Einsatzgruppe Ostereich for Austria in 1938, Czechoslovakia had *Einsatzgruppe Dresden*, and *Einsatzgruppe* II Brünn in 1938.

Poland was the first time the *Einsatzgruppen* had operated in country whose people were seen as less than human. In June 1939 Hitler spoke to Baldur von Schirach[5] and Hans Frank[6] about his vision of slavery for the Polish people:[7]

> "The ideal picture is this: a Pole may possess only small holdings in the Government General which will to a certain extent provide him and his family with food. The money required by him for clothes, etc., he must earn in Germany by work. The Government General must become a centre for supplying unskilled labor, particularly agricultural labor. The subsistence of these workmen will be fully guaranteed because they can always be made use of for cheap labor."

Two months later speaking to his generals he said:

> "Everybody shall have to make a point of it that we were determined from the beginning to fight the Western Powers. Struggle for life or death ... destruction of Poland in the foreground. The aim is elimination of living forces, not the arrival at a certain line. Even if war should break out in the West, the destruction of Poland shall be the primary objective. I shall give a propagandist cause for starting the war never mind whether it be plausible or not. The victor shall not be asked later on whether we told the truth or not.[8]

The *Einsatzgruppen* entered Poland in 1939 behind the German army with a dual agenda. The first and public version that they sold to the *Wehrmacht* was that they were there to provide rear area security. The army was worried about partisan activity with legitimate reason. Poland and Germany after the First World War had skirmished repeatedly on their borders and Poland maintained militias, especially in the Danzig area. Also with the recent changes in the army's deployment strategy almost all forces were concentrated at the front leaving little army presence in the overrun territory behind them.

These worries were what Himmler and Heydrich played upon in order to get the freedom of action to implement their actual agenda as outlined in Operation Tannenburg. This, for the army, was yet another deal with the devil that would lead them one-step closer to collaboration in mass murder. The army knew that methods the SS would use would be brutal yet by agreeing they would be able to tell themselves that none of the blood that was shed was on their hands. Perhaps the large estates given to them from confiscated land and the cash bonuses paid to the generals authorized by Hitler at the conclusion of the Polish campaign also helped ease their minds.

I do not believe at this stage of the war the generals of the army understood exactly what they were agreeing to. A pogrom or two was fine with them. The seizing of assets for the benefit of the victor was historically what one did after conquering a country. The idea of killing every Jew an almost every Pole was something that I hope would of have been at least somewhat repugnant to them at this point of the war.

Einsatzgruppen mission parameters did not just include what was discussed above; the intellectual decapitation of a state using extreme methods. They were also given orders to chase the Jews when ever possible out of the German zone and into the Russian zone. On the surface this seems contradictory to Heydrich's order that stated the need to concentrate them in urban areas close to transportation hubs. I believe it was a ruse, allowing Heydrich, Himmler, and Hitler time to absorb Poland without disclosing to the army what their real intentions were.

One of the techniques used by the z.b.V. and other *Einsatzgruppen* to spread terror into the Jewish population was to shoot a few of the prominent members of the community. This was not the large scale shooting to come; rather it was used as a way of motivating the community to relocate. Another popular method of expressing the Reich's displeasure with their presence was burning down their synagogues. Burning down synagogues was a technique that had been successfully refined over the years in Germany. In Poland it was taken a step further by the including of Jews inside the synagogue. The death toll in these actions never equaled what the police would accomplish in a day after the invasion of the Soviet Union. The burning of buildings with people trapped inside would become standard police operating procedure later in the war as part of the antipartisan campaign. There they would burn synagogues with hundreds of people inside and shot people by the tens of thousands.

The head of the Special Operations Group (z.b.V) was *SS-Obergruppenführer* Udo von Woyrsch. His group's activities irritated the Army enough that they asked for his court martial. Not that they were appalled by his actions rather it was the how he accomplished his assignment that so upset them. The German army put a very strong emphasis on troop discipline and Udo's men who engaged in looting, raping, and burning down synagogues deeply offended their sense of order. Himmler's reply to Udo's critics and their demand for his courtmartial was to confirm Udo as a special commander of the police on September 12, 1939.

The special operations group continued with its campaign to terrorize Jews into fleeing by burning down synagogues in a number of towns. In Dynow on September 20, 1939 they burned the local synagogue down with twelve people inside it. By September 24, 1939 at least 500 Jewish men and an unknown number of Poles had been killed by the Special Operations group. Their unique way of impressing the locals with the Reich's displeasure about their continued existence continued to make them unpopular with the army and they were transferred to Katowice on September 22, 1939 to pacify the German generals.

The assault on the Polish people would continue for years to come but in a relatively brief amount of time the *Einsatzgruppen* successfully proved what they were capable of doing. It was a model that with minor refinements would be used in the Soviet Union. In this brief period of time over 500 towns and villages were burned and 16,376 people were shot in mass executions. Many of these shootings were the result of the pre invasion compilation of names that the SD had arranged.

The German police duties in Poland were not limited to the activities described above. Hitler's plans called for the destruction of Poland as a nation, the surviving people kept alive only to provide bodies for manual labor. The Poles themselves were considered barely a step above the Jews in the National Socialist racial hierarchy. The Poles were divided into five racial categories; Nordic, Sub Nordic, Dinarian, Praeslavic, and Oriental. Only three percent of the Poles examined by the SS race specialists were found to be biologically suitable or human. Poland lost almost sixteen percent of its population during the war. Not even the Soviet Union lost as many people. The professional class in Poland was slaughtered with forty five percent of the doctors, fifty seven percent of the lawyers, and forty percent of the professors killed.[9]

A large portion of western Poland following its conquest by the Germans was renamed *Reichsgau Wartheland*. The area had a sizeable German minority (16%) and was selected to be the first resettlement and Germanization zone for the new Reich. Germans and people of German ancestry (*Volksdeutche*) were moved to this area and provided with homes and land.

In order for these new settlers to occupy their promised homesteads the Poles that occupied them had to be evicted. This is what a number of German police battalions found themselves doing. They were assisted by the Polish born *Volksdeutche* who were formed into police auxiliary (*Selbschutze*) units. These units were in existence only a short time as they were found to be too corrupt and undisiplined by German standards but during their short existence they proved to be effective as murderous thugs.

The new settlers included Baltic *Volksdeutche* who were less than enthusiastic with their new accommodations, as Poland's soil was not as fertile as the land they had left behind. To their surprise their Polish neighbors who had not been evicted proved to be less than welcoming. The Poles that had been evicted were moved to camps were they could be sorted for use as labor back in the Reich or in the fields and factories of Poland. The police were assigned to find and escort these people to their new accommodations and provide camp security.

Poland, at least for a few more years, had the largest Jewish population in Europe. Heydrich on September 21, 1939 ordered that all Jewish communities with populations of less than five hundred were to be transferred to the urban ghettos. The German police battalions were split into company size or smaller units and fanned out across Poland to round up Jews from the villages and consolidate them into the ghettos established in larger towns with rail transportation. On a number of occasions the decision was made that it would be easier to march them a short distance out of town and into a hastily dug ditch and shoot them. I found it interesting that a few days before this order was issued all Jews were forbidden to own radios anywhere in the Reich.

In the next few years some Jews managed to cling to life in labor camps while the majority found themselves locked down inside the numerous ghettos. There they fought to stay alive while disease, starvation, and periodic selective purges reduced the numbers of survivors until the ghettos were completely liquidated. Once again the police were there to help round them up and provide security for the trains that took them to the death camps. Some of the Jews managed to escape and form partisan bands or join existing Polish ones where they fought the German Police Regiments assigned to antipartisan operations.

Polish 1939 Police Group Composition

Police Group 1: This group was assigned to AOK 14
Police Battalion I /1: Later became Police Battalion 92
Police Battalion II/1: Later became Police Battalion 63
Police Battalion III/1: Later became Police Battalion 171
Police Battalion IV/1: Later became Police Battalion 81
Police Battalion V/1: Later became Police Battalion 62

Police Group 2: This group was assigned to AOK 10.
Police Battalion I/2: Later became Police Battalion 101
Police Battalion II/2: Later became Police Battalion 102
Police Battalion III/2: Later became Police Battalion 103
Police Battalion IV/2: Later became Police Battalion 42
Police Battalion V/2: Later became Police Battalion 71

Police Group 3: This group was assigned to AOK 8.
Police Battalion I/3: Later became Police Battalion 41

Police Group 4: z.b.V (Special Operations).
Police Battalion I/4: Later became Police Battalion 61
Or the following Police Battalions; 62, 63, 81, 92, and 171. I tend to agree with Alexander B. Rossino and Wolfgang Curilla that Police Group z.b.V. was an *Einsatzgruppen* staffed with *Schutzpolizei* and SD and detailed to murder Poles as part of Operation "Tannenburg." Police Group z.b.V. was a logical progression and the precursor to what was to come in the Soviet Union.

Police Group 5: This battalion was assigned to AOK 4.
Police Battalion I/5: Later became Police Battalion 1

Police Group 6
Police Battalion I/6: Later became Police Battalion 2
Police Battalion II/6: Later became Police Battalion 3
Police Battalion III/6: Later became Police Battalion 4
Police Battalion IV/6: Later became Police Battalion 91

Top: 1938 Meeting of SS Totenkopf, Police, Gestapo in Berlin prior to the Invasion of Poland.

Above: Poles being deported for Forced Labor.

Right: Polish POWs being rounded up in 1939.

Above: Men of German descent were hired to work as Police Auxiliaries (Selbschultz) in Poland.

Left: Poland 1939, police conducting a stop and search at a checkpoint.

Below: Refugees leaving Zacsze, a suburb of Bialystok in 1939. The Schupo (PB 92/93) is working with a Polish police officer from the newly created and German controlled Polish police.

Above: Police officers from the 1 to 9 series police battalions in Poland in 1940.

Right: A women and her children await resettlement.

Right: A church in Warsaw, Plac Trzech Krzyzy, in 1940.

Below: Polish Police or the "Navy Blues" pose for a group photo. While formed by the Germans a significant percentage collaborated with the resistance.

CHAPTER THREE

INTO RUSSIA

When the German *Wehrmacht* launched Operation Barbarossa on June 22, 1941 it was not the type of war western civilization had grown accustomed to. This invasion, like that of Poland was not about absorbing the conquered into the victors system of government and creating a larger and wealthier state. This was a war of ideological extermination. The losers in this conflict would either be slaves or dead, their land taken and resettled by the victor.

Historians have mentioned the sheer waste of manpower and other resources involved in implementing and continuing the genocidal policy of the Nazis. Why didn't the German high command realize the insanity of using boxcars to move Jews to camps rather than using them to move munitions and troops? Why tie up so many men who were desperately needed elsewhere? The reason is that the invasion of Russia was the continuation of Nazi party philosophy as stated years earlier by Adolf Hitler in his book *Mein Kampf* and repeated continuously in the years since. The *Wehrmacht*'s only role was to take the territory. The governing of the new lands would be done by the Nazi party whose core beliefs were the extermination or enslavement of racially inferior people and the taking of their lands for use by Germans or those of German blood. Genocide was an integral part of that. Insanity in the context of Nazi party philosophy would be not killing them. Even when retreating it was seen as the correct option if not the most important goal of the party.

In 1941 the police battalions followed the army into Russia with the same dual mission as in Poland. Officially the *Einsatzgruppen* that went into Russia totaled 3,000 personnel of which approximately 500 were German police. I use the word official in the sense that they were assigned to actual *Einsatzgruppen* that existed on an organizational chart in Berlin. When it came to conducting actual operations these *Einsatzgruppen* were a skeleton that was fleshed out by temporarily assigned police battalions and indigenous auxiliary police units. MacLean's *The Field Men* estimates that with rotation and transfers at least 10,000 German police served with the *Einsatzgruppen* and accounted for 492,000 or one-third of the estimated deaths. That equals forty-nine victims per police officer. That number actually may be too low when you factor in the number of casualties that occurred during a police battalion antipartisan operation.

These units went into Russia with official approval to kill. It would not take the General who read the order below very long to figure out what was being said between the lines. Especially after Poland the message in (paragraph b) would be very clear:

> Order #21 Signed By Keitel Concerning Jurisdiction of Military, SS, and Police Forces During Barbarossa.[1]
>
> The Russian territory that is to be occupied shall be divided up into individual states with governments of their own, according to special orders, as soon as military operations are concluded. From this the following is inferred:
>
> a. The area of operations, created through the advance of the Army beyond the frontiers of the Reich and the neighboring countries is to be limited in depth as far as possible. The Supreme Commander of the Army has the

right to exercise the executive power in this area, and may transfer his authority onto the Supreme Commanders of the Army Groups and Armies.

b. In the area of operations, the *Reichsführer-SS* is, on behalf of the *Führer*, entrusted with special tasks for the preparation of the political administration, tasks that result from the struggle which has to be carried out between two opposing political systems. Within the realm of these tasks, the *Reichsführer-SS* shall act independently and under his own responsibility. The executive power invested in the Supreme Commander of the Army (OKH), and in agencies determined by him shall not be affected by this. It is the responsibility of the *Reichsführer-SS* that through the execution of his tasks military operations shall not be disturbed. Details shall be arranged directly through the OKH with the *Reichsführer-SS*.

c. As soon as the area of operations has reached sufficient depth, it is to be limited in the rear. The newly occupied territory in the rear of the area of operations is to be given its own political administration. For the present, it is to be divided, according to its genealogic basis and to the positions of the Army Groups, into North (Baltic countries), Center (White Russia) and South (Ukraine). In these territories the political administration is taken care of by Commissioners of the Reich who receive their orders from the *Führer*.

The following two orders make it even plainer.[2]

On May 13, 1941 Keitel, as Chief of OKW, signed an order from the *Führer*'s Headquarters providing that Russian civilians suspected of offenses against German troops should be shot or ruthlessly punished without a military trial, and that prosecution of German soldiers for offenses against Russian civilians was not required. On 27 July 1941 he ordered that all copies of this decree should be destroyed, but without affecting its validity.

On July 23, 1941 Keitel signed an order concerning the administration of occupied Russia. This order provided that legal punishments were inadequate in so great an area and that the troops should use terrorism in crushing the population's will to resist.

When the German army entered Russia regions such as the Ukraine and the Baltic's were willing to greet them as friends and liberators. The army may have been willing but as the orders quoted above state; they had no authority to engage the people of the lands they rolled across as anything but scenery. What these people, left behind in the wake of the army received was a civil administration based on the Nazi philosophy of race and exploitation. It did not take long for them to alienate the populace.

The result was Poland on a much larger scale. For the first year the police battalions were able to concentrate on the "special tasks for the preparation of the political administration." This can be summed up as rounding up and shooting Jews, communists, and anyone's whose attitude was found wanting. The first year saw the creation of the ghettos and the transportation and consolidation of the Jews in them. It was also the beginning of the mass executions of Jews by firing squads.

The winter of 1942 and the Soviet counter offensive found many battalions in the front lines where they were primarily used as reserves or to augment regular army divisions. Army Group North especially had need of their help outside of Leningrad. The spring of 1942 saw them released from front line duty. This was the final year for large-scale executions by squads equipped with rifles or machine guns. It also saw the rise of indigenous police units created and attached to regular German police battalions. The indigenous units carried out much of the mass murder under German supervision. It was easier on the German personnel mental an emotional state of mind and the local volunteers were inexpensive, being paid in plunder, and plentiful. Never the less Himmler after witnessing executions near Minsk by members of a police battalion and an *Einsatzkommando* realized more efficient methods were needed.

As a result of the German occupation policies the problems with partisan activity increased exponentially. Part of this was because the communist party had planned for partisan warfare. The rest resulted from the barbaric treatment the population received. The partisans in time grew in size enough to field small armies. Antipartisan operations where the Germans fielded tens of thousands of men supported by armor were increasingly common towards the end of the war. Partisan warfare was brutal and among Soviet partisan groups women were included in the ranks. Of these women only four in a hundred would survive to the wars end.[3]

German policies and the war itself were very hard on the people in the countries that made up the Soviet Union. The casualty figures were huge and the effect on the Soviet Unions demographics is still felt today. Belarus lost over twenty percent of its population. The Soviet Union as a whole lost over twenty-five million dead. Russian POWs taken by the Germans usually died as the fatality rate was almost sixty percent. The siege of Leningrad killed over a million and a half people alone. In this one battle more Russians died than the total casualties of the United States and the United Kingdom for the entire war.

The final year of the war in the east would find the police on the front lines fighting in *Kampfgruppen* (battle groups) trying to stop the Soviet army. The only police battalions with a realistic chance of survival were those that were fortunate enough to be in the Adriatic region or in Europe. Those that did survive and were lucky enough to go into captivity on the Allied side were fortunate as the Nürnberg trials did not consider the police a criminal organization.[4]

Left: The grave of a thirty-two year old Wachtmeister who died in Romonowka and was buried in Senhow on December 22, 1941. A number of his comrades died with him in what must have been a sharp skirmish.

Below: Russian POWs march into captivity, one woman marches with them.

Bottom: A Russian villages population is rounded up for deportation to the Reich as forced labor.

CHAPTER FOUR

THE PARTISANS

Stalin may have been the only communist official surprised by the German invasion. While Stalin was recovering his poise the Soviet Union was stripping the countryside in front of the advancing German army and shipping its industrial capacity to the Ural Mountains where it was hoped it would be safe. The struggles of the average Soviet worker in recreating their countries factories in the middle of nowhere is worthy in itself of a book.

While the communist party had made plans for partisan warfare and the continuance of the party no one had thought the front would approach so quickly, let alone advance to such depth in the Soviet heartland. The party's plan was to go underground, establishing itself in each village, town, and city. In the Ukraine underground warehouses were dug and camouflaged. These were stocked with food and supplies. The typical supply dump was almost ten feet deep and about 115 square feet with the walls reinforced by heavy logs. It had a rammed dirt floor that was then covered in branches to absorb moisture. The roof would be leveled with the ground and covered with dirt. Then small bushes and grass would be planted on top. The Chernigov Region in the Ukraine had almost two hundred of these dumps built in its various districts.[1]

Soviet partisans in the Ukraine were organized at a district level with each district providing men and women for the partisans and informants inside the villages. Another source of partisan manpower was the bypassed groups of Red Army soldiers who took to the woods and swamplands. Once the front had stabilized short of Moscow and Leningrad the Soviet army began actively encouraging and supporting these detachments. Supplies and men were dropped by parachute and small temporary airfields began to appear in partisan held areas.

The German army besides having to contend with the Soviet sponsored and supplied partisan groups also found themselves fighting partisan groups with nationalist aspirations such as the Polish Home Army. A number of these groups did not quietly disperse with the end of the war in 1945. Instead they continued to fight the Soviets who were still tracking them down and killing them into the 1950s.

The German army did not have enough men to garrison every village or small town nor was it their responsibility. They had security divisions that were responsible for *Koriicks* (Sectors) behind the front but these troops were second rate and rarely motorized which was a bit of a drawback in a country the size of Russia. For the entire Soviet Union there were only nine Security Divisions available. The *koriicks* were sectors in the Army Group rear area of operations. Each security division was responsible for an area that in the USSR varied in size from 5,000 to 10,000 square miles. These sectors were broken down into smaller administrative areas that at the smallest were the responsibility of company-sized units. *Gendarmerie* troops were used to garrison small villages and static *Schupo* units were assigned to the larger towns and cities.

Police battalions were assigned to the three army groups that invaded the Soviet Union and were assigned to work with Security Divisions. For Army Group North in 1941 and the beginning of 1942 Police Battalion 2 was assigned to Security Division 281; Police Battalion 105 was assigned to Security Division 207; Police Battalion 65 was assigned to Security Division 285. For Army Group Center Police Battalion 131 was assigned to Security Division 403; Police Battalion 317 was assigned to Security Division 286; Police Battalion 309 was assigned to Security Division 221. For Army Group South Police Battalion 318 was assigned to Security Division 213; Police Battalion 311 was assigned to Security Division 444; Police Battalion 82 was assigned to Security Division 454.[2]

Policing an antipartisan operations were increasingly done as the war continued by indigenous units officered by German SS and Police, and the police battalions formed as regiments. In the early years of the war, especially when it looked as if they might win, there were minimal problems in raising indigenous units who were willing to kill their former neighbors for pay. Some volunteered because they hated the communists or thought that in time they would be able to help create a semiautonomous state inside the Reich. For others it was the same motivation that has created mercenaries for centuries. The SS and the Police were more than happy to use them as cannon fodder and executioners.

The partisans were a major thorn in the Germans side as partisan attacks were extremely disruptive to the supply and support of units operating far from the Reich. Especially damaging was the continual attacks on the railroads that were the arteries of the *Wehrmacht* in Russia. The rail lines were extremely important because of the lack of hard surface roads or in many places roads at all. The Germans required that all railroad lines have all trees and brush cleared at least 300 yards on each side. They built an elaborate series of guard posts and police battalions spent a great deal of time patrolling roads and rail lines. Police battalions were usually stationed in towns that were key railroad and road junctions. An example of the importance of the railroads to the German Army was the II Panzer Army that in early 1943 consisted of approximately thirty-five divisions. Their primary supply line was one double track railroad line.

The effectiveness of the partisan attacks presented a serious problem as seen in the following statement made in the introduction of *The Underground Committee Carries On* by Alexei Fyodorov: "The unit under my command exterminated alone more than 25,000 German invaders and their accomplices. It derailed 683 trains carrying enemy troops and tanks, planes, trucks and ordnance. Eight armored trains and their crews also flew into the air. The dynamiters of our unit blasted forty-seven railway bridges, 35,000 meters of railway bed, twenty-six oil bases and fuel stores, and thirty-nine ammunition and outfit depots; mines planted by our partisans destroyed twelve tanks and eighty-seven trucks." This was in the Cherigov and Volhynia region of the Ukraine. Even allowing for the possibility of exaggeration it is an impressive total of destruction.

Broadly defined there were three kinds of antipartisan actions that the police battalions found themselves consistently involved in. The first would was the regular patrolling of a defined area. This was the making the rounds of the villages and checking to see if anything looked out of place and also check in with the local members of the German sponsored puppet government. They would do routine weapon and paper searches.

The second would be an HSSPF (Higher SS Police *Führer*) organized punitive action that would involve battalions, regiments and indigenous units. These were "search and destroy" operations and they would have an operational name. Many of them, especially in the Slovenia area were named after food such as Operation "Roast Mutton." Or they would reflect the coarse humor of the men commanding them such as "Harvest Festival" for a large-scale slaughter action. These operations were marked by their extreme brutality. The goal was to remove any support for partisans by killing everyone in a village or area who could provide that support. Any grain livestock, food, or farm machinery would be taken. Often these operations would include the seizing of people for use in the Reich as slave labor.

The third operation was an actual military operation. These operations were when the Police, SS, and the regular army along with indigenous support troops would actually attempt to close and engage armed partisan bands. These operations usually did not amount to much as most partisan bands preferred to wait until the odds were in their favor before engaging in combat.

Above: A captured Soviet partisan probably minutes before his execution.

Top right: A partisan destroyed locomotive in the Ukraine.

Right: Postcard for the German public showing the police as the equal to soldiers. Author's copy.

Above: Warning sign that the area ahead was not safe for less than two vehicles because of partisans.

Below: A railroad security post. These were built at intervals along the railroad in a futile attempt to stop the partisans.

Above: Partisans being brought in. The officer is Wehrmacht but behind him can be glimpsed an auxiliary wearing an armband.

Below: Hunting Bandits in Russian in 1942. Note the auxiliary with the armband behind the truck.

CHAPTER FIVE

THE AUXILIARIES

The creation and use of paramilitary groups or auxiliary police did not begin with the invasion of Russia in 1941. They had been used previously in Poland with varying degrees of success. In Poland the *Selbutschutz* were formed as a paramilitary formation from men of German descent. They were disbanded because their behavior was more of a liability then the services they provided. Although the use of murderous, raping, and looting thugs did continue, it was with those who could maintain minimal discipline.

The use of auxiliaries was driven by the needs of the Reich as the war progressed. The SS managed to get past its distaste for those who were not fortunate enough to be born in western and northern Europe. Enough so that by the end of the war divisions created with non-Germans outnumbered the German ones. For the police the progression was somewhat different. Beginning with the invasion of Poland the use of indigenous personnel to support SS and Police units was seen as essential. They helped point out the local Jews and other undesirables and were more than willing to assist in killing them for a share of the plunder.

It was recognized early on that prolonged shooting of men, women, and children was hard on the average German policeman. There was also the problem of the sheer number of people who needed shooting. There was just not enough time in the day for the police in concert with the SS to kill as many people as required. On July 25, 1941 Himmler ordered the formation of auxiliary police units using preferably ethnic Germans or reliable non-communist elements from the locals. These units were named *Schutzmannschaften* (defense units) or *Schuma*. Indigenous battalions were created using the one company for every two ethnic ones raised. The officers and NCOs were usually German.

I believe many police battalions after the invasion of Russia worked with several attached companies of auxiliary police. The companies were separate from the *Schuma* battalions and while never officially on the battalion rolls were fed, clothed, and paid by the battalion. The battalions, especially those involved in mass executions needed the extra manpower, and when it came time for the actual executions they were the preferred shooters. Later they were needed to fill gaps in the frontlines, battle partisans, and provide security for the roads and rail lines. When a company was assigned ghetto security and watch duties the auxiliaries stood the night watches. The pay may not have been good but for the auxiliaries the opportunities for looting were outstanding.

While not a police formation the SS *Sonder* (Special) Battalion Dirlewanger operated extensively with the police battalions and after 1942 had a large number of Ukrainian and Russian personnel serving with it. This battalion, named after its commander Dr. Oskar Dirlewanger was infamous for its conduct and brutality during the war. While the total number of civilians killed, looted or raped will never be known it is safe to estimate the total in the tens of thousands.

Almost every occupied country contributed personnel to the German Police, some far more than others. Poland, who suffered the most under German rule, contributed the smallest number. The Polish Police (*Polnische Polizei*) never amounted to more than 15,000 at their peak. The Ukraine by 1941 had fielded eighteen *Schutzmannschaft* battalions at approximately five hundred men each. These battalions were commanded by

German Police officers and used extensively in the eradication of the Jews and later civilians during antipartisan operations. Estonia contributed twelve police battalions that were used extensively in Poland. Lithuanian fielded at least twenty battalions, one of which was attached to Police Battalion 11. Their help was essential to the liquidation of the Jewish population of Eastern Europe.

Above: Auxiliaries outside of Krakow in the Winter of 1942.

Right: A police auxiliary in Riga, Latvia in 1942.

Below: Yugoslavian SS/Police Auxiliaries outside of their barracks.

CHAPTER SIX

THE HOLOCAUST

The role of the police in the process of the Holocaust was to provide the National Socialist leadership with the men to pull the trigger. The difference in this process between the police and the SS running the camps amounted to the difference between your thumb and index finger. Different, yet both belong to the same hand and both are required to make a fist.

When you read about the police battalions in the next section of this book please realize that each man who served in one is as guilty as any man who worked in the death or labor camps run by the SS. Like any guard at Auschwitz they organized, processed, and if need be executed the enemies of the Reich in numbers that still have the power to stun the imagination. Soldiers can at least say that they killed other armed and trained men who sought to kill them. What excuse does the man standing in a pit filled with bodies; two thirds of them women and children use?

To write and think about, even casually, the Holocaust leads one to the question of why? Why did they kill so many innocent people and why did so many allow themselves to be killed? Why did they stand there passively waiting with the sounds of rifle fire audible to all but the deaf? Why did they assemble in the town squares across Eastern Europe an allow themselves to be marched off in orderly columns after being stripped of their belongings?

They did resist but only after far too many had perished. In the beginning they did not because who could of imagined what awaited them. Yes, I am sure some suspected but what were they to do? Run off and leave the elderly and the children behind? Where would they go when the Germans were everywhere and most had never traveled father than thirty miles from their place of birth.

It is difficult for us today to understand how isolated many of these people were then. They did not own cars, phones, or television sets. Many did not even own a radio. Once the Germans arrived the printing presses were shut down or converted to printing only German propaganda. The Jews were already segregated in their own sections of town and that segregation was enforced with draconian ruthlessness once the Germans arrived. They were effectively marooned on an island and surrounded by a sea of hostile or indifferent populace.

Since so many of the police battalions listed in this book participated in actions designed to either control, transport or eliminate the Jews it might be helpful to describe a fictional account of an action synthesized from actual events.

The town of Nicolowa had existed since the early 11th century in the Ukraine and by the 1800s had become a minor center of Jewish learning based on the teachings of Rabbi Ben Cohen. In 1941 the town had a population of 6,023 of which 2,201 were Jews. The suddenness of the German advance caught the town by surprise and very few were able to successfully flee with the retreating Soviet army.

The German army passed through Nicolowa with very little impact on the town itself. True, some of the townspeople had welcomed them and there were a few incidents with the soldiers. The soldiers had forced the Goldstein boys to their knees and shaved their beards off to the amusement of many in the town. When the eldest boy had protested they had beaten him until he was unconscious but it wasn't like incidents such as this had not happened before. The older Jewish men reassured everyone by recounting stories about the German occupation of the town in the first war and how it had not been that bad. The Germans were civilized people, and besides they could not be any worse than the communists.

Two days later the bulk of the German army units had moved on. The towns Jewish Rabbis and leading merchants were summoned to the new national socialist administrative building in what had been the communist party headquarters to meet the new administration. Here they were presented with a list of all the Jewish residents of the town, conveniently left behind by the communist party officials who had taken a census of the town a few years earlier. They were asked to update it and return it in forty-eight hours. They were surprised by the hostile reception they received and when Rabbi Tocsin who at seventy-two did not move quick enough to leave he was kicked in the rear and propelled out the door to the great amusement of the Germans. Afterward in their discussion of the events of the day the Jews decided that these men were German political officers and the equivalent of the previous administrations NKVD men. In other words the only thing that had changed in was the uniforms.

Two days later a convoy of trucks arrived in town carrying a platoon of *Schupo* and a number of Ukrainian auxiliaries who were promptly billeted in the local school. Later that day some of the trucks and men were seen surveying the anti-tank ditch that had been built in a hurry the previous year and had proven to be totally useless. That same day the Jewish leaders were summoned and told to have everyone report the next morning at 0700 in the town square with no more than twenty pounds of personal possessions as they were going to be relocated two hundred miles to the east where they would be all working on a former collective farm growing cabbage. The elders began arguing vehemently with the SD officer in charge. This subsided immediately when the officer shot the loudest in the head.

The idea of an entire segment of a town being given less than twenty-four hours to relocate may seem utter lunacy but during this time period in Ukrainian history large population movements were not unusual, especially ones at gunpoint. Stalin, in his paranoia over the possibility of a German fifth column and in implementing his agricultural policies had already moved millions of people in the region with as little regard to the effect on the people.

The Jews assembled as ordered the next morning at 0700 in the town square where their identification was checked against the master list and then they were segregated into groups based on age and sex. The men over sixteen an under fifty were grouped at a distance of a hundred yards from the main mass of people. Meanwhile a search of the Jewish quarter had begun as the police began looking for stragglers. Those gathered in the marketplace could hear shots ringing out as they were found.

At 1030 without any warning the police opened fire on the group of men who had been separated using two heavy machine guns and police formed in ranks delivering methodical volley fire into the seated group of men. A police officer and several men walked among the bodies fifteen minutes later delivering shots to the head to anyone suspected of being alive. The survivors in the other groups began wailing and those that were too loud and in convenient reach of the police were silenced with a gun butt to the head. The remaining people were quickly formed into a column of five abreast and marched out of town all the while being screamed at by the police to Move! Move!

They were halted in a clearing outside of the woods that screened the anti tank ditch and told to stack their belongings in a pile to the side. Then in groups of twenty five they were led down a path lined with police an auxiliaries who were screaming at them to move and lashing out at them with clubs. They were stopped abruptly and told to strip. Any sign of resistance was meet with a blow of a club or rifle butt. They were then lead in single file in groups of ten out to the edge of the anti tank ditch and stopped. Facing them were ten police armed with rifles who on command then shot them, the impact of the bullets knocking them down into the ditch where Ukrainian auxiliaries waited to shoot any who had not died immediately and to arrange the bodies in orderly rows. By nightfall the town of Nicolowa no longer had any Jews left and many of their former neighbors had begun moving into their homes.

An anti-tank ditch. They were perfect for the mass executions the SS and Police committed. Already dug in many cases, large enough to hold a number of bodies, and a firing parapet already built along the top. This photo was taken by a member of the Police.

A Jewish man fetches water from a well while a laughing German police man stands by.

A Jewish man in the Warsaw ghetto. It is highly unlikely he was still alive a year later.

A Jewish child in the Warsaw ghetto. German police stand behind her. She was probably singled out for the photos because of her blonde Aryan looks.

An unknown Polish Jew in early 1940.

People dig their own graves as an police auxiliary watches.

Right: A Totenkopf SS officer conducting a selection. His name was Heinrich, and he began his career at Dachau in the early 1930s and later transferred to Buchenwald. Based on other photos in the set he was very likely attached to an Einsatzgruppe.

Below: A man whose job title was "Kicker" cleans the edge of a mass grave of bodies. Courtesy: USHM.

APPENDICES

Appendix 1
The Battalions: Regular and Reserve

Police Battalion 1 (Reserve)
The battalion was formed with personnel from Berlin, Germany in 1939.
Field Post Number(s): 35937. Later the battalion formed Police *Shützen* (Rifle) Regiment 36 on June 24, 1943 that disbanded in 1944.[1] Staff Field Post Number: 57850, I Battalion 59603, II Battalion 56319, III Battalion 58066, Gesch. Battr. 14617.
The battalion was formed in Berlin an active in Poland in 1939 as the I/Police Regiment 5 and was attached to Police Group 5, AOK (Army Over Command) 4. The Fourth Army was in reserve and consisted primarily of border police (*Grenze*) units. The other two battalions of the regiment were Ukrainian *Schuma* with each battalion having a German company.[2]

Regiment/Battalion Locations & Activities
January 1944: The battalion was in Volozhin where Police Battalion 12 was also stationed.

August 30, 1944: The battalion (now Police *Shützen* Regiment 36) was destroyed in the Molodechno[3] area when the Soviet army shattered Army Group Center with "Operation Bagration" that began on June 22, 1944. Out of the German divisions that opposed the Soviets over twenty-five were completely destroyed.[4]

Police Battalion 2 (Reserve)
The battalion was formed with personnel from Berlin, Germany in 1939.
Field Post Number(s): 31274, 40848
Commanding Officer(s): Major Richard Röhrborn (1941 to 1942), Major Hassler (1942 to ?)
Major Richard Röhrborn: NSDAP Member July 1, 1941. SS Member May 1, 1939. SS Number: 327 319. He was awarded: KVK 2nd Class with Swords; The 1939 *spange* to his 1914 Iron Cross Second Class; The Commemorative Medal of March 13, 1938 for the annexation of Austria; The Wound Badge in Black. His fitness reports remarked repeatedly on his "National Socialist worldview."[1]

This battalion was active in Poland in 1939 as the I/Police Regiment 6. In December 1939 it was attached to Police Regiment Warsaw.[2]

The battalion formed the I/Police Regiment 1 in July 1942 and was sent to the Army Group North area of operations.[3]

In January 1943 it helped form SS Police Regiment "*Griese*" in Marseille, France. Later in March 1943 it helped form the second version of the I/SS Police Regiment 14. In March 1945 the entire regiment was transferred to the newly formed 35 SS Division and redesignated as the 91 SS and Police Grenadier Regiment.

Regiment/Battalion Locations & Activities
May 15 to December 31, 1941: The battalion along with Security Division 281 is conducting anti-partisan operations in Army Group North area of operations.

November 1941: Army Group North, composed of the 16th and 18th armies, had almost completely encircled the Russian city of Leningrad. These two armies had a total of twenty-eight divisions, most of them under strength, and ill prepared for the Russian winter while having to defend a 372-mile front.

Police Battalion 2 had been rushed to the Staraya Russa (Leningrad) area in December 1941 as Soviet partisans in preparation for the Russian counteroffensive increased their activities behind German lines. By the end of January the partisans had killed 196 German soldiers, destroyed twenty-three trucks, and blew up three bridges.[4]

February 1942: The battalion headquarters staff and the 2nd Company of Police Battalion 2 were attached to X Army Corps/AOK 16 in the Straya Russa area which is south of Lake Ilmen. Straya Russa was X Army Corp headquarters, and the 2nd Company probably was being used for local security. The remaining companies of the battalion were conducting anti-partisan operations.

April 1942: The 1st Company of Police Battalion 2 was located in Dedovichi, protecting the railway line that runs south from Leningrad toward Vitebsk. The German garrison there had been destroyed previously by partisans in July, 1941. The German army took rail security seriously as roads in Russia were often worthless due to snow or mud. All railroad lines that ran through forest or wooded areas were cleared to 300 yards on each side. A series of sentry posts were built at intervals along the railway lines in a futile attempt to protect them from partisan activity.

April 12, 1942: Major Röhrborn receives his Wound Badge (*Verwundetenabzeichen*) in Szobolawa when a grenade explodes in a wood pile next to him.

July 1942: At the creation of the regiment the battalion was in North Russia.

January 1943: The battalion arrived in Marseille, France to help form SS Police Regiment "*Griese*."

March 1943: The battalion was used to create the second version of the I/SS Police Regiment 14.

June 1943: The battalion arrived in Slovenia.

Croatians welcome the Germans to their town.

August 25-27, 1943: The entire regiment was now in Virovitica, Croatia, having moved there from Slovenia.

September 9, 1943: The regiment is ordered by the III SS Panzer Corps to advance from Zagreb to Karlovac, and then to Ogulin to help disarm the Italian units in the area following Italy's capitulation the previous day.

September 19, 1943: The battalion is detached and in Ozalj.

October 20, 1943: The regiment is reassigned from III SS Panzer Corps to II SS Panzer Corps.

January 1944: The battalion is guarding the rail line in and around Novo Mesto.

March 16, 1944: The battalion skirmished with partisans in the vicinity of Sentjernej.

November 14-16, 1944: The battalion along with the III Battalion attacked partisan concentrations around Crnomelj.

March 16, 1945: Most of the regiment was redesignated SS and Police Grenadier Regiment 91 of the new 35 SS Division and the remainder were disbanded. The remainder most likely meaning any of the indigenous volunteers.

March 20, 1945: The 35 SS Division is near Guben on the Oder except for this battalion, which was still in Slovenia and located in Krsko until March 29, 1945 when it departed to join the rest of the regiment at Guben. The division was badly damaged at the battle for Seelow Heights and destroyed during the Halbe breakout during April 1945. A few men of the battalion may have survived to surrender to the Americans.[5]

Police Battalion 3 (Reserve)

The battalion was formed with personnel from Berlin in 1939.

Field Post Number(s): 36381. The 3rd company while operating with *Einsatzgruppe* D used field post number 47540.

Commanding Officer(s): Major Richard Röhrborn (September 12, 1939 to April 2, 1940), Major Friedrich Boch (1940 to ?).

Other Officer(s): The 1st Company Commander was Captain Hans Siegling.[1] The 2nd Company commander was Captain Franz Zipperling.

The 1st company in 1943 helped form *Schuma* Battalion 57 in Riga, Latvia that was a battalion in Police *Schützen* Regiment 36.

The battalion arrived in Poland in 1939 as the II/6 Police Regiment where they were attached to Police Group 6, AOK 4. AOK 4 was held in reserve as it mainly consisted mostly of border (*Grenze*) police units. In December 1939 it was part of Police Regiment Warsaw.[2] The battalion formed the I/Police Regiment 1 in July 1942.

Einsatzgruppen/Atrocity Actions

This battalion participated in numerous executions as documented in East and West German court cases and other sources. The following is not the entire list of atrocities – rather I have used a sample that lists their locations.

The battalion arrived in Russia in July of 1941 and was

active with *Einsatzgruppe* B, C and D and the battalion companies were used individually in support of SD operations through July 1942.[3]

The 1st company (*Klemp* 2005) was responsible for the death of 48,000 people. This company was active with *Einsatzgruppe* B and *Einsatzkommando* 8 in 1941. The 1st company replaced the 2nd company, Police Battalion 9 in the *Einsatzgruppe*. Einsatzgruppe B had approximately 655 men assigned to it. The group headquarters staff had seventy-one men. The group was broken down in to commandos. *Sonderkommando* 7a had ninety-three men, 7b had ninety-one men, *Einsatzkommando* 8 had 241 men, and *Einsatzkommando* 9 had 186 men.

The 2nd company worked with *Einsatzgruppe* C. The 3rd company was active with *Einsatzgruppe* D. The 4th company worked with *Einsatzgruppe* A and was stationed in Krasnogwardeisk. The battalion was often working with elements of Police Battalion 9 who also contributed men to each of these *Einsatzgruppes*.

The known operations include "actions" (a German euphemism for killing) in the summer of 1942 in Krainy, and in December in Bellinitsche.

January 1942: The 1st and 3rd companies killed 4,000 to 5,000 Jews in Mogilev.

November 1942: The following is from a report written on 3rd companies activities by Police Inspector Preuss. Inspector Preuss in his report (November 5, 1942) writes about his regret in the delayed filing of his report as he has been to busy since August to sit in his chair back in the office. The 3rd company until July was active with *Einsatzgruppe* D in Simferopol and in August they were in Taganrog. *Einsatzgruppe* D and its commandos were extensive users of the gas vans. Gas vans were especially modified portable gas chambers that pumped carbon monoxide into the back compartment. The vans came in two models, one that held eighty and one that held sixty people. The company, together with *Einsatzgruppe* D then moved on to Woroschilowsk. An advance team (*Vorkommando*) was sent to Kisslowdsk. The SD was using small squad size units (*Teilkommandos*) and one man from the company would be detailed to it was sent out to conduct an action.[4]

March-June 1943: The 3rd company of Police Battalion 3 was active in the Pripet Marshes with "*Kampfgruppe Bierkamp*." *Einsatzgruppe* D was commanded by *SS-Brigadeführer* Dr. Walter Bierkamp from July 1942 until March 1943 when it was renamed as *Kampfgruppe "Bierkamp*."[5] This *kampfgruppe* was disbanded in May 1943.

This battalion's total number of victims including deportations was 62,542 men, women, and children.[8]

Regiment/Battalion Locations & Activities.

April to October 1940: The battalion was stationed in Drontheim, Norway.[6]

September 10-12, 1941: The battalion was active in the Mogilev area conducting partisan sweeps.

April 1943: The battalion was in the Borisow and Minsk area.

May 1943: The battalion took part in operation "Blitz," an anti-partisan operation in the area near Horodytsche.

May 23, to June 25, 1943: The battalion took part in operation "Cottbus" an anti-partisan operation in the Palikee area of Belorussia. Cottbus was an especially bloody operation. The official body count was 9,800 people of which 2,000-3,000 in one report were listed as having died while "clearing mines."

October 28, 1943 to January 18, 1944: Operating southwest of Newel.

May-June 1944: Operating in the Beresinosu swamp area on anti-partisan operations.

October-November 1944: Listed by Army Group South as being available for the defense of Budapest.

December 28, 1944: The entire regiment is defending Budapest in the Kispest area of the city along with the 22 SS *Freiwilligen* Cavalry Division Maria Theresa. Since only 170 men of the 22nd made it out of Budapest I think it would be safe to assume that SS Police Regiment 1 existence ended here. Officially the regiment was disbanded in March 1945.[7]

Police Battalion 4 (Reserve)

The battalion was formed with personnel from the Berlin area.

Field Post Number(s): 26800

The battalion was active in Poland in 1939 as the III/6 Police Regiment and was attached to Police Group 6, AOK 4. In December 1939 it is recorded as being part of Police Regiment Warsaw. Tessin writes that it may have become part of SS Police Division 4.

Police Battalion 5 (Reserve)
The battalion was formed with personnel from Berlin in 1939.
Field Post Number(s): 36187
The battalion was listed as active in Poland in 1939 and part of Police Regiment Cracow.

Regiment/Battalion Locations & Activities.
October 1939 to March 1940: In Poland.

April 1940 to January 1940: The battalion returns to Berlin.

January 1941 to April 1943: Stationed in the Warthegau.[1] Stefan Klemps book mentions the Möhne catastrophe in connection with this battalion. They may have been providing security for the dams such as the ones on Möhne and Heve rivers. These dams were the target of the famous British dam busters raid. It is interesting to note that 749 Ukrainian POWs were listed as being killed as part of this raid in 1943 which could explain the presence of this police battalion.

Police Battalion 6 (Reserve)
The battalion was formed from personnel from Berlin in September 1939.
Field Post Number(s): 03316
Commanding Officer(s): Major Mulverstedt, Major Richard Dröge (1942 to ?), Major Otto Schroeder (1945).[1]
Other Officers: Lieutenant Lothar Allisat, 1st Company (September 1, 1939 to December 12, 1940)[2]
Major Richard Dröge was later the commander of the SS Police Jäger Regiment 50 in 1945. This was a short lived formation that was used to help form the 1st SS Police Jäger Division in March 1945. The battalion was active in Poland in 1939 and in December 1939 it was the VI/Police Regiment Warsaw. In May 1942 the battalion was active as the I/Police Regiment Center.[3] In July 1942 the battalion became the I/13 Police Regiment.

Einsatzgruppen/Atrocity Activity
On September 5, 1939 the military commander of Bydgoszcz, Brigadier General Eccard *Freiherr* von Gablenz ordered the city to be pacified due to continuing attacks on German military personnel and previous attacks on people of German ancestry who lived there.

The town was searched by men from Police Battalion 6 and the Security Police. This was a house to house search and they had orders to shoot anyone who was found with a weapon. The definition of what constituted a weapon was rather broadly defined as including bayonets and firearms regardless if they were operable or not. They were also looking for anyone they considered looked "suspicious" which I am sure had as broad as definition as their firearms policy.

Local Nazi sympathizers had created lists of the people in town whom they believed would not view the German occupation as an occasion for rejoicing. Undoubtedly a few old scores were also settled in those lists as well. These lists had been created all over Poland and forwarded to the SD who then created master lists and distributed them to *Einsatzgruppen* commanders and others who they thought could make proper use of them.

The "suspicious" people discovered during the search were taken to a former Polish artillery barracks and sorted. Those who weren't on any lists or who could prove German ancestry (*Volksdeutche*) were freed. The remaining group of approximately 500 people was held until locally conscripted Jews had finished digging a trench. They were then led in groups to the trench and shot.

After this a warning was issued that any more attacks on German soldiers or local ethnic Germans would result in hostages being shot. On September 8, a Polish civilian shot and wounded a German soldier. In reprisal Police Battalion 6 assisted by Security Police and regular German troops shot at least 400 local people who had previously been taken hostage in the town square.

September 10, 1939: As the area was seen as a hotbed of resistance Police Battalion 6 and members of *Einsatzgruppe* IV were assigned to "Action *Schwedehohe*." This was a sweep of the town and nearby areas for "suspicious people." They then shot another 120 Poles in an antitank ditch outside of Bydgoszcz.[4]

January 28, 1943: The regiment is assigned to Operation Erntefest (Harvest Festival) II carried out west of the Minsk

A group of Police, SS, and auxiliaries conduct a search in Bydgoszcz. Courtesy: USHM.

to Slutsk highway between January 28, and February 9, 1943. According to a German report, 2,400 partisans were killed and 2,300 partisan helpers or sympathizers were executed."[5]

Regiment/Battalion Location and Activities
April 1940: In Lysa Gora near Radom.

September 1940: The battalion returns to Berlin after its tour of duty in Poland.

May-July 1942: The battalion returns to the East and is in Smolensk.

July 1942: In Kardymoma

August 17-29, 1942: The entire regiment is participating in Operation "Grief" along with the Police Regiment 14. This operation took place in the Witebsk/Orscha area. The operation resulted in the deaths of 498 "partisans" and 123 captured. German losses were fourteen dead and sixteen wounded.

January 1943: In Mogilev.

February 8, 1943: The battalion is assigned to SS and Police *Kampfgruppe* "von dem Bach" in Belorussia and conducting anti-partisan operations.

February 8-26 1943: This battalion helped form *Kampfgruppe* "West." It, along with three other *Kampfgruppes* were used for Operation "Hornung." *Kampfgruppe* "West" also included Police Battalion 85 and *Schuma* Battalion 18. For further details on Operation "Hornung" see Police Battalion 13.

March 25, 1943: The battalion is in Plissa.

March 31, to April 7, 1943: The regiment was divided between SS and Police *Kampfgruppe* "Schimana" and "Kuntze" in Belorussia for Operation "Lenz Süd" (Spring South) against several thousand partisans in the Sloboda area twelve miles northeast of Bobruisk.

July-August 1943: The regiment belonged to a force of four SS Police regiments plus other units that were brought up to attack the partisan Kovpak Brigade lead by Brigadier General Sydor Kovpak that was active in Ukraine and Galicia. See Police Battalion 85.

September 1943: In the Lublin, Poland area.

October 25, to November 15, 1943: Participating in Operation "Heinrich." The battalion with the rest of the regiment minus the II which was in Smolensk plus twenty-eight battalions of police, Schuma battalions, and German security troops, police tank companies and support units surrounded and attacked a huge concentration of partisans (estimated by the Germans at more than 16,000) in the swampy, heavily wooded lake district between Nevel and the Latvian border. Before the operation made any progress Soviet breakthroughs in the vicinity forced the troops to end "Heinrich" and switch over to a defensive role against the oncoming regular units of the Red Army. They did not do very well against the Soviet army and took heavy causalities.

December 30, 1943 to January 1944: The entire regiment (2,239 men) were on the front line between Polotsk and Nevel under SS and Police *Kampfgruppe* "von Gottberg" (total strength 8,132).

March 1, 1944: This battalion and the III were part of SS and Police *Kampfgruppe* "von Gottberg." Also attached to this *Kampfgruppe* during this period was the Kaminski Brigade.

April 1944: The regiment was transferred from Belorussia to Klagenfurt, Austria and then to Oberkrain in Slovenia to reinforce the anti-partisan units under the HSSPF in Wehrkreis XVIII. Most sources state that the regiment was billeted in Austria just across the border from Slovenia and returned to these garrisons after each anti-partisan operation in Slovenia concluded.

June-July 1944: The battalion was conducting offensive sweeps and patrols in the area between Bleiburg and Solcava.

December 11, 1944: The regiment assembled in Crna and with the SS Police Regiment 28 and the Lehr Regiment Brandenburg in Kamnik. The combined force advanced on the Gornja Savinja Valley to destroy elements of the Partisan 14th Division that had been occupying the villages of Luce, Ljubno as well as other communities along the valley. Several days after the operation began a column from SS Police Regiment 25 and strong elements from Reserve *Gebirgsjäger* (Mountain Troops) Regiment 18 and Landesschützen (Reserve Rifle) Regiment 18 moved forward from the east and south, driving the partisans from most of the valley.

March 20, 1945: The battalion was stationed in Bleiburg, Austria.

April 1945: The battalion is helping to protect the rail line and route of withdrawal around Bled.

Police Battalion 8 (Reserve)
The battalion was formed with personnel from Berlin on September 30, 1939
Field Post Number(s): 28488

Regiment/Battalion Location and Activities
November 1939: In Prague, Czechoslovakia

December 1939: The battalion returned to Berlin.[1]

January 1940: In Warsaw, Poland

July 1940: In Lublin and Biala Podlaska to October 1940.[2]

In July 1940 the German Police began transporting Jewish men from Biala Podlaska to the Belzec concentration camp. There were also a number of work camps established during this time period employing Jews in the area that lasted until the liquidation of the ghetto.

November 14, 1940: The battalion is transferred to Norway.[3]

July 1941: The battalion has returned to Berlin

April 16, 1942: The battalion is cannibalized for men to make up for losses in the east.

Police Battalion 9 (Reserve)
This battalion was formed with personnel from Berlin in September 1939.

Field Post Number(s): 38393, 32850
Battalion Commander(s): Major Paulus Meier, Major Seidel (1941 to 1942), Major Wilhelm Haack. After the war Major Meier was employed by the Hamburg Police.
The 1st company commanding officer was Captain Peter Clausen. The 1st Platoon leader was Helmet Keil (rank unknown).

The 2nd company commanding officer was Captain Dr. Helmet Gantz.[1]

The 1st Platoon leader was 1st Lt. Paul Dinter.

The 2nd Platoon leader was 1st Lt. Dölle.

The 3rd Platoon Leader was Sergeant Richard Neubert.

The commanding office of 3rd company was Captain Walter Krumme.

The 1st Platoon leader was 1st Lt. Fritz Sperhake.

The 2nd Platoon leader was 2nd Lt. Paul Hecker.

The commanding officer of 4th company was Captain Hans Gabel.

In July 1942 the battalion became the III/Police Regiment 27.

Einsatzgruppen/Atrocity Activity
This battalion participated in numerous executions as documented in East and West German court cases and other sources. The following is just a small sample that I have used to place their locations.

Spring 1941: Four companies were assigned to three different *Einsatzgruppen*.

The 1st company was assigned to *Einsatzgruppen* A. *Einsatzgruppen* A operated in the Baltic area and was headquartered in Riga in 1941. The 1st company split its platoons with one going to *Einsatzkommando* 2; the second platoon to *Einsatzkommando* 3, and the 3rd platoon along with the company commander went to the headquarters of *Einsatzgruppe* A.

The 1st platoon was active in Libau (June 29, 1941) and Windau. They also visited Siauliai in July 1941. From Siauliai they went to Mitau and ended up in Riga where the 3rd platoon and the company commander were. In November they were in Tosno. The 2nd platoon was in Kovno in July 1941 and sent a squad of men to Dünaberg, Ostrow, and Pleskau. The 3rd Platoon and company commander were stationed in Krasnogwardeisk which was the headquarters of *Einsatzgruppe* A. In November the 3rd platoon was still in Riga.

Einsatzgruppen A was also assisted by the Arajis *Kommando* named after its Latvian creator Viktors Arajs. Together with the 1st and 2nd platoon of the 1st company they were employed as part of *Einsatzkommando* 2 and busy killing Jews and communists in the Hochwald/Bickernicker Wood. During July and August 1941 they killed at least 5,000 people. The 1st company, SD, Security Police, and the Arajis commando continued executions in these woods through December 1941.

September 24, 1941: The 1st company, eight *Gendarmerie*, and SD personnel visited a hospital for the mentally ill in Krasnogwardeisk were they assisted in the death of 500 to 800 patients by lethal injection.

Einsatzgruppe A killed 250,000 Jews in ten months.

The 2nd company was assigned to *Einsatzgruppen* B that worked in the Minsk area. The company headquarters staff consisted of one officer, ten NCOs' and eight enlisted. The 2nd company, 1st and 2nd platoon were in Mogilew working with *Einsatzkommando* 8. The 1st platoon participated in 7 or 8 actions. Both platoons participated in a large action with Police Battalion 316 in Mogilew where 3,726 Jews were killed.

The 2nd company was in Tschernjowka, Stolpce, and Tscherwen in August and September 1941 where they were busy killing Jews. They killed over 400 Jewish men, women, and children. September and October 1941 found the 2nd company killing people in Iwenez (fifty Jews), (632) patients in a hospital in Minsk, Krugloje (thirty-one Jews), Marina Gorka (seventy) Usbeken, Tatars, and Jews, Schidow (627 Jews). In November 1941 they killed 900 Jews in Mstislawl and in Rudnja 835 Jews. They then returned to Mogilew where they continued killing Jews.

The 1st Platoon leader was 1st Lt. Paul Dinter. This platoon (aprox. twenty men) worked with *Einsatzkommando* 8 and *Sonderkommando* 1b. He was an SS member (1941) and later battalion commander of the I/SS Police Regiment 14.

The 2nd Platoon leader was 1st Lt. Dölle. His platoon worked with *Einsatzkommando* 8 and *Vorkommando* Moscow. *Einsatzkommando* 8 was in Bialystok, Slonim and Baranovichi. From August 6 to September 9, 1941 it was in Minsk and then moved to Mogilev which became its headquarters. It operated in southern Byelorussia and sent units like these platoons to Bobruisk, Gomel, Roslavl, and Klinzy. The 2nd company also worked with Army Security Division 221.

The 2nd Platoon was active in Kovno. Kovno was and is still ringed with forts in the northwest area of the city built by the Russians to defend the approaches from invasion from the west. These forts served a number of purposes for the Germans with the primary one being a holding area for executions. At least 80,000 people died here, most of them Jews. The forts are numbered and the most infamous ones are IV, VII, and IX. The 2nd Platoon beginning July 1941 began executing a large number of those 80,000 people.

The 2nd platoon was assigned to a squad-sized unit in *Einsatzkommando* 3 and along with SD personnel and others killed 9,012 Jews and 573 communists in Pogulanka from July 7, 1941 to August 21, 1941

The 3rd platoon of the 2nd company was assigned to *Einsatzkommando* 9 that had a strength of 120-150 personnel. This consisted of; 12-15 SS officers; 30-40 Gestapo, Criminal Police, and SD; 15-20 support staff; one platoon of Waffen-SS (Reserve); this platoon consisted of thirty men under Sergeant Richard Neubert.

The 3rd platoon was in Minsk and on August 15, 1941 was working with *Einsatzkommando* 8 shooting people. They participated in a number of large actions. They were shooting Jews, White Russians, Bolsheviks, and 11 Asians. By September 1941 they had shot at least 5,000 people.

The 3rd company was assigned to *Einsatzkommando* 6, and *Einsatzgruppe* C, in Lvov. *Einsatzgruppe* C was headquartered in Novo Ukrainka and later Kiev and Poltava.

The 2nd Platoon leader was 2nd Lt. Paul Hecker. This platoon was active with *Einsatzkommando* 6. *Einsatzkommando* 6 was active in Krivoi Bog, and the towns of Dnepropetrovsk and Zaporoshye. In November 1941, it was stationed in Stalino. Later 3rd Company replaced 4th company in December 1941 and split into *Einsatzkommandos* and continued the work of killing civilians with *Einsatzgruppe* D until January 1943.

The 4th company was assigned to *Einsatzgruppe* D. *Einsatzgruppe* D was active in the Caucasus and the Black Sea area. The 4th company was transported by rail to Duben, northeast of Leipzig with all its vehicles and weapons. They then traveled by truck to Romania in July 1941. There the company was split into five *Einsatzkommandos* and a HQ guard staff.[2]

April 1942: In Tosno the 4th company executed twenty-five Jewish men.

In December 1941, the 4th Company was recalled, as were all the various commandos now based in the Crimea and around the north shores of the Sea of Azov. They assembled in Cherson, and traveled by rail to Poland for R&R in the ski resort of Zakopane. Afterwards they were then posted to Norway where they finished the war as the III/Police Regiment 27.[3]

Reichsführer-SS Heinrich Himmler witnessed his first live execution in Minsk on August 15th, 1941. Himmler had not seen combat during World War I so this was his first known time seeing people shot at close range. Most accounts written of this encounter have stated that he did not find it to be a pleasant experience. This battalion and *Einsatzkommando* 8 provided the shooters for the event.

After watching the executions he realized that his men needed a more humane way of dispatching their victims. Not out of concern for the victims of course, rather to alleviate the toll it was taking on the Germans who were pulling the trigger. History shows us that his "humane" solution was the gas chamber.

Police Battalion 9's war diary records over 186,735 victims either killed or deported to concentration camps.

Regiment/Battalion Location and Activities
1939: Prague, Czechoslovakia

May 1940: In Oslo, Norway and then transferred to Poland in June 1940.

July 1942: Back in Oslo, Norway. Although Curilla has the entire regiment participating in Operation "Adler" until August 1942.

1944: Kongsvinor, Norway.

1945: At the end of the war the men of the battalion were interned in a British POW camp.

January 17, 1947: The British transferred 247 men of the battalion to the Soviet Union where 170 of them received a 10-25 year sentence in a work camp.

Police Battalion 10 (Reserve)
The battalion was formed from personnel from Berlin in August 1939.

Field Post Number(s): Unknown
Battalion Commander(s): Major Küstner (1939 to 1942), Major Theodore Stahr (May 1942 to ?),[1] Major Woytewitz (1942 to ?)
Other Officer(s): The 1st company commander was 1st Lieutenant Rehbein in 1942.
This battalion formed III/ Police Regiment 1 in July 1942.

In July, 1943 the battalion helped form SS Police Regiment "*Griese*" in Marseille, France.

Regiment/Battalion Locations & Activities
In December 1939: The battalion was part of Police Regiment Warsaw.

1939: The battalion was in the following cities; Ostrow, Siedlice, Warsaw; and Lublin.

July, 1940: In Warsaw, Poland.[2]

January 1942: The battalion was transferred to Oberkrain between Ljubljana and Kranj where it joined Police Battalions 171 and 181.

June 30, 1942: Elements of the battalion were supporting an Italian anti-partisan operation in the Horjul area about 7 miles west of Ljubljana, Slovenia.

July 13, to August 1942: The battalion participated in Operation "Enzian" whose mission was to search for and destroy partisan bands from the mountains and forests west of Ljubljana centered on the Horjul area. For the most part, the partisans evaded the sweep.

July 1942: The battalion was stationed in Kamnik, Slovenia.

August 1 1942: The battalion is in Stein. Stein was where Police Regiment 19 was also stationed. The 1st company is in Luowitz. The 2nd company is in Obertuchein. The 3rd company is in Streina.

November 11, 1942: The battalion participated in a partisan sweep of the Vransko area that is northwest of Trbovlje in the Celje area.[3]

Police Battalion 11 (Reserve)
The battalion was formed with personnel from the Konigsberg area in September 1939. This was a four company battalion.
Field Post Number(s): 47450, 25505
Commanding Officer(s): Major Franz Lechthaler (1941-1942).[1]

The 1st company commander was Captain Vans Low.

The 1st company platoon leader was Sergeant Willy Schuischel (1942)

The 2nd company commander was Captain Willy Papenkort.[2]

Also a Captain Hans Timm is listed as this company's commander.[3]

The 2nd company platoon leader was Sergeant Heinrich Pasternack.

The 3rd company commander was Captain Alfred Tornbaum.

The 4th company (NSKK) commander was *SS-Obersturmführer* Ludwig Vick (1942)

The battalion on May 5, 1941 was equipped with 4 Model 1908 machine guns.[4]

The battalion helped form the I/Police Regiment 2 in July 1942 in Tilsit, Eastern Prussia.

Einsatzgruppen/Atrocity Activity
November 1939: In Ostrow where the 2nd company killed 156 men, and 208 women and children.

July 1941: The battalion arrived in Kovno, Lithuania and raised 3 companies of Lithuanian auxiliary police (12th Lithuanian *Schutzmannschaft* Battalion or *Schuma*).[5] Two of the four companies of the battalion left for Minsk in September, 1941 taking the auxiliary police with them.

June 1941: The battalion staff is in Kovno. The 1st company is approximately thirty miles from Kovno. The 2nd company is in Kovno quartered in a school. The 3rd company is in Kovno and quartered in the University. The 3rd company detached a platoon for guarding Russian POWs in East Prussia for about six weeks during this time period. This platoon returned in August after spending a day in Pilviskiai (approximately thirty miles from Kovno) during the return trip. While not listed as being present it is highly probable that they participated in what is quoted below. Especially considering 3rd companies history over the next few years:

"On August 27th 1941, early in the morning, all men aged 14-70 years old were rounded up in the market square, the sick being brought on carts. They were kept under heavy guard by armed Lithuanians, who maltreated them during the day. At nine o'clock in the evening they were led back to the barn.

"The next day, Thursday the 28th, at three o'clock before dawn, all men were taken out of the barn. The ten artisans were sent to the sewing shop, whereas 200 were given spades and told that they were being sent to Germany for digging peat. They were taken to a place about 1.5 km from town and ordered to dig two big pits. After completing the job they were shot by order of the local police commander and buried in the pits they had just dug. On Friday, the 29th of August, 500 men including Jews from neighboring villages and twenty young intelligent women from Pilvishok, were shot too. Among the victims was Dr. Moshe Dembovsky, a reserve Colonel of the Lithuanian army, who had fought during the Lithuanian independence war. Before he was shot he told the Lithuanian murderers that their crimes would not be forgotten and that the blood of the innocent victims would forever call for revenge, in response to which the Lithuanians cracked his head with the butts of their rifles. All the victims were piled into one of the pits, the other was left empty. The Lithuanians took the valuables of the victims for themselves." Total number of dead is approximately 800 Jews.

July 1941: The 1st company is stationed in Mariampol, Lithuania until December 1941.

September 1941: The 3rd company was operating in Mlawa and Kovno. The 1st or 2nd platoon returned to Pilviskiai in September 1941 to finish killing the Jews:

"On September 14th it was rumored that the next day something was about to happen. Seventy women escaped and hid in surrounding villages. On the next day, the 15th of September 1941 (23rd of Elul 5701) the women and children were ordered to leave their houses and for each to take a small parcel with them, having been told that they were going to be transferred to the Kovno Ghetto. They were assembled in the market square, the ten men who worked for the German "Kommantantur" and the rest of the men were also included. Among them was also the pharmacist Bolnik, who guessed what was going to happen and swallowed the poison he had prepared before. All, including the two Rabbis, were led to the empty pit. While being beaten, they were forced to undress and then they were shot, and the children were thrown into the pit alive. By evening the murderers returned to the town singing the Lithuanian anthem."[10]

September 1941: The 3rd company guarded the Kovno ghetto assisted by Lithuanian auxiliaries.

In Slutsk where the battalion working with *Einsatzkommando* 3 killed at least 1,000 people.[6] This battalion was constantly providing men to *Einsatzkommando* 3 for actions during the next year.

October 6, 1941 to December 1941: The 3rd company supported by Lithuanian auxiliary police units, a GFP 640 (Secret Field Police) unit, and Pioneer Company 707 in Minsk were they killed 19,000 civilians during this period.

October 1941: In Rudensk Uzlany where they killed another 800 "partisans, Communists, Jews, and other suspicious riffraff" were killed. They were assisted in this by the GFP 640 and two companies of Lithuanian police auxiliaries.

October 6, 1941 to December 1941: Assisted in killing at least 1,300 people in the community of Smilowicze.

October 6, 1941 to December 1941: Assisted in killing 625 civilian prisoners killed at a prison camp in Minsk.

October 6, 1941 to December 1941: The 2nd and 4th company killed 1,150 Communists in another camp near Minsk.

October 6, 1941 to December 1941: Elements of the battalion kill 1,000 Jews in Koydanov.

October 6, 1941 to December 1941: Approximately 5,000 Jews were herded into ditches outside the city of Slutsk and executed.

October 6, 1941 to December 1941: The battalion assists in killing approximately 6,600 Jews in the Minsk ghetto in order to make room for Jews arriving from Germany.

The total death count for this battalion is estimated to be 37,346.

Regiment/Battalion Locations & Actions
1939: The battalion staff and the 1st company are in Pultusk, Poland. The 2nd company is in Ostrolenka. The 3rd company is in Mlawa.

January 1942: The battalion minus the 3rd company which remains in Kovno is needed to help contain the Soviet counter offensive and is on the front line in the Newel, Welikije Luky, and Toropez area. They were in this area until April or May 1942.

May 1942: The 2nd company is fighting partisans near Klitschew and Suscha.

January-February 1943: Elements of the battalion are providing security for the Minsk to Slutsk road.

February 8, 1943: Active with SS and Police *Kampfgruppe* "von dem Bach." Active in Operation "Hornung," and "Cottbus."[7] This battalion formed *Kampfgruppe* "East" together with three other *kampfgruppes* were used for Operation "Hornung." *Kampfgruppe* "West" also included Police Battalion 13 (II/1), and 22 (III/2), 1st SS Infantry Brigade, and the Druzhina SS. For further details on Operation "Hornung" see the entry for Police Battalion 13.

March 31, 1943: Active with SS and Police *Kampfgruppe* "Schimana." During this period they were conducting anti-partisan operations in the swampy area near Beresina north of Borissow.

April 17-24, 1943: The regiment participates in Operation "*Zauberflöte*" (Magic Flute). See Police Battalion 85 for more details.

August 5-15, 1943: They participated in Operation "Herman" in the Naliboki Forest area west of Minsk. The Naliboki Forest area was home to a well-organized resistance. Among the resistance forces a large Jewish partisan force established itself with the ranks filled with Jews who had managed to escape the Germans and survive their encounters with other partisan groups who often saw them as enemies. Of the partisans the Bielski Brothers had organized a well run and equipped base in the forest. This base was more of a small town including a Synagogue and from it they were able to conduct numerous raids on the Germans.

Units participating were: The entire regiment (2nd), Police Rifle Regiment 31, *Gendarmerie Kommando* z.b.V. Kreikenbom, part of an unknown Police Panzer Company, *Gendarmerie* platoons 7, 13, 19, and 21. Partisan and civilian casualties were 4,280 which included six "bandit" leaders and two Soviet Commissars'. Civilians seized for forced labor was 9,065 men, 7,701 women, and 4,178 children. German casualties were forty-six dead, 112 wounded which included nine officers.

January 20, to March 1, 1944: Active with SS and Police *Kampfgruppe* "von Gottberg." The end of March found them in the Polotsk area.

April 16, 1944 to May 10, 1944: with *Kampfgruppe* "Anhalt" south of the Polotsk area.

November 1944: In Brandenburg.

Police Battalion 12 (Reserve)
Field Post Number(s): 37822
Commanding Officer(s):

Regiment/Battalion Locations & Actions
July, 1942: In Minsk, Russia

Police Battalion 13 (Reserve)
The battalion was formed with personnel from the Konigsberg area in 1939. This was a four company battalion.
Field Post Number(s): 09571 as II/Police Regiment 2.
Commanding Officer(s): Major Hans Griep
2nd Company commander(s): George Rosenstock, 1930 NSDAP Member, 1931 Member SA, 1941 Member SS.
Captain Gustav Adam, 1st company commander. Awarded German Cross in Gold: July 21, 1944

The battalion formed the II/Police Regiment 2 in July 1942 in Tilsit, East Prussia.

Einsatzgruppen/Atrocity Activity
February 1940 to September 1941: The battalion is active with the SS and Gestapo in assisting in the deaths of 16,000

to 18,000 Jews and Poles near Kammersdorf and Bialuty, Poland.

May 1940: Elements of the battalion shot an unknown number of Poles in the woods by Bursz, Poland.[1]

July 19, 1941: The 2nd and 3rd company are stationed in Plock and detailed to ghetto security. Here they were active processing Poles per Operation "Tannenbaum" for transportation to the camps. A platoon of the 2nd company was detached and sent to Königsberg and then Riga.

July 22, 1941: The 2nd company arrives in Libau. The company at this time had a strength of 120 men and a contingent of 75 Volksdeutche attached as auxiliaries. The company was detailed to the SD and began mass executions. These executions were filmed by an amateur photographer, Reinhard Wiener (Marine FlakAbt. 707) and used as evidence in the 2nd company commanders trial.

September-October 1941: The 2nd company detached a platoon for duties in Hajnowka.

November-December 1942: In the Mlawa District, Poland. This battalion helped kill 12,000 Jews during the liquidation of the Mlawa ghetto.[2] This was a roundup and transportation action for the battalion and it took place in phases.

The first phase began on November 10, 1942 with a consolidation of the Jews from surrounding areas. All work outside the ghetto had been stopped and the Jews were returned from the labor camps in Ciechanow to the Mlawa ghetto. The elderly and sick of other ghettos were transported to the Mlawa ghetto. Most of these elderly and sick were from Stzegowo ghetto. They were probably deported to Treblinka.

The second phase took place from November 13-17, 1942. This transport was split into two deportations and was sent to Auschwitz. Before these deportations were carried out, the Germans conducted a "selection." The "candidates" for deportation who were being held at the flourmill inside the ghetto were forced to run by the police. Those who did not run as quickly as the police thought they could were shot on the spot or executed near the mill wall. During this selection process the Germans also stripped and robbed the Jews of all their valuables and money.

The third phase which effectively emptied the ghetto took place during the week of November 24, leaving the Mlawa ghetto with only had a couple hundred Jews at most. On November 18, 1942 approximately 5,000 Jews from Makow Mazowiecki were shipped to the nearly empty Mlawa ghetto. They were joined on November 24th 1942 by at least a 1,000 Jews from Stzegowo. They were then shipped to Auschwitz. This took place over several days or weeks.

June 30, 1940: The 3rd company is in Slonim as was *Einsatzkommando* 8.

December 1942: In Plohnen where the battalion assisted in killing 5,000 people.

Regiment/Battalion Locations & Actions
1939: The battalion is in Latvia.

March 1940: The battalion was assembling in Schrottersburg, Germany.[3]

April 1940: In Ploczk, Poland were the battalion was briefly stationed.

August 1941 to Summer 1942: On ghetto guard duty in Bialystok. The battalion staff, 1st, and 3rd company are stationed here. The 2nd company was stationed in Libau, Latvia and later Hajnowka, Poland.

August 1-5, 1942: Participated in Operation "North Pole II" in the Syro Lipki area north of Smolensk. This was an anti-partisan search and destroy operation.

September 24, 1942: The 1st company is in Litowsk where they received four heavy machine guns. They were providing security for the ghetto in Milejczyce. The company was split up with one officer and twenty-three men assigned to the ghetto. This ghetto had a deportation of 1,000 Jews to Treblinka in November. The ghetto in Wysokie/Litowsk was assigned forty men and the ghetto in Kleszczele fourteen men. The Kleszczele ghetto had 400 Jews deported to Treblinka during this time period. These ghettos were consolidated into one ghetto in Litowsk which was then emptied by deportation to Treblinka.

November 1942: A squad from 1st company is in Bialystok and working as an execution squad. The rest of the battalion is in Slonim where the 1st company is detached for Operation "Hamburg."

1943: In Minsk

February 8, 1943: Active with SS and Police *Kampfgruppe* "von dem Bach." Active in Operation "Hornung," "Cottbus" and "Altona."[7] This battalion formed *Kampfgruppe* "East" which together with three other *Kampfgruppes* were used for Operation "Hornung." *Kampfgrupppe* "West" also included Police Battalion 11 (I/1), and 22 (III/2), 1st SS Infantry Brigade, and the Druzhina SS. They were also joined by Special Battalion "Dirlewanger," *Schuma* Battalion 57, Police Signal Company 112, and Police Panzer Company 12.

The operations goal was the elimination of partisan bands in the Pripet Marshes between Slutsk and Gomel and the Brest to Litovsk highway. According to a German report, 2,219 partisans and 7,378 partisan sympathizers were killed as well as 3,300 Jews. The latter may have been hiding out in the marshes with the partisans. German and indigenous auxiliary losses were twenty-nine dead and thirty-eight wounded. The operation confiscated; 9,578 cattle, 844 pigs, 5,700 sheep, 559 horses, and 223 tons of grain. The total number of weapon seized was fourteen pistols and 172 rifles.

August 1943: In Gleboki where they helped kill 3,000 Jews. The entire regiment was then operating with *Kampfgruppe* "Gottberg" along with other units. The *Kampfgruppe* was divided into sections or task groups with the regiment assigned to *Einsatzkommando* "Dirlewanger." They began on August 1, 1943 at 0500 hours and proceeded to Izledz, then Rudnia, Nalibocka, and to Zaborze and Ciechanowszozyzna. Also assigned to the *Kampfgruppe* were SS Police Regiment 2 and Police *Shützen* Regiment 31. They arrived at Gleboki on August 8, 1943.[4]

March 1944: On the front lines near Polozk. The 4 SS Police Division was also in the area fighting as Kampfgroup SS Polizei.

November 1944: In Brandenburg.

February 1945: With the 9th Army.

March 1945: With the 4th Panzer Army.

Police Battalion 22 (Reserve)

This battalion was formed from personnel in the Stettin, Germany area in October 1939. Many of the reservists called to active duty were from Pomerania and Mecklenburg.

Field Post Number(s): 20525, 47348

Commanding Officer(s): Major and SS-*Sturmbannführer* Bruno Walden, Major Ewald Sternagel (1941-1942), Dr. and SS-*Sturmbannführer* Heinrich Kupetz (1942 to ?).

Major Walden was decorated with the Knight's Cross on January 1, 1945 and the German Cross in Gold on November 11, 1944.

Other Officer(s): The 1st company commander was Wilhelm Steinberg (rank unknown)[1]

The battalion formed the III/Police Regiment 2 in July 1942 in Tilsit, East Prussia.

Einsatzgruppen/Atrocity Activity

1940: In Thorn, where they guarded Jewish and Polish prisoners in Fort 7 and they were also assisting the Gestapo with raids and arrests. They also participated in the shooting of prisoners and hostages Thorn had a large POW camp that at its peak held 20,000 men.

September 1941: The battalion had returned to Stettin previously and now was returning to the east for another tour of duty. On September 17, 1941 the battalion reported that its companies were distributed to the following cities. The 1st company was in Frauenburg and Goldingen. The Jews of Goldingen (Latvia) were eliminated in two mass executions by the end of 1941. Most of the young men had been conscripted into Soviet Army so those left behind for execution were the elderly women and children. The first and largest execution began by having the Jews assemble in the towns' synagogue where they were then marched into the Padura Forest about two miles from town where they were shot and then buried in a pit. The 2nd company was in Riga. The 3rd company and the battalion staff were in Mitau.

November-December 1941: The battalion was in Riga, Lithuania were it assisted in executing 25,000 people.[2] The Rumbula forest was used as the killing site. The 2nd and 3rd company provided the German manpower for assembling the Jews, checking their homes to make sure no one was hiding, and marching them to the killing site. The 3rd company also provided security at the site during the killing.

February 1943: In Slutsk where the battalion assisted in executing 3,000 people, most of them were women and children.

August 1943: In Gleboki, Poland where as part of SS and Police *Kampfgruppe* "von Gottberg" they assisted in killing at least 3,000 Jews. See Police Battalion 13 for more details.

Regiment/Battalion Locations & Actions
1939: The battalion is in Poland.

November 1941: The 3rd company was stationed in Jelgava, Latvia.

September 1941 to January 1942: The battalion was in North Russia and Latvia. The companies were split among Mitau, Riga, and Frauenberg. Mitau had 1,500 Jews killed in August 1941. Frauenberg was also the site of a small work camp.[3]

January-September 1942: The battalion was on the front line and in combat with Police Regiment North and the 81st Infantry division. Their sector was in the Ilmensee/Straja (Leningrad) area near the village of Selishchenskoe.

October 1942: The battalion operating in the Stalino area.

January 5-14, 1943: This battalion, the 307, and all of Police Regiment 13 participated in Operation "Franz" which was primarily a labor sweep for bodies to be sent back to the Reich for forced labor work.

February 1943: The battalion participated in Operation "Hornung," along with the rest of the regiment, the 1st SS infantry, and the Druzhina SS as part of *Kampfgruppe* "East." This operation was similar to any other German anti-partisan operation in that the primary casualties were civilians. See Police Battalion 13 for further details.

March 2-21, 1943: This battalion along with Police Battalion 307 participated in Operation "Föhn I and II" (Warm Winter Wind) south of the Brest to Slutsk highway. This was primarily a roundup of people to be used for forced labor. Approximately 1,226 people were deported.

May 2-7, 1943: The battalion, along with part of unknown Police Panzer Company engaged in Operation "Gunther" near Lagoisk and Rudnja in the Manyly Forest area.

March 1944: In Polozk on the front lines.

November 1944: In Brandenburg.

(See Police Battalion 13 for 1945.)

Police Battalion 32 (Reserve)
The battalion was created using personnel from Berlin in Minsk in December 1942.
Field Post Number(s): 27969
Commanding Officer: Major Leo von Braunschweig (1941-1942), Major Siegfried Binz (1942 to 1943). The major was awarded the German Cross in Gold on May 26, 1943.[1]
They were originally assigned to Police Regiment Böhmen. On December 22, 1941 they were assigned to Police Regiment Center. Later they became the I/Police Regiment 21.

Einsatzgruppen/Atrocity Activity
September 1941: In Lvov where the battalion shot at least 1,000 people.[2]

Regiment/Battalion Locations & Activities
December 1941: The battalion arrived in Minsk.

1941: In Lvov.

January 19, 1941: The battalion was in Juchnow.

April 1941: In Prague, Czechoslovakia.

August 1941: Police Regiment Center is ordered to take up positions east of Slutsk. Here with the 252 Infantry Division they stopped the breakout attempt of the 12 Russian Infantry Division.[3]

April 1942: Part of a *Kampfgruppe* sent to relieve an encircled German army unit in Beresina, Russia.

May 16, 1942: The battalion was dissolved, possibly as a result of its encounter with a Soviet paratroop regiment or division on January 23, 1942. Any men fit for field duty were transferred to Police Battalion 308.

Police Battalion 33 (Reserve)
Field Post Number: 47797
Commanding Officer(s): Major Dall, Lt. Colonel H. Braschnevitz.[1]
This battalion used Baltic Germans extensively to fill its ranks.

Einsatzgruppen/Atrocity Activity
July 14, 1942: The battalion or elements of it provided security along with Ukrainian auxiliaries for a transport of Jews from the Riga ghetto to the rail station using wagons.

Summer 1942: The battalion was in Rowno and Kiev. In Rowno they were on ghetto watch duty.

Regiment/Battalion Locations & Actions
July 1941: The 1st company was in Frankfurt. The rest of the battalion was in Lvov and Rowno. Later the 1st company was transferred to Police Battalion 320 and was stationed in Rowno from 1942-1943. It may have ended up becoming Police Company Rowno.[2]

October 1941: Sent to Lvov, Poland.

August-October 1941: Active as Reserve Police Battalion "Ostland." Later the battalion was renamed Police Battalion 33 in the summer of 1941 and it was then active in the Baltic area.
July 1942: Arrived in Riga.

February 1943: In Revel, Estonia with Police Battalion 293.

March to July 1944: Police Watch Battalion, Revel, Estonia.

Police Battalion 41 (Reserve)
The battalion is formed from Leipzig, Dresden, Halle, and Chemnitz area personnel in October 1939.
Field Post Number(s): 32649
Commanding Officer(s): Major Sternhagel, Major Kopka, Major Walter Seltz.[1]
2nd Company, 1st Platoon: 2nd Lieutenant Kurt Bruckner, 1st Lieutenant Henrich.[2]

The battalion was in Poland in 1939 as the I/ Police Regiment 3 and attached to Police Group 3, AOK 8. The battalion formed the I/Police Regiment 22 in July 1942 in Warsaw.

Part of the battalion was used to form the I/25 Police Regiment. They had a mounted police squad or platoon.

Einsatzgruppen/Atrocity Activity
September 18, 1939: In Przemysl, Poland. The battalion executed seven men during a partisan sweep.[3] Przemysl fell to the Germans on September 15, 1939 an *Einsatzkommando* 1 was active there almost immediately killing Jews and members of the Polish intelligentsia per Heydrichs Operation "Tannenburg" orders.

September-October 1939: In Lodz were members of the battalion as stated in the DDR War Crimes trials "Participation in the execution of a total of 107 Polish men in the course of three execution operations as well as participation in the public hanging of three Polish men."

November 1941 to February 1942: The 1st company was on ghetto duty in Kutno.

June 1942: The 3rd platoon of the 1st company killed 40-50 women outside of Krasnik in a wooded area. The 1st company shot ten Polish men.

August 1942: The 3rd platoon of the 1st company shot ten women and children in Krasnik. The women were from 30-60 years old and the children's ages 4-6 years old.

November 1942: The battalion or elements of it assisted in a ghetto action in Krasnik where 200 Jews died. The Jewish ghetto in Krasnik was completely liquidated by November 1942. The 5,000 Jews who lived in it were shipped in a series of actions starting in April 1942 to Belzec concentration camp. The 1st company killed approximately 100 men and women and provided security for the march to the train station for the deportation. They were assisted by Ukrainian auxiliaries, SD, and motorcycle gendarmerie personnel.[4]

April 19 to May 8, 1943: The battalion is in Warsaw providing security and assisting in the deportation of Jews from the ghetto to the train station. The 1st company provided 40-50 men that killed 3,587 people during this action which was the third and final stage of ghetto liquidation. The battalion remained in Warsaw until June 9, 1943.

November 1943: The battalion assisted in Operation "*Erntefest*" (Harvest Festival) which began at dawn on

November 3, 1943. The Trawniki and Poniatowa labor camps were surrounded by SS and police units. Jews were then taken out of the camps in groups and shot in nearby pits dug for this purpose. At Majdanek, Jews were first separated from the other prisoners. They were then taken in groups to nearby trenches and shot. Jews from other labor camps in the Lublin area were also taken to Majdanek and shot. Music was played through loudspeakers at both Majdanek and Trawniki to drown out the noise of the mass shooting. The killing operation was completed in a single day at Majdanek and Trawniki. At Poniatowa the shootings took two days. Approximately 42,000 Jews were killed during "*Erntefest*." They were assisted by the 101st Motorized *Gendarmerie* Battalion and a mounted police squad from their regiment.[5]

Regiment/Battalion Locations & Actions

June 3, 1939: The battalion was assigned two armored car platoons while in Amsterdam. The armored cars stayed in Amsterdam when the battalion rotated out and were used by the incoming battalion (PB 254).[6]

September 9, 1939: The battalion was commended for its actions in the capture of Lodz, and the protection of 8th Army's flank.

September 1939 to December 1940: The battalion was stationed in Lodz.

December 1940 to March 1941: The battalion returned to Leipzig.

March 3, 1941 to April 30, 1942: Attached to Police Headquarters and stationed in Posen.

June 1942: The 1st company has a platoon each in Krasnik, Zaklikow, and Janow. The 3rd platoon was in Warsaw before being transferred to Krasnik.

June 1942: Elements of the battalion are in Zamosc.

July 1942: The battalion is in Warsaw.

June 10, 1943: The 3rd platoon is in Chlewiska and the 1st platoon and company commander in Konskie.

July 1944: The battalion was destroyed in Russia (Army Group Center) and disbanded December 21, 1944 in Danzig. See Police Battalion 61 for more details.

Police Battalion 42 (Reserve)

Battalion formed with personnel from the Leipzig, Dresden, Halle, and Chemnitz area.
Field Post Number(s): 31338, 03634
Active in Poland in 1939 as the IV/Police Regiment 2 and attached to Police Group 2, AOK 10.[1]
Later they were attached to Police Regiment Radom.
The battalion formed Police Regiment I/17 in July 1942 in Northern Russia.

Regiment/Battalion Locations & Actions

August 1941: The battalion is in Eindhoven, Netherlands.

July 1942: In Russia in the Army Group North area of operations. This battalion is under operational control of HSSPF Russia North until November 1942.

October 27-29, 1943: In the Starachovice, Poland area.

February 1944: Active in the Ukraine.

June 1944: In Warsaw, Poland.

July 2-12, 1944: The entire regiment was attached to SS *Kampfgruppe* "von Gottberg." The rapid advance of Soviet forces compelled a withdrawal southwest toward Grodno before the end of the day. Campaign maps show SS Police Regiment 17 in an ever-shrinking defensive line just north of Grodno until the city had to be given up.[2]

August-October 1944: The regiment was engaged fighting against the Resistance (Polish Home Army) in Warsaw.

September 1944: The battalion was attached to the 73rd Infantry Division that was part of the 9th Army. This was the 2nd version of the 73rd Infantry. The original division was destroyed in Sevastopol in May 1944. This version lasted until September 1944 when it was destroyed by the Soviets during their assault on the Praga suburb of Warsaw.

November 1944: The entire regiment, or what was left of it, was ordered to transfer from Warsaw, to Slovenia.

November 1944: This battalion was transferred to Slovenia and by November 27, 1944 was engaged in operations in the mountains north of Sostanj, about eleven miles northwest of Celje. This was the only unit of the regiment in Slovenia at this time, with the remainder arriving during December.

March 20, 1945: The battalion was stationed in Slovenska Bistrica, which is about fourteen miles northeast of Celje, Slovenia.

March 30, 1945: The battalion is moved from Slovenska Bistrica to Kranj, which is north of Ljubljana in Oberkrain.

April 22, 1945: The entire regiment is engaged against the Partisan 7th Corps units around Grcarice just to the west of Kocevje.

Police Battalion 43 (Reserve)
Field Post Number(s): Unknown
Regiment/Battalion Locations and Activities
December 1939: In Lublin, an assigned to Police Regiment Lublin.
August 1940: The battalion is transferred to Warsaw.

Police Battalion 44 (Reserve)
The battalion was formed with personnel from Leipzig and Halle area in 1939.
Field Post Number(s): 39202, 33345
The battalion was in Lodz, Poland in 1939.
The battalion was issued eight Model 1908 machine guns on May 5, 1941.[1]
The battalion formed IV/ Police Regiment 27 in 1942. In June 1943 it became the I/SS Police Regiment 27.

Einsatzgruppen/Atrocity Activity
November 11-24, 1939: In Lodz where members of the battalion killed seventy-seven Poles and Jews in two execution operations at a rifle range near Lodz.[2]

Regiment/Battalion Location and Activities
May 1940: In Lodz.

April 1941: In Dresden, Germany.

December 1941: The battalion was transferred from Germany to Skofja Loka, which is about five miles southwest of Kranj in Oberkrain.[3]

December 27, 1941 to January 12, 1942: The battalion together with Police Battalions 93, 171, 181, 325, and *Landesschützen* Battalion 322 and 857, took part in the first large anti-partisan operation in Slovenia. It occurred in the mountains and wooded terrain between Ljubljana and Kranj and was aimed at destroying the Gorenjski Partisan Battalion which had been recruiting in the area and raiding the German garrison towns.

July 1942: Transferred to Oslo, Norway.

June 1943: This battalion is still in Oslo while the other two battalions of the regiment are in Halden and Konigvinger.

Police Battalion 45 (Reserve)
The battalion is formed in the Aussig, Germany area primarily with reserves from the Sudetenland.
Field Post Number(s): 37718
Commanding Officer(s): Major Franz (1941), Major Martin Besser (1941 to ?), Major Rosenbauer (?)
2nd Company Commander(s): Captain Englebert Kreuzer

The battalion was active in Poland in 1939.

The battalion was attached to Police Regiment South in 1941.

In July 1942 the battalion became the I/ Police Regiment 10.

Einsatzgruppen/Atrocity Activity
July 28, 1941: In Schepetovka, Ukraine. At least seventy Jews were killed here. Stefan Klemps book states at least seventy while the Simon Wiesenthal Center lists the Jewish population of Schepetovka as 3,916 in 1926. The Center records that all Jews who had not fled by the summer of 1941 were killed.

September 1941: In Slawuta where they assisted in killing 522 people.

September 1941: In Sudylow where they killed 471 people.[2]

September 1941: In Berdichev, Ukraine where the number of victims was reported at 272 to 1,000. In this action they provided cordon security, escorts, and shooters. An unknown

SS Regiment was flown in by Junker 52s to do most of the shooting, HSSPF Jeckeln was in attendance. He was a mass murderer who called his method of killing "*Sardinenpackung*" or sardine packing. This is because he would have the victims lie down and then shoot them. Then the next group would be escorted in and then he would have them lie down on top of them. By the end of August 1941 he had personally supervised the murder of 44,000 human beings.

The following description of what happened is taken from the account written by Russian author Vasily Grossman whose mother was one of the casualties of this action:[3]

> "This action like many other ones took place over a period of a couple weeks. Berdichevs Jews had been forced into the ghetto a week earlier. On September 4, 1941 the Germans ordered 1,500 young Jews to prepare for an agricultural work assignment. They were assembled and told if they were good they might be able to bring a few potatoes back to the ghetto when they completed the work. They were then marched off and shot between Lysaya Gora and the village of Khazina."

On September 14, 1942 units from an SS Regiment arrived. On September 15, the SS and Police drove the inhabitants of the ghetto into the market square. Those who were too old or crippled were shot inside their houses. The remaining people were herded into the market square. Pits had already been dug in preparation at the end of Brodskaya Street. Then four hundred people were selected, taken to the pits, and shot.

September 1941 Babi Yar, Ukrainian auxiliary police assisted this battalion in the shooting of 33,000 Jews. They were also assisted by Police Battalion 303.[4]

This battalion is responsible for the deaths of 65,045 people.[5]

Regiment/Battalion Locations & Activities

January 1942: The battalion was in Poltava. Poltava at this time was the headquarters of Army Group South.

1943: In Kupiansk, Ukraine.

May 12, to June 18, 1943: The entire regiment, SS Police Regiment 11, 10 Police Panzer Company, *Einsatzgruppe* D *Kampfgruppe* "Bierkamp", and a Slovakian Security Division participated in Operation "Weichsel I and II" in the Dnjepr/Pripjet Marsh area. This was a labor roundup and rear area zone clearance operation. The totals were 10,442 people evacuated and 18,860 people sent into forced labor. There were 1,114 "bandits" killed with eighty-nine camps found in the woods, 105 bunkers, and a 115 field positions cleared.

August 2, 1943: Operating as part of *Kampfgruppe* "von dem Bach."

1944: In Rovno, Ukraine.

January-February 1944: Operating near Kustyn, Ukraine.

March 15, 1944: In Brody.

April 1944: In Kostopol, Ukraine.

May 1944: In Stanislawczik, Poland.

August 1944: The battalion was transferred to Slovenia.[6]

Police Battalion 51 (Reserve)

The battalion was formed with personnel from the Stuttgart area in September 1940 in Strasburg.
Field Post Number(s): 09414
Commanding Officer(s): Major Fritz Walkhoff
The battalion had one armored car platoon assigned to it in June 1940.[1]
The battalion formed the I/14th Police Regiment in 1942. On November 3, 1942 troops from the battalion, eighty-four Ukrainians, and 226 Russians from *Schutzmannschaft* Front Battalion 53 were used to create *Schutzmannschaft* Front Battalion 55 under the command of this battalion.

Einsatzgruppen/Atrocity Activity

June 15, 1942: The battalion is working with *Einsatzkommando* 8 and *Sonderkommando* Dirlewanger in Borki and the area around it. On June 26, 1942 they were in Belynitschi Golowtschin.[2]

Regiment/Battalion Locations and Activities

December 1939: In Radom, Poland.

June 1940: The battalion is in Pionki.

September 1940: The battalion returns to Strasburg.

May 1941: The battalion was in Czechoslovakia.

April 1942: The battalion was in Rzeszow.

August 17-29, 1942: The entire regiment is participating in Operation "Grief" along with the Police Regiment 13. See Police Battalion 6 for more details.

November 7, 1942: The battalion stormed and captured a partisan base near Slutsk after thirty-four hours of continuous fighting. The battalion lost eighteen police and one tank in this engagement.

November 13, 1942: The battalion returns to Minsk.[3]

November 1942: On the frontline with the Italian division "Tridentino."

December 1942: The battalion was operating near Iwanowka, Poland.

June 15, 1942: The battalion is participating in Operation "Potsdam" along with *Sonderkommando* Dirlewanger north of Bobruisk.

June 26, 1942: Participated in an unnamed operation near Gorodok.

September 1942: In Mogilew where they were stationed.

October 10-24, 1942: The entire regiment participated in Operation "Karlsbad" near Borissow, Orscha, and Tscherwen along with the 2 Police Panzer Company. Enemy casualties were 546 dead and fifty-five prisoners. German casualties were twenty-seven dead and sixty-four wounded.

November 27, 1942: This battalion and the III/14 (PB 313) moved to the front and into the sector occupied by the 8th Italian Alpini Army Corp and established contact with the Italian Division Tridentino near Bassawka on the Don River. They were assigned a 15cm howitzer battery, two mortar companies, and one panzer hunter company to provide additional support.

December 15, 1942: The battalion is ordered to Iwanowka to join Wehrmacht units (385 I.D.) who are engaged in fighting the Russians. They are accompanied by the II/14 (Police Battalion 122) that had a machine gun platoon and a PAK platoon. They also had the 14th Panzer company (Police) and a communications company attached. The regimental headquarters staff and commander caught up with them on December 17, 1942 when they were approximately five miles to the east of Iwanowka. They continued to move towards the town along with Italian units who were being rushed to the front in piecemeal fashion. They then engaged Russian forces that overran them. The regiments involved lost 50% of their officers and men in one day here. The regimental commander, Lt. Colonel Buckman was captured on December 19, 1942 and the regiment shattered.

What was left of the regiment regrouped in Mitrofanowka where they were used to help form *Kampfgruppe* "Grimm." They were joined on December 25, 1942 by the remainders of the I/6. The II/14 was then attached to *Kampfgruppe* "Führer Begleit Battalion *Grossdeutschland*." The remaining pieces of the regiment had reformed and received a new regimental commander Lt. Col. Peter. By the end of January the regiment was by Kupjansk. Police Regiment 15 was also in the same area and had also been shattered. What was left of the 15th regiment was collected in Kharkov and sent to *Kampfgruppe* "Josten" on January 8, 1943. By the middle of January 1943 the remnants of 14th Police Regiment, 15th Police Regiment, and the 6th Police Regiment were formed into *Kampfgruppe* "Josten." Two weeks later the same units formed *Kampfgruppe* "Nord" in or around Kupjansk and then took up positions near Dwuretschnaja.

The positions were held briefly as the regiments were pulled off the front line. Police Regiment 14, or what was left of it (a company) returned to Mogilew where they had a brief rest period before becoming the new I/24 in February 1943. On February 2, 1943 Lt. Col. Valtin, the commander of the 6th Police Regiment took command of the remaining remnants of the 14th, the 6th, 15th, and II/8 which was then ordered to Berditschew. They were then ordered to back to Aldershorst, Germany to form a new 14th regiment using Police Lehrbattalion III and the regimental staff of the old 6th Police Regiment.

The regiment was accused of performing poorly by the 8th Italian Army while under attack from an inferior force. The German army sent Himmler a report stating that, "the regiment performed badly, allowing itself to be surrounded and only escaped after discarding most of its equipment. It then took up a defensive position where it employed primitive tactics and preparedness; it was surprised and beaten by two Russian companies." It is unclear whether the surviving officers were courtmartialed.

On April 4, 1943 the new SS Police Regiment 14 left for Marseille to join SS Police Regiment "Griese." The new 14th besides its regular companies had a mortar and tank hunter company. The new I/SS Police Regiment 14 was still being assembled in September 1943 in Stuttgart under its new commander Lt. Col. Hemminger.[4]

1944: Fighting partisans in Slovenia.

April 1945: Helped form 35th SS Division.

Police Battalion 53 (Reserve)
The battalion was formed with personnel from the Mullhausen and/or the Stuttgart area.
Field Post Number(s): 39947
Commanding Officer(s): Major Fechner (1941-1942), Major Schöppe (1942 to May 1943)
The battalion formed the III/Police Regiment 22 in July 1942 in Warsaw, Poland.
The battalion was responsible for the deaths of 7,000 people and the deportations of 5,529.[1]

Regiment/Battalion Locations & Activities
May 1941: The battalion was in Czechoslovakia.[2]

October 26, 1941: Operating with the IV Panzer Army.

July 1941: Listed as serving briefly with Police Regiment North in the Riga area.

January 1942: Transferred to the front in the area of Pleskau, and then moved near Staraja Russa where they stayed until September.

January-June 1942: The first company is with Police Battalion 65 in Cholm.[3]

September 1942: The battalion is in Warsaw.

Summer/Fall 1943 to Summer 1944: The battalion is stationed in Warsaw with 3rd company active in Grodzisk and Brwinow. The 1st company is active in Sokolow, Lochow, and Ostrow. The 3rd company was active in the Grodzisk and Brwinow area near Warsaw.

July 1944: Destroyed in Russia and disbanded in December 1944 in Danzig, Germany. See Police Battalion 61 for more details.

Police Battalion 56
This battalion was formed with personnel from the Stuttgart area.
Field Post Number(s): 23418
Commanding Officer: Major Stoetzer, Major Herbert Furck (September 1943 to ?)
The battalion became the I/Police Regiment 16 in November, 1942. In 1943 they helped form the I/SS Police Regiment 3 in the Nederlands.

Regiment Locations & Activities
October 1941: Attached to Police headquarters (BdO) in Prague, Czechoslovakia.

February 17, 1942: The battalion was assigned to *Kampfgruppe* "Jeckeln" to help stop the advance of the Soviet army in the winter of 1941. They, along with troops from V/1 SS Division (LSSAH), and four other Police Battalions were airlifted to the front near Leningrad (Staraja Russa) where they were active with the 122nd Infantry Division.

October 25, to November 15, 1943: Participated in Operation "Heinrich" in the swampy, heavily wooded Lake District between Nevel and the Latvian border. This battalion was assigned to *Kampfgruppe* "Wachtel."[2] The section also included Police Battalion 102, *Ausbildung* Battalion IV, Police Panzer Company 16, Police Regiment Riga, a Police Panzer *Jäger* company, and a SD *Einsatzkommando*. Also attached were two companies of Lithuanian Police, three flak troops, and five PAK (anti-tank) troops. This operation was halted due to a Soviet offensive and the troops assigned instead found themselves fighting the Red Army.[2]

Police Battalion 61 (Reserve)

This battalion was formed with personnel from the Dortmund and Recklinghausen area. The 1st and 2nd companies were all active duty police from Dortmund. The 3rd and 4th company's officers and NCOs' were regulars from Recklinghausen while the rest were reservists who had been called to active duty.

Field Post Number(s): 34383, 06545

Commanding Officer: Major Friedrich Dederky (1939-1942)

1st Company Commander(s): Captain Erich Mehr[1]

2nd Company Commander(s): Captain Julius Wannamacher

3rd Company Commander(s): Captain Hans Kärgel

Active in Poland in 1939 as the I/4 Police Battalion where it was assigned to Police Group 4 in Posen. The battalion helped form the I/Police Regiment 9 in 1942. In 1944 the regiment was destroyed and the remnants were sent to SS Police Regiment 16 in the Balkans.

Einsatzgruppen/Atrocity Activity

October 1939: The battalion was in Kalisch, Poland and assisting in the deportations of Poles as part of the resettlement program.[2]

1940: The 1st company is on guard duty for the Warsaw ghetto.[3]

January-October 1942: Stationed in Warsaw, Poland. Here they were doing ghetto roundups and providing security for the deportations from the train station. They also had their own bar on Krochmalna Street in Warsaw that was decorated with a Jewish star over the bar. The walls had crude anti-semitic drawings of the police and Jews interacting behind the barbed wire.

Regiment/Battalion Locations and Activities

August-September 1939: The battalion was in Gleiwitz. This is where the incident that Hitler used to justify the war with Poland occurred. On August 31, 1939 a radio station was seized by the Germans in Gleiwitz, and an anti-German propaganda broadcast was broadcast over the airwaves. The SS killed a German Polish sympathizer and left his body in front of the station to make it look like the Poles had attacked and seized the radio station to broadcast the propaganda.

September-June 1940: The battalion is working out of Posen.

June 1940: The battalion returned to Germany.

A woman in the Warsaw Ghetto in 1941.

October 1942: The battalion is assigned to the 281 Security Division and fighting partisans in the rear of Army Group North.

October 25, to November 15, 1943: Participated in Operation "Heinrich" in the swampy, heavily wooded lake district between Nevel and the Latvian border. These battalions along with the rest of its regiment were assigned to Section Möller. Also assigned were Estonian Police Battalions 286, 288, 289 and various support units.[4]

July 1944: The regiment was assigned to Army Group North and destroyed in Russia in. This is when Army Group North was crushed by the Soviet Army with the beginning of their offensive on June 22, 1944. Various available Police Regiments and other units were pulled together to form *Kampfgruppe* "Jecklin" near Vydziai. They filled a gap between the 215th Infantry Division and the 3rd Panzer Army and were in action on July 4, 1944. Remnants of the regiment after this battle went to SS Police Regiment 16 in the Balkans.

Police Battalion 62 (Motorized) (Reserve)

The battalion was formed with personnel from the Essen area in 1939.

Field Post Number(s): 20382, 40113

Commanding Officer(s): Major Franz Keller, Major Fritz Kösterbeck, Major Wilhelm Ney

Major Wilhelm Ney took command sometime in 1942 and his Operations Officer (Ia) were Captains Hans Müller and later Captain Matrow.

Other Officers(s): 1st Company Commander: Captain Hans Vogel

2nd Company Commander: 1st Lt. Helmut Bornhöfft. 3rd Company Commander was 1st Lt. Franz Hessel.

Active in Poland in 1939 as the V/Police Regiment 1 where it was assigned to Police Group 1. In December 1939 the battalion became part of Police Regiment Cracow in Poland. Some of the personnel were transferred to Police Battalion 69.

The battalion formed the III/Police Regiment 4 in August 1942.[1]

Later the battalion formed the I/Police Regiment 28 in November 1942.

Regiment/Battalion Locations & Activities
February-September 1940: The battalion is in Königshütte.

October 1940: Part of the battalion was in or near Lille, France. The 1st company was stationed in La Panne, and the 4th company in Hazebrouck, France.

March 1941: The battalion was stationed in Lorient and Le Poldu, France.

September 1941: The battalion was providing security for the building of Atlantic wall.

April-May 1942: The 1st company was in the Netherlands in Hengelo.

November 1942: This battalion was in Brest, France. The II battalion of the regiment was stationed in Riga, Latvia. The III Battalion was stationed in Poltava, Ukraine that was also headquarters of Einsatzgruppe C.[2]

April-May 1943: The 1st company was in the Netherlands in Hengelo. The 2nd company was in Almelo, Netherlands. The 3rd company was in Enshede, Netherlands.

August 1943: All battalions were sent to Marseilles, France.

February 1944: The regiment was transferred from France to Slovenia with the staff in Strazisce, a suburb of Kranj, and the battalion in Kamnik.

April 11-28, 1944: Together with the *Landesschützen* Regiment 184 and other units totaling some 6,000 men, the regiment carried out an operation in the Smartno area to the east of Kamnik, but with little success. As usual, the partisans managed to slip through the cordon and avoid direct confrontation.

August 19, 1944: The regiment and Lehr Regiment Brandenburg set out from Domdale which is about five miles from Ljubljana in five columns in a failed effort to bring two brigades belonging to the Partisan 4th Operations Zone to battle in the Moravska Valley.

October 20-25, 1944: SS Police Regiment 28 "Todt", Lehr Regiment Brandenburg and a battalion of Cossacks swept along the road from Kamnik north to Kamniska Bistrica, but the partisans had dispersed and there was little contact.

December 11, 1944: SS Police Regiment 28 "Todt" and Lehr Regiment Brandenburg assembled in Kamnik, and SS Police Regiment 13 assembled in Crna. The combined force then advanced on the Gornja Savinja Valley to destroy elements of the Partisan 14th Division that had been occupying the villages of Luce, Ljubno as well as other communities along the valley. Several days after the operation began a column from SS Police Regiment 25 and strong elements from Reserve *Gebirgsjäger* Regiment 18 and *Landesschützen* Regiment 18 moved forward from the east and south, driving the partisans from most of the valley.

February-April 1945: The regiment operations were shifted from east of Kranj to the west of Kranj and Ljubljana with sweeps and patrols of the mountains and woods in the vicinity of Skofja Loka, Selca, and Podbrdo.

March 20, 1945: The battalion is in Domdale.

Police Battalion 63 (Reserve)
This battalion was formed with personnel from the Wuppertal area in 1939.
Field Post Number(s): 04703
Commanding Officer: Major Willing (1939-1940), Major Bolte (March-June 1940), Major Hans Scheurenberg (June 1940 to July 1942), Major Hutter (August 1942 to ?)
Other Officer(s): 1st company commander: Captain Greschuchna, 3rd Company, 1st Platoon, 1st Lieutenant August Demling (1940)
Active in Poland in 1939 as the II/Police Battalion 1 with

Police Group 1, AOK 14. In December, 1939 the battalion was assigned to Police Regiment Cracow.
The battalion strength in 1940 was 574 men.

The battalion was scheduled to form the II/Police Regiment 14 in November 1942. Instead Police Battalion 122 took its place and this battalion stayed in Wismar. Police Regiment 14 was formed twice as the original regiment was destroyed in battle. The battalion on December 24, 1942 was assigned to Police Regiment Griese and in April 1943 became the II/SS Police Regiment 14.

Regiment/Battalion Locations & Activities
April-June 1939: The battalion was stationed in Katowice.

September 1939: The 1st company is stationed in Sambor. They would only be in Sambor a brief time as it was turned over to the Soviets as part of the agreement Stalin and Hitler made for the carving up of Poland. The 2nd company was in Auschwitz. The 3rd company was in Lvov.

June 1940: The battalion is in France. A platoon is stationed in Calais. The 1st company is in Lille. The second company is in Douai. The 3rd company is in Arras.

September 1940 to Summer 1941: The battalion is in Metz and quartered in a castle.

August 1941 to March 1942: The battalion is stationed in Essen.

July 1942: The battalion is now in The Hague, Holland.

January 1943: The old Police Regiment 14 is destroyed with the exception of the II/14 (PB 122). The battalion becomes the new II/SS Police Regiment 14 and the entire regiment is in Slovenia on June 3, 1943.

June 4, 1943: The battalion is stationed in Litija east of Ljubljana to counter partisan incursions in the Sava Valley and attacks on the rail line that ran along it.

September 9, 1943: The entire regiment is ordered by III SS Panzer Corps to advance from Zagreb to Karlovac and then to Ogulin to help disarm the Italian units in the area following Italy's capitulation the previous day. The lead elements of the regiment reach Ogulin on September 14, 1943.

October 12, 1943: The battalion and elements of the Panzer Grenadier *Versuchs* (Experimental) Regiment (Motorized) 901 attacked units of the Partisan 8th Division NOVJ (Yugoslav National Liberation Army), in the villages of Josipdol and Skradnik and drove them out. This was the opening phase of a much larger operation called "Wolkenbruch III" that was intended to drive the partisans out of an area they had liberated around Delnice. Included in this operation were elements of the 71 Infantry Division, 1 SS Panzer Division 1st Regiment, 11 SS Panzer Grenadier Division, 162 (Turkish) Infantry Division, the "Hermann Göring" Division, SS Police Regiment 19, and 1,200 Slovene Domobrans. This was a large operation using at least 50,000 men and 110 tanks over four phases with this regiment participating in the 3rd and 4th phases. By the time the operation ended on November 15, the regiment was operating around Kocevje. Operation "Wolkenbruch" was conducted with the usual brutality and many civilians were summarily executed on the spot and their homes and villages burned to the ground.

October 20, 1943: The regiment is reassigned from the III SS Panzer Corps to II SS Panzer Corps.

June 1944: The battalion is in Celje.

February 2, 1945: The battalion.was attacked by partisans in the Stranice area.[2]

March 16, 1945: Most of the regiment was designated SS and Police Grenadier Regiment 91 of the new 35 SS Division and the remainders were disbanded. The remainders were probably the non-German members.

March 20, 1945: The entire regiment is with the 35 SS Division near Guben on the Oder except for I Battalion, which was still in Krsko, Slovenia until March 29, when it departed to join the rest of the Regiment at Guben.

April 27, 1945: The 35 SS Police Grenadier Division had his headquarters overrun near Halbe and was encircled along with other units of the 9th Army. Survivors of the regiment form a *kampfgruppe*, and with the remnants of the 9th Army broke out of the encirclement and headed for American lines about thirty-four miles away to surrender. Some of the battalion may have made it to the Americans while others went into Soviet captivity.

Police Battalion 64 (Reserve)

This battalion formed with personnel from the Essen area in Cologne on October 12, 1939.

Field Post Number(s): 32932, 22732

Commanding Officer(s): Major Adolf Josten (1941-1945)

Other Officer(s): 1st Company commander was 1st Lieutenant Adolf Gross.

2nd Company: 1st Lt./Captain August Huft. 2rd Company: Captain Wilhelm Denker, 3rd Company commander was Captain Otto Ehrmann. 4th Company: 1st Lieutenant Johannes Wirth

This battalion was issued two Model 1908 machine guns on May 5 1941.[1]

This battalion was active in Poland in 1939 were it was being stationed in Wloclawek, Poland.

The battalion formed the I/Police Regiment 5 in July 1942 in Belgrade. The regiment was motorized and it was the primary police unit for the HSSPF in Serbia. Apparently they were not very busy the first year there as the resistance movement was in its infancy.[2]

Einsatzgruppen/Atrocity Activities

In 1939 this battalion was rarely together as the companies were constantly split off with at least two of them operating under the control of BdO, Danzig. Later in November 1939 three companies were active with SS-*Brigadeführer* Christoph Diehm and Friedrich Class who commanded *Einsatzgruppe* V in Poland.[3]

June 1941: In the Belgrade area and attached to *Einsatzgruppe* E.

August 1941: In Skela, Serbia where the 3rd company commander, Lt. Otto Ehrmann and three Police NCOs' were killed by partisans. Skela was burned the next day in retaliation. The following is a quote describing this event is from "The Trials of Major German War Criminals, Volume 7" at Nuremberg, Germany from nizkor.org:

> "In the village of Skela, a communist detachment opened fire at a German military truck. It was established that several of the inhabitants had been watching and saw the preparations for this attack. It was further established that these inhabitants could have warned the nearest station of the Serbian gendarmerie. It was also established that they could have secretly warned the German military trucks against the imminent attempt. The inhabitants did not profit by the opportunity and had thus placed themselves on the side of the criminals. The village of Skela was burned to the ground. Supplies of ammunition exploded in several houses during the fire and this was accepted as a proof of complicity on the part of the inhabitants. All the male inhabitants of the village whose participation in the attack had been proved were shot, and 50 communists were hanged on the spot."

What is interesting is "supplies of ammunition exploded in several houses during the fire..." I can only imagine how this convinced the men of the company of the duplicity of the locals and served to justify in their minds the action taken there and later when conducting searches of other villages.

September 1941: The 1st and 3rd company is stationed in Sabac where they provided security for the concentration camp. The 1st company is recorded as making 400 Jews do a fifteen-mile forced march to Sabac. The Jews were turned over to the 1st company by a German infantry unit. Making their captives do forced marches was not unusual as the Nuremburg trials records several instances were it was used in this area. This quote is taken from the same testimony as above about the burning of the village of Skela:

> "I omit the next five paragraphs and invite the attention of the Tribunal to a short part of the report of the Yugoslav Government dealing with the so called "death march" or "march of blood," that march of dire fame to the camp of Yarak. I quote that particular part which deals with this atrocious crime of the Hitlerites.
>
> "In the beginning of September, 1941, a large German punitive expedition rounded up all the male population between the ages of fourteen and seventy years and drove them from Shabatka across the Sava River into the settlement of Yarak in Sirinya. That was the so called 'death march'. About 5,000 men had to run a distance of twenty-three kilometers and back again. Those who could not stand the pace and fell by the way were ruthlessly shot on the spot. Because many were old and weak, the number of victims was great, especially while crossing the bridge over the Sava."

I conclude this and I continue with the next paragraph:

> "On the way back they met another group of 800 peasants who had to cover the same distance, but the treatment of this group was still more brutal. They had to run with their arms raised over their heads. They were systematically murdered on the way. Only 300 men of the group reached Yarak alive."

While this is not the same incident that 1st company is recorded to have committed it is not unreasonable to assume that it resembles it, and that it was not an uncommon practice of police units in Slovenia.

September 26, 1941: In Sajmiste, Serbia where the battalion helped kill 6,000 Jews.

This battalion was primarily an execution battalion continuing the same type of work they performed in Poland in 1939 but on a much larger scale. During their time in Serbia the battalion once again had their companies split off and put under the operational control of the SS to conduct killing operations. They were active with Einsatzgruppe E which was run from Belgrade and commanded by SS Brigadeführer Wilhelm Fuchs.

October 4, 1941: Elements of the battalion possibly participated in the execution of 2,100 Jews and communists from the Šabac concentration camp in retaliation for the deaths of 21 German soldiers on October 2, 1941.[4]

October 12-13, 1941: Elements of the battalion possibly participated in the execution of 1,000 or more Jewish men at the Zasavica camp in Šabac.

October 17, 1941: The battalion is tasked to shoot 600 Jewish and Gypsy hostages in a holding camp in Belgrade, but it is unclear if the battalion actually participated. This may have been the Seniak camp where a number of gypsies were being held during this time period.

April-May 1942: Elements of the battalion took part in guarding the arrival of and emptying of a poison gas van from the Semlin camp in which 40-50 Jews were gassed per trip. The bodies were dumped at the Avala shooting range near Belgrade. Stefan Klemps book has it starting earlier in March with 7,500 being killed. He states that 6,280 were killed in the gas wagon and most of these were women and children. The rest died of starvation or from exposure to the cold.[5]

March-May 1942: The battalion is proving security for the Sabac concentration camp.

Regiment/Battalion Locations & Activities

September 1939: The 1st and 3rd companies are in Gdynia. The 2nd company was in Lipno. The 4th company was in Leslau.

May 28, 1940: The battalion returned to Essen after finishing its tour in Poland.

June 22, 1941: The battalion was ordered to transfer from Essen to Belgrade and arrived there on June 30, 1941: The battalion was used for anti-partisan operations, reprisal executions and various guard duty assignments in Serbia, including the camp for Jews at Semlin, across the river from Belgrade. This was an unusual camp as it, along with the camp at Chelmno pioneered the use of specially modified vans that were used to kill Jews and other "undesirables." These vans were mobile gas chambers that pumped carbon monoxide into a closed compartment into which people had been packed. The camp at Semlin killed at least 15,000 people this way.

Summer, 1941: Lieutenant Wilhem Denker was the 2nd company commander. His company was quartered in the Podolska School in Belgrade. In June 1941 the 3rd company under the command of Lieutenant Otto Ehrmann was also quartered in the school.

July 1941: The 1st company spent four weeks conducting anti-partisan operations in Uzice, Serbia. Uzice is in western Serbia and became a major partisan resistance area. They then returned to Belgrade. Partisans later that year declared the short-lived "Republic of Uzice." The ratio for reprisals here was for every German soldier killed one hundred locals would be shot. This was extremely effective in creating a hostile populace.

July 1941: The 2nd company was in Valjevo on anti-partisan duty. Valjevo is about seventy miles from Belgrade. The 3rd company was in Obrenovac, a suburb of Belgrade.

September 1941: The 3rd company returns to Belgrade sometime in late September where it remained until late July, 1942.

October 10, 1941: Fifteen officers and fifty NCOs from various Order Police units in Germany were ordered to Belgrade and told to report to the commander of Police Battalion 64 to begin training 1,000 auxiliary police comprised of ethnic Germans from the Banat, Yugoslavia.

The decision to form the auxiliaries in Serbia was due to regular German police battalions being urgently needed for the occupied eastern territories. The training of 1,000 Banat *Volksdeutsch* began on October in Kikinda (Police *Ausbildungs* (Training) Company 1), Betschkerek, (Police *Ausbildungs* Company 2), Pancevo (Police *Ausbildungs* Company 3), Versac, (Police *Ausbildungs* Company 4), and Weisskirchen (Police *Ausbildungs* Company 5), all these being towns in the Banat (Vojvodina) area north of Belgrade.

December 1941: The 1st and 2nd company returns to Belgrade and its new quarters in Castle Dedinje. That is how my translation of the German text describes it but I believe it was the old royal palace in the Dedinje area of Belgrade.

June 1942: The 3rd company is detached and sent to Greece sometime during this period.

June 1942: The battalion is in Nischka Banja and Jagodina on anti-partisan operations.

August 19, 1943: The entire regiment is ordered to move from Kragujevac to Arandelovac in order to make barracks space available for arriving units.

September 1, 1943: The regimental staff and the battalion are in Belgrade.

September 24, 1943: The battalion is transferred from Belgrade to Cacak.

October 3-8, 1943: The battalion, along with the rest of the regiment participated in Operation "Maisekolben" (Corn Cob) against guerrilla organizations in the mountains between Valjevo and Cacak. Other units participating were the Bulgarian 24th Division, elements of Panzer Company z.b.V. 12, and SFK (Serbian Volunteer Corp) battalions. The results were disappointing for the Germans with about 100 partisans killed and 500 suspects arrested.

October 10-20, 1943: The regiment swept the area from Cacak through Uzice to Bajina Basta on the Drina together with elements of the Bulgarian 24th Division in an attempt to catch insurgents fleeing toward East Bosnia after Operation "Maiskolben."

October 31 to November 5, 1943: The regiment carried out Operation "Hammelbraten" (Roast Mutton) about twelve miles south of Cacak against Chetniks; the enemy had abandoned their camp in the woods and there was little contact. The regiment transferred to Kragujevac to rest and refit after the operation.

January 29, 1944: The entire regiment set out from Celic and over the next several days swept the road past Koraj toward Bijeljina, encountering numerous road blocks and fought several skirmishes with the strengthening partisan forces.

March 1944: The entire regiment leaves Serbia for Operation "Cannae" (Occupation of Hungary). They returned to Serbia, possibly in May 1944. There they were working with the II/SS Police Regiment.

May 14, 1944: The battalion is in Cacak and was patrolling the road between Draglica and Negbina.

May 29, 1944: The battalion is in Usce and responsible for the defense of the Ibar Valley from Raska to just south of Kraljevo due to an increasing threat from the Sandjak region. The Battalion Commander was given command over the III/SFK 3, and the I and II/SFK 5 for this purpose.

July 1944: The entire regiment participated in the anti-partisan operation "Trumpf" in the West Morava Valley along with the Bulgarian 27th Division, all five regiments of the SFK, Chetniks and other German units. The objective was to block the northern movement of four partisan divisions (21st, 22d, 24th and 25th) that had just been formed in southern Serbia.

July-August 1944: Almost immediately following the conclusion of "Trumpf" at the end of July, the regiment was employed in Operation "Draufgänger" (Daredevil) aimed at destroying partisan forces in Montenegro to prevent their penetration into Serbia. The enemy formations were delayed but not destroyed.

August 1944: The 3rd Company of the battalion is detached and sent to northeast Greece under regiment command of the "Demotika"/LXXXXI Army Corp. The company was detached for a long time because it was given its own Feldpost number (20898).

October 12, 1944: The entire regiment is now in Obrenovac, about fourteen miles southwest of Belgrade as part of the defensive ring around the Serbian capital. The city was liberated on October 20, 1944 by units of the Soviet 3rd Ukrainian Front and partisan forces. The regiment and other remnants of the German defense retreated across the Sava into Syrmia.

October 13, 1944: The regiment had been part of the forces assigned to "Brückenkopf Obrenovac", part of the defensive ring on the southwest side of Belgrade. The bridgehead was evacuated during the night of October 13, and this battalion, *Feldgendarmerie* Troop 861, *Sturmgeschutz* (Infantry Support Weapon) Company "Gewitter" and a Luftwaffe Alarm Battalion were ordered to Semlin and reassigned to *Kampfkommandant* Belgrade.

October 22, 1944: The entire regiment is engaged in the Semlin area as part of z.b.V. Stephan, which was a mixed collection of miscellaneous units evacuated out of the Belgrade area.

January-April 1945: Regimental staff, this battalion and the II are in the Vocin area of Slavonska Pozega in Croatia where many police units were engaged in central and eastern Slovenia under z.b.V. Geiger (z.b.V. Stephan).

April-May 1945: The main body of the regiment withdrew toward Zagreb in the latter part of April and surrendered in the Celje area on May 13, 1945.

Post War
On April 11, 1947 Major Adolf Josten, the battalion commander was executed for war crimes in Belgrade.

Police Battalion 65 "Cholm" (Reserve) (Motorized)
The battalion was formed with personel from the Recklinghausen area in September 1939. The officers and NCOs' were active duty regulars while the rest were reservists. This was a four company battalion with the 4th company having two machine gun platoons and a PAK (antitank) platoon.[1]

Field Post Number: 38608
Commanding Officer: Major Ernst Weis (September 1939 to November 1939), Major Barkhold (1941-1942). Major Joachim Kleine, Major Otto Dippelhofer.[2]
Other Officers(s): The 3rd company commander was Walter Schmidt (Rank Unknown)
The battalion formed the I/Police Regiment 25 in Lublin in July 1942. In July 1942 they received men from Police Battalion 41.

Einsatzgruppen/Atrocity Activities
June 1941: In Siauliai where the 3rd Company assisted in the killing of 3,000 Jews. This was before the creation of the Vilna ghetto.

June-December 1942: The battalion was active with roundups and transport of Cracow, Poland Jews to Auschwitz and Belzec concentration camps. They also shot the patients of a Jewish hospital in the woods near Cracow.

This battalion killed an estimated 1,689 people and deported 10,000 to the camps.[3]

Regiment/Battalion Locations & Actions
May 1940: The battalion is in the Nederlands.

May 26, 1941: The battalion is in Heilsberg, East Prussia.

June 22, 1941: In Tilsit, East Prussia

June 26th, 1941: The 1st and 2nd company is stationed in Kovno. The 3rd company was stationed in Siauliai, and the battalion staff was stationed in Luga, Lithuania. The entire battalion ended up in Luga where they were stationed for their winter quarters.

January-June 1942: The battalion was part of *Kampfgruppe* "Scherrer" around Cholm where the battalion along with other elements of the German army was encircled and in continuous combat for 107 days. Major General Scherrer, the commanding officer of the 281 Security Division was put in charge of "Fortress Cholm" a city of 12,000 people. Cholm was extremely important to the 16th Army who if it had fallen would have been in danger of being overrun. The city defenders were supplied by air, the second air bridge of the war with the first being Demjansk. There were 467 police at

Cholm with 80% of them getting an Iron Cross 2nd Class and all of them getting an Infantry Assault Badge.[4]

The survivors received the Cholm shield and the battalion received the honor name of "Cholm". The Cholm Shield design was done by Sergeant Schlimmer who was a member of the battalion. After he turned in the design minor changes were made to it by Professor Klein and the final design was approved by Adolf Hitler.

June 1942 to January 1943: In Brunowice, Poland for reset and refitting.

January-February 1943: The battalion staff was headquartered in Lublin and the companies were stationed in Krasnik, Krasnystaw, and Lubartow. Krasnik was about three miles from a labor camp run by the Hermann Göring Werke that included a Heinkel aircraft factory. There was a mass escape attempt in the winter of 1943.

February 2-11, 1943: The regiment along with *Gendarmerie* Battalion 1 (motorized) and *Landesschützen* units from the Heer carried out an unnamed anti-partisan operation in the Zamosc/Bilgoraj area south of Lublin against an estimated 400 Polish communist partisans, killing 159 and burning down 156 farms. This was followed by four more small anti-partisan operations to the end of the year in the vicinity of Parczew. The Parczew forest was home for units of the Polish Peoples Army and a Jewish partisan band led by Yehiel Grynszpan.

May 1943: The battalion was in Copenhagen providing security for the transportation of Jews and Danes to Theresienstadt and Oranienburg concentration camps.

January 4-10, 1944: The entire regiment and an unknown *Landesschützen* unit carried out Operation "Wintersport" against the Polish Home Army battalions in the Opole Lubelskie area about twenty-two miles west of Lublin.

March 1944: The battalion was transferred from Poland to Slovenia.

March 27, 1944: A motorized column from the battalion was attacked by 1st Brigade/Partisan 14th Division while enroute from Mozirje to Ljubno northwest of Celje and forced to turn back.

April 9-27, 1944: The regiment along with Police Battalion 203 and a Landesschützen unit, participated in Operation "Immergrün" (Evergreen) in the Chelm area against both Polish and Soviet partisans.

May 14-25, 1944: The battalion along with SS Police Regiments 13 and 14, *Landesschützen* Regiment 18, *Gebirgsjäger* Regiment 134, Artillery Regiment 112 and a large number of *Steirischen Wehrmannschaft* (indigenous German militia from Styria) carried out anti-partisan Operation "Anton I." Assembling in Kamnik, Celje, Sostanj, Crna and Slovenjgradec, the surrounding German forces attacked the four brigades of the Partisan 4th Operations Zone in their mountain hideout. According to postwar Yugoslav accounts the partisans were able to evade their attackers and there were few casualties on either side.

July 30 1944: The battalion was in action to the northeast of Kamnik.

August 1944: The battalion was transferred to Cilli and Ljubjana and in 1945 in the area of Krajina, Yugoslavia.

February 13, 1945: The battalion was transferred to Novo Mesto.

March 13, 1945: The battalion was still garrisoned in Novo Mesto, although its mail address was in Ljubljana.

April 9, 1945: The battalion was operating in the Kocevje and Novo Mesto area and continued in that area until the end of April.

May 1945: The battalion withdrew from Novo Mesto via Zidani. Most of the battalion went to Celje where it was surrendered on May 14, 1945 and went into captivity at the British POW camp in Klagenfurt.[5]

Police Battalion 66 (Reserve)

The battalion was formed with personnel from Cologne in June 1940.

Field Post Number(s): Unknown

Commanding Officer(s): Major Olfenius, Major Richard Sonnenberg, Major Hübner, Major Fischer.

The battalion formed the I/Police Regiment 3 in May, 1942 in the Nederlands. Some of the battalion personnel were used to form Police Battalion 69 "Todt".

The battalion took the place of Police Battalion 105 in the regiment or of a battalion formed in Oranienburg and never sent. Regardless it became the III/SS Police Regiment 5 in 1944.[1]

Regiment/Battalion Locations & Activities

June 1940: The battalion was in Darmstadt.

August 1940: In Diedenhofen.

June 1941 to May 1942: Returned to Germany and stationed in Cologne.

July 1942: The Hague.

March 1943: In Krusevac.

September 1, 1943: The battalion is moved to Nis in order to free up barrack space for arriving units.

September 17, 1943: HSSPF Serbian requested that SS Police Regiment 5 with its three battalions assemble in Topola, Kragujevac and Krusevac as a mobile reserve for operations against guerrilla infested areas in cooperation with the Bulgarian 24th Division. The SFK (Serbian Volunteer Corp) had the 2nd Regiment in Kragujevac and the 10th Regiment in Krusevac at this time also. These regiments were well equipped for indigenous regiments and were considered very good troops by the Germans.

October 10-20, 1943: The entire regiment swept the area from Cacak through Uzice to Bajina Basta on the Drina together with elements of the Bulgarian 24th Division in an attempt to catch insurgents fleeing toward East Bosnia after Operation "Maiskolben (Corn Cob)".

October 31 to November 5, 1943: The Regiment carried out Operation "Hammelbraten (Roast Mutton)"about twelve miles south of Cacak against Chetniks; the enemy had abandoned their camp in the woods and there was little contact. The regiment transferred to Kragujevac to rest and refit after the operation.

December 10, 1943: The battalion is ordered to Valjevo to counter the possible movement of Partisan 5th Division in that direction.

January 1, 1944: The battalion is in Krusevac.

January 17, 1944: The battalion is transferred from Krusevac to Zvornik on the Serbian side of the Drina River.

March 1944: The entire regiment departed Serbia for Operation "Cannae" (Occupation of Hungary).

July 1944: The regiment participated in anti-partisan Operation "Trumpf" in the West Morava Valley along with the Bulgarian 27th Division, all five regiments of the Serbian Volunteer Corps (SFK), Chetniks, and other German units. The objective was to block the northern movement of four Partisans divisions (21st, 22nd, 24th and 25th) that had just been formed in southern Serbia.

July-August 1944: Almost immediately following the conclusion of "Trumpf" at the end of July, the regiment was employed in Operation "Draufgänger (Daredevil)" aimed at destroying partisan forces in Montenegro to prevent their penetration into Serbia. The enemy formations were delayed but not destroyed and the German forces took heavy casualties. The 21st SS Division 'Skenderbeg' was shattered. The "Skenderbeg" was formed with predominately Muslim Albanians.

October 12, 1944: The entire regiment is now in Obrenovac as part of the defensive ring around the Serbian capital Belgrade. The city was liberated on October 20, 1944 by units of the Soviet 3rd Ukrainian Front and partisan forces. The regiment and other remnants of the German defense retreated across the Sava into Syrmia.

October 13, 1944: The regiment had been part of the forces assigned to "Brückenkopf Obrenovac," part of the defensive ring on the southwest side of Belgrade. The bridgehead was evacuated during the night of October 13th and SS Police Regiment 5, *Feldgendarmerie* Troop 861, *Sturmgeschütz* (Infantry Heavy Weapon Support) Company "Gewitter" and a Luftwaffe Alarm Battalion were ordered to Semlin and reassigned to the *Kampfkommandant* Belgrade.

January-April 1945: The battalion is separated from the rest of the regiment and located in Rogaska Slatina from January to May 1945.[2]

Police Battalion 67 (Reserve)
This Battalion was formed from the Essen area in May 1940.
Field Post Number(s): Unknown
Commanding Officer(s): Major Wilhelm Gabriel, (December 1943 to February 1944), Major Johannes Korda (February 1944 to ?), Major Kurt Sack.[1]
The battalion formed the II/Police Regiment 25 in Lublin, Poland on May 28, 1942.

Einsatzgruppen/Atrocity activity
Fall 1941: In Szczbrzeszyn, Poland where the battalion assisted in killing 1,000 people.[2]

1942: In Zamosc, Poland where 2,000 people were killed. This may have been a Jewish roundup and deportation action from the ghetto in Zamosc. Records for the Belzec Concentration camp record 3,000 Jews being transported on April 11, 1942.[3]

Zamosc was in the "First Resettlement Area" of the *Generalgouvernement* and in November, 1942, was subject to Police and SS operations to remove "undesirables" to make room for German nationals or *Volksdeutche*. Tens of thousands of Poles were deported to labor or extermination camps, or killed outright, while others were singled out to be "Germanized" and resettled in the Reich. Himmler visited Zamosc, and thought it was a lovely town. He planned on renaming it Himmlerstadt after it was resettled and properly "Germanized."[4]

The following quote is from: *"Szczebrzeszyn" Encyclopedia of Jewish Communities in Poland*, Volume VII, (Poland), Translation of "Szczebrzeszyn" chapter from Pinkas Hakehillot Polin. Published by Yad Vashem, Published in Jerusalem:

> "Acts of murder and deportation to the camps began in S in May 1942, and continued throughout the summer. On May 8th, the Gestapo arrested two men and two women in the middle of the night, took them to nearby Zwierzyniec and there killed them. In the morning Gestapo personnel arrived in S from Zamosc. They rounded up some 2,000 Jews in the town square and opened fire on them. About a hundred Jews were killed and many others wounded. **When the firing had ceased the Germans demanded from the Judenrat three kilograms of coffee and 2,000 zloty "to cover the cost of the bullets used"**. [Bold by Author] At the end of May the Germans sent some 300

German Police in Litzmannstadt in March 1942.

Bodies lie in a Jewish Cemetery near Bydgoszcz. Courtesy USHM.

Jews from S to the extermination camp at Belzec. On June 23rd the Germans arrested scores of Jews and led them in the direction of Bilgoraj. Their fate remains unknown. Another 20 Jews held in the local jail were murdered the same day in a field outside the town. On August 8th some 400 Jews were taken to the railway station, crammed into goods wagons and sent to Belzec. Another 200 elderly Jews were taken that same day outside the town and there shot to death. A few days later the Germans sent some 700 Jews to the labor camp near Chelm, where they too were killed."

1942: In Bilgoraj, Poland were the 3rd company assisted in 1,200 deaths. This was probably the first action in Bilgoraj that took place in August 1942. This was not an execution action; rather it was a roundup and transportation operation. The 3rd company was stationed in Bilgoraj at this time:

"The first action in Bilgoraj took place in August 1942. The leaders of the *Judenrat* were summoned to the district office and ordered to prepare a list of a thousand Jews who, according to the Germans, were to be sent to a labor camp in Ukraine. The deportees were allowed to take a small quantity of personal items and a little money with them. The members of the *Judenrat* and workers in German service were exempt from being registered. On the allotted day the thousand deportees assembled in the market square in accordance with the list prepared by the *Judenrat*, together with members of their family. The number present thus exceeded that demanded by the Germans. Polish carters and their wagons came to transport the deportees. Since there was a surplus of the latter present no check was carried out on the basis of the *Judenrat's* list.

"On August 9th the convoy left Bilgoraj escorted by a reserve contingent of the German *Schupo* Police brought to the town for this purpose. The convoy consisted of 25 wagons loaded with equipment and the more than thousand Jews. It arrived at Swir, where it was joined by a group of Jews expelled from Tarnogrod. All were then transported to the railway station at Czernuszewce, where they were put on board goods wagons and taken to the extermination camp at Belzec."[6]

November 3-4, 1943: Participated in Action "*Erntefest*" (Harvest Festival) which began at dawn on November 3, 1943. "The Trawniki and Poniatowa labor camps were surrounded by SS and police units. Jews were then taken out of the camps in groups and shot in nearby pits dug for this purpose. At Majdanek, Jews were first separated from the other prisoners. They were then taken in groups to nearby trenches and shot. Jews from other labor camps in the Lublin area were also taken to Majdanek and shot. Music was played through loudspeakers

German police publicly humiliate Jews in the yard of the Szczebrzeszyn town council. Courtesy USHM.

at both Majdanek and Trawniki to drown out the noise of the mass shooting. The killing operation was completed in a single day at Majdanek and Trawniki. At Poniatowa the shootings took two days. Approximately 42,000 Jews were killed during "Erntefest ."[7]

Regiment/Battalion Locations & Actions
May 1940 to 1942: In Holland.

February-May 1942: The battalion returned to and was stationed in Essen.

February 1943: Operating in the Lublin, Zamoscz, and Bilgoraj districts.

April 11, 1943: The 1st company of the battalion helped put down a prisoner uprising in the Belzec, concentration camp.

April 1943: In the Ostrov, Lubelski, Zamoscz, and Bilgoraj districts.

June 1943: In the Parczew, Poland area. The Parczew Forest area was home to both Jewish and Communist partisans. The communist partisans briefly held Ostrov in late 1943 until driven out by the Germans.

April 1944: Chelmno, Poland area. The Chelmno death camp was active until March 1943 when it was shut down. In April 1944 it was reactivated in order to liquidate the remaining Jews of the Lodz ghetto. Approximately 25,000 Jews were killed in this period.

November 17, 1944: The battalion was in Szczekociny. The battalion strength was nine officers, 375 men. The battalion and the III/25 operated in Western Poland until 1945.[8]

Police Battalion 68 (Reserve)
Battalion formed with personnel from the Cologne area
Field Post Number(s): Unknown
Commanding Officer(s): Major Robert Wieprecht (June 1940 to ?), Major Hans Kärgel. He joined NSDAP in 1932 and the SS in 1940. The battalion formed the II/Police Regiment 3 on July 3, 1942 in Holland.

Regiment/Battalion Locations & Actions
December 15, 1940 to April 23, 1941: The battalion is in Assen an under the operational control of BdO Hague.

April 24 to July 10, 1941: The battalion is in Rotterdam.

July 11, 1941 to May 7, 1945: Based in Amsterdam, Holland.

Police Battalion 69 (Reserve)

The battalion was formed with personnel from the Cologne area on August 18, 1941. The battalion was formed using staff from Police Battalion 62 and 66. The rest of the battalion was a mix of ethnic Germans, Croats, and Ukrainians. This was an unusually large battalion as it had five companies rather than the usual three.

Field Post Number(s): 40937

Commanding Officer(s): Major Richard Sonnenberg, Major Paul Bernickel (June 1943 to ?)[1]

Other Officers(s): The 4th company commander was 1st Lieutenant August Huft.

The battalion formed the III/Police Regiment 17 in July 1942 in Riga, Latvia. The battalion contributed one company to the new II/SS Police Regiment "Todt" 28 in 1943. Another source (Curilla. pg.609) has the battalion forming the II/28 in November 1942 with Police Battalion 62 filling out the rest of the German strength of the regiment.

Einsatzgruppen/Atrocity Activity

September 1941: The 1st and 2nd companies were sent to Army Group South. The 3rd company was sent Army Group Center. The 4th and 5th companies were sent to Army Group North.

The 1st company was in Nikolajew, home of *Einsatzgruppen* D, an operating under SD command. This *Einsatzgruppen* reported that as of November 5, 1941 they had executed 31,767 people.[2] In September the company was in Winniza.

September 1941: The 2nd company was in Kiev and Kharkov. The company killed a number of mentally ill patients in a hospital in Poltawa during this time period.

September 1941: The 3rd company was in Brest Litowsk, Mogilew, Minsk, Slonim, Baronowicze, and Smolensk. They were operating as a mobile execution squad. This was the route *Einsatzcommando* 7a/b was following. This company operated under SD control along with Lithuanian and Latvian auxiliaries until November 1941. They killed 12 people in Brest Litowsk in September.

The 3rd platoon, 3rd company was in Slonim in September and October 1941 where they executed three men and one woman. On November 14, 1941 the platoon along with the 6th company, 727 Infantry Regiment, *Gendarmerie*, and *Schupo* stationed in Slonim assisted in killing 7,000-9,000 Jews near Czepilow.

September 1941: The 4th company was in Vilna. Two ghettos; the big and the little were formed there in early September. The company killed 1,000 Jews in Radoszkowice; 1,000 Jews in Luninetz; 500 Jews in Lachwa. The Jews of Luninetz were marched approximately three miles out of town and shot.

September 1942: A platoon from the 4th company is in Lachwa conducting a ghetto action with the SD, a squad from 2nd company, Police Battalion 306, and 200 auxiliary police. The death toll was reported at 1,946 men, 698 women, and 724 children. This Jews here fought back in the first uprising in a ghetto. On September 2, the people inside the ghetto learned that the Germans were digging pits outside of town. When told to line up for deportation later that day they attacked the Germans and their auxiliaries as they entered the ghetto with axes, sticks and whatever else they could find. At least a 1,000 Jews were able to escape although most of them were later tracked down and shot.

September 1941: The 5th company was in Pleskau, Luga, and outside Leningrad.

May-September 1942: The 4th company was in Luninetz, Mikaszewicze, Schitkowicze, and Staruchi.

This battalion is responsible for the deaths of 18,255 people.[3]

Regiment/Battalion Locations & Activities

Winter 1941: The 3rd company was in Bobruiska conducting joint anti-partisan operations with army units. During this time frame 1,013 Jews were shot in an action in the area.

August 1942: Elements of 3rd company were patrolling the Minsk to Smolensk road.

October 1942: Elements of the 3rd company are stationed in Roslawl.

January 1943: The battalion is sent to Holland.

February 1943: The battalion is in France possibly for the creation of the regiment. Sometime afterwards they return to Germany.

February 1944: The battalion is transferred to Yugoslavia.

Police Battalion 71 (Reserve)
This battalion was formed with personnel from Munich.
Field Post Number(s): 20020
Active in Poland in 1939 as the V/Police Regiment 2 and attached to Police Group 2, AOK 10.

Regiment/Battalion Locations & Activities
December 1939: Attached to Police Regiment Radom.

Police Battalion 72 (Reserve)
This battalion was formed with personnel from Munich area in 1939.
Field Post Number(s): Unknown
Commanding Officer(s): Major Richard Maiwald (? to 1943), Major W. Fischer (December 1943 to ?). Major Maiwald was a member of NSDAP (Number 4 262 696), and the SS (Number 367 701). His decorations were: Iron Cross 2nd class (1914), The Iron Cross 1st Class (1939) and Spange to his Iron Cross 2nd Class (1914). He later became the commander of the 2nd version of SS Police Regiment 6 in 1944.
Other Officers: 1st Lieutenant Wilden. 1st Platoon, 1st Company leader.
In December 1939 the battalion was part of Police Regiment Radom.

The battalion became the I/Police Regiment 19 in July 1942 in Veldes, Slovenia.

Regiment/Battalion Locations & Activities
February 1940: Stationed in Czenstochau, Poland. The 3rd company helped relieve (plunder) the Jews of Czenstochau of any possessions of value.[1]

April-September 1940: The battalion is in Warsaw. Heinrich Himmler visited the battalion on April 28 and 29.

April 1941: The battalion is back in Munich refitting.

April 15, 1941: Transferred to Slovenia during the second half of April a week or two after the Germans had occupied Yugoslavia with garrisons in Krsko (Staff), Brezice, Rogaska Slatina and Ptuj. The battalion was reinforced with Reserve Police Company "Vienna" and 1st Company Reserve Police Battalion 124, with both of these stationed in Maribor. The 1st Company may have been stationed in Dobrna during this time period.

Their initial task in Slovenia was the maintenance of order and the deportation of Slovenes from what was now part of the Reich. This was not a small-scale deportation as the battalion assisted in deporting at least 40,000 Slovenes.

August 1941: In Marburg, Slovenia.

August 8-9, 1941: Took part in the first German operation against partisans in Slovenia with a sweep in the mountains southwest of Radovljica.

August 10, 1941: One company from the battalion was transferred from Krsko to Bled.

September 20, 1941: The 1st company engaged partisans sabotaging the railway line south of Sostan. The 3rd company was also in Cilly operating with the 1st company of Police Battalion 124.

April 1942: The battalion is operating in the Trbovlje, Bled, and Kamnik area against partisans to the north and east of Ljubljana.

July 1942: In Veldes.

September 29, 1942: The battalion is conducting an anti-partisan operation in the Trbovlje and Prebold area.

January 1943: The entire regiment took part in a sweep of the mountains around Kropa.

February 25, 1943: The battalion along with the III carried out a limited sweep of the Marija Reka area to the north of Trbovlje.

June 13, 1943: The battalion and *Grenadier* Reserve Company Alpenland 3 (Motorized) engaged partisans in the Kamnik area.

August 1943: The battalion is on detached operations about 22 miles to the east between Kamnik and Trbovlje.

December 9-10, 1943: The 2nd company of the battalion along with SS Police Regiment 14 was in Kocevje when attacked at night by 3 or 4 brigades of partisans. They were saved when reinforcements arrived the next day. Kocevje was a 14th century German settlement and the police units in the area probably considered it an oasis in hostile territory.

October 1943: The battalion took part in operation "Wolkenbruch" near Lubijana.

February 6, 1944: The battalion took part in an operation in the vicinity of Kamnik.

June 1944: In Grenoble, and then in Paris in June 1944. They were transferred to Grenoble in France to reinforce security operations against French partisans.

September 1944: In Langres.[2]

December 1944: Released from its attachment to the 16 Volksgrenadier Division, the regiment began returning to Slovenia during the second half of December.

March 20, 1945: The entire regiment was now using Celje as its permanent garrison, although the battalions and companies were deployed in the field on operations.

April 25, 1945: The battalion is operating along both sides of the Celje to Maribor road which was soon to be the main route of withdrawal north toward Austria for the hundreds of thousands of German and Croatian troops in Croatia.

May 10, 1945: The battalion whose strength was less than sixty men are interned in Klagenfurt POW camp after surrendering to the English.

Police Battalion 74 (Reserve)

This battalion was formed from the Augsberg area in July 1940.

Field Post Number(s): 07708

In October 1941 the 2nd company was transferred to Police Battalion 310 in Lvov.

The battalion formed the II/Police Regiment 17 on July 1942.

Regiment/Battalion Locations & Activities

June to October 1940: In Strasbourg, France.

October 1940: In Alsace, France.

March 1941: Transferred to Cracow, Poland.

1943: In the Starachovice, Poland area.

February 1944: In the Ukraine.

June 1944: Warsaw, Poland.

Police Battalion 81 (Reserve)

This battalion was formed from the Breslau area.

Field Post Number(s): 16695+

This battalion was active in Poland in 1939 as the IV/Police Regiment 1 and attached to Police Group 1, AOK 14. In December 1939 it was attached to Police Regiment Warsaw.[1]

Regiment/Battalion Locations & Activities

1940-1942: Possibly a company each in Beuthen, Olmütz, Brünn.

1942: The battalion was dissolved.

Police Battalion 82 (Motorized) (Reserve)

The battalion was formed with men from the Leibnitz, Oppeln, and Breslau area. The men from Leibnitz created two companies with men from Oppeln and Breslau each creating a company. Each company had three platoons, and the battalion itself had four companies. The officers were all active duty while the rest were reservists with the exceptions of an unknown number of NCOs'. In 1941 a SMG platoon was created and a large number of machine pistols were issued to the troops.

Field Post Number: 37330

Commanding Officer(s): Major Walter Kegel (1939 to March 1941), Major Rudolf Ebert (March 1941 to May 1942), Major Ewald Denninghaus (May 1942 to ?).[1]

Battalion Adjutant: 1st Lt. Johannes Piehl then Captain on January 30, 1942 and 1st Company commander. Captain Piehl joined NSDAP on May 1, 1933 and was awarded the Iron Cross 2nd and 1st class and the Infantry Assault badge.

The battalion was in Kattowitz in 1939. By the end of 1940 this battalion was completely motorized. The battalion formed the I/Police Regiment 6 in July 1942.

Einsatzgruppen/Atrocity Activity
March to April 1940: The battalion staff is stationed in Karwin and working with the SD finding and killing Polish civilians who had been identified as part of Operation "Tannenburg."

1940-1942: Listed as operating in the following towns or areas during this time period; Chrzanow, Kolzowka, Krasnij Ugol, Krasnij Bor, Maloje Polpino, Orlowka, Rshaniza, Sjelzo, Staraja Lawschina, Subowka, Suchodol, Tscherwonoje, Tschitschkowo, Werchnjaja Rshaniza as well as unknown towns in the Brjansk, Gremjatsch, Kattowitz, Shitomir, Shirjatino and Ssineserki areas.

In the trial summary for Johannes Piehl, a member of this battalion who was sentenced to life imprisonment the court had this to say about the battalion activities in his trial summary:[2]

> "Arrest of members of the Polish intelligentsia. Deportation of at least 300 Poles to Germany as forced laborers. Shooting of 65 Jews as a "reprisal" for the bombing of an airport by Soviet planes. Shooting of men and women who had been arrested as suspected of partisan activities during "cleansing and pacification operations" as well as shooting of captured partisans. Burning down of villages, confiscation of cattle and food supplies and expulsion or arrest of the town inhabitants ... in many cases accompanied by mishandling and killing ... within the context of anti-partisan warfare in the Soviet Union."

December 1940 to May 1941: The 1st and 2nd company is stationed in Chrzanow which was ten miles from Auschwitz. Chrzanow was almost eighty percent Jewish and had a large ghetto where roundups to collect people for the work camps happened frequently during this time period.

Spring 1940: 1st company and battalion staff is in Karwin, Austria. The 2nd company is in Saybusch, Silesia. The area was undergoing "Germanization" operations and an estimated 20,000 Poles at a minimum were deported from the Saysbusch area in 1940. The 3rd company is in Chrzanow. Chrzanow at this time was being used as a holding area for Jews from the surrounding area.

July-August 1941: The battalion is stationed in Shitomir. They were conducting anti-partisan operations in the area of Polonje and Shitomir with the 454 Security Division. While they were in the area they were also shooting Jews as a reprisal for an airport bombing. Some of the Jews were children.

February 26, 1942: The 1st company shot fourteen partisans. They were working with their Ukrainian auxiliaries doing sweeps of the Brjansk to Rosalawl road.

March 1, 1942: The 1st company is working with Police Battalion 309 near Rshaniza.

March 1-10, 1942: Part of the battalion participates in Operation "Anton." The units participating in "Anton" were broken up into *Kampfgruppes* with the battalion as part of *Kampfgruppe* II under the command of Major Ebert. They began "Anton" on March 3, 1942 in Shukowka. On March 4th, 1942 they were hunting partisans in the woods near Starja Lawschina where they killed eighteen of them. On March 5, in Suchodol they burned down fifteen houses. On March 6, they killed about thirty more partisans and burned down houses.

April 2, 1942: The battalion was fighting partisans near Kolowka where they killed fifteen partisans and set fire to about eighty houses.

January 1943: The battalion burned down the villages of Shurinitsch, Beshan, Podswjatoje, and Rosnowo.

Regiment/Battalion Locations & Actions
May 1941: The 2nd company is in Pilna working with the 454 Security Division.

September-October 1941: Conducting anti-partisan operations in the area of Korosten and Fastow in the rear of the 2nd Panzer Army (Korück 532) until July 1942. The 1st company is stationed in Brjansk and providing support to ongoing "Large Actions."

September-December 1941: Working with Police Battalion 309, and Ukrainian auxiliaries in the Maloje Polpins area.

February-June 1942: The battalion is in the Brjansk area in support of the II Panzer Army. They were doing partisan sweeps, providing rail security, and guarding POWs.

March 3, 1942: In Orlowka.

March 4, 1942: The 1st company is fighting partisans in the forest by Starja Lawschina. A few days later they burned down thirty houses.

April-May 1942: The 1st company is conducting anti-partisan patrols near Krasnij Rog.

July, 1942: The battalion was sixty miles from and southwest of Brjansk near Gremjatsch.

January 1943: The regiment was destroyed during the fighting near the Don River with remnants making it to Gdynia, Poland in March 1943. See Police Battalion 51 for more details. A second SS Police Regiment was created in 1944 and was commanded by Lt. Col. Maiwald, the former commander of Police Battalion 72.

Police Battalion 83

The battalion was formed from the Upper Silesia area. Originally the battalion was formed with men from the town of Gleiwitz but the manpower demands of the war quickly made it necessary for the recruiting pool to be drawn from a larger area.[1]

Field Post Number(s): 35103, 35206

Commanding Officer(s): Major Eugen Seim, Major Widder (1943)[2]

Other Officer(s): The commander of the 1st company was Captain Walter Gustke. He was also commissioned a captain in the SS in 1941.

The 3rd company in October 1941 was sent to Police Battalion 310 in Lvov.

The battalion formed the I/Police Regiment 24 in Lvov in July, 1942. The regimental staff was not formed until April 21, 1943 and may have been the staff of the former Police Regiment Radom.

Einsatzgruppen/Atrocity Activity

January 7-14, 1943: SS Police Regiment 10, 13, and 24 along with Police Panzer Company 5 comprised SS and Police *Kampfgruppe* "von Gottberg" for anti-partisan operation "Franz" against several thousand partisans in the area between Minsk and the Berezina River. According to the after action report, 1,143 partisans were killed plus a further 882 suspects or sympathizers, and 1,000 locals deported for forced labor.

Regiment /Battalion Locations & Activities

October 1941: In Breslau, Poland.

July 1942: In Lvov where they had been stationed for at least a year.

August 21, 1942: The battalion is in Lagoisk getting ready for large operations against partisans in the area. They are conducting operations with the Latvian 26 *Schuma* Battalion.[3]

January 1943: The regiment is transferred to Krajina, Slovenia

1943: This battalion and the II battalion were in Mogiliev in 1943 while the III battalion was sent to France.

February 5-10, 1943: The regiment is conducting Operation "Albert" with II/SS Police Regiment 14 (PB 122) and the *Sicherungs* Battalion 555. The goal was to cut off and destroy partisan units to the east of Uzda, but the operation was relatively unsuccessful. It did save the II/14 as the other two battalions of its regiment were destroyed in combat during this same time period.

March 1943: Active in support of the II Panzer Army in stopping a Soviet army breakthrough near Bryansk.

March 31, 1943: Operating with SS and Police *Kampfgruppe* "Kuntz."

March 1, 1944: Active with SS and Police *Kampfgruppe* "von Gottberg."

October 25 to November 15, 1943: Participating in Operation "Heinrich" with 28 battalions of police, *Schuma*, security troops, police tank companies, and support units who surrounded and attacked a huge concentration of partisans (estimated by the Germans at more than 16,000) in the swampy, heavily wooded lake district between Nevel and the Latvian border. Before the operation made any progress, Soviet breakthroughs in the vicinity forced the anti-partisan troops to end "Heinrich" and switch over to a defensive role against the oncoming regular units of the Red Army. Heavy losses were sustained over the next several weeks.

April 1944: Active with SS and Police *Kampfgruppe* "von Gottberg" and operating south of Polotsk.

April 16, to May 10, 1944: Operating as part of *Kampfgruppe* "Anhalt" under SS-*Obersturmbannführer* Günther Anhalt.

March 26 to April 16, 1944: Participating in Operation "Regenschauer" (Rain Shower) with thousands of other SS and Police and Army troops under the overall command of Panzer AOK 3. They attacked the "Ushachi Partisan Republic" located in a thirty-two-mile stretch of territory between Polotsk and Lepel where an estimated 17,500 partisans were encamped. The partisans were a threat to the Orsha to Lepel rail line that Panzer AOK 3 depended on to bring up supplies to the Vitebsk to Orsha sector of the front. The partisans withdrew from the perimeter as the Germans moved in and there was little fighting.

April 16 to May 10, 1944: Participating in Operation "Frühlingsfest" (Spring Festival) and continuing "Regenschauer" (Rain Shower) in the same area against the same partisans, but now heavily reinforced with additional SS, Police, and Army troops. This time they succeeded in closing the net and over the course of the two operations they killed 7,011 partisans, captured 6,928 and brought in 349 deserters.

May 22 to June 20, 1944: Participating in Operation "Kormoran" (Cormorant) with SS and Police *Kampfgruppe* "von Gottberg" with SS Police Regiments 2, 13, and Police Panzer Companies 1, 9 and 12, a number of *Schuma* battalions along with elements of 221 Security Division and 391 *Feldausbildungs* Division. They drove an estimated 15,000 to 16,000 partisans into a swampy area near Molodechno and destroyed them. The Germans claimed enemy losses to be 7,697 killed, 5,286 captured, and 342 camps and 900 bunkers destroyed.

June 22, 1944 to July 8, 1944: The regiment along with the rest of SS and Police *Kampfgruppe* "von Gottberg," carried out a fighting withdrawal along the Molodechno to Lida line (fifty-one miles) following the commencement of the massive Soviet Belorussian offensive on June 22, 1944. By July 13, the regiment is no longer shown as being under *Kampfgruppe* "von Gottberg" and had possibly had been withdrawn into Poland to refit.

November 1944: In the Kattowitz and Hindenburg area in Silesia being rebuilt following heavy losses in Poland.

1945: Possibly in Silesia.[4]

Police Battalion 84 (Reserve)

This battalion was formed from the Holleshau and Gleiwitz area in early 1940 with most of the men being over the age of thirty.

Field Post Number(s): 35103, 35206

Commanding Officer(s) Major Reifflin (1941-1942)

The battalion was part of Police Regiment Mähren.

Regiment /Battalion Locations & Activities

June 1940: The battalion is transferred to Böhemia with elements left behind in Holleschau.

January 1941: The 2nd company is in Mährisch Ostrau and later joins the rest of the battalion in Iglau.

April 1942: The battalion is flown in Ju 52s to Wyriza to reinforce Police Rifle Regiment 1 of the SS Police Division after the losses incurred from the Soviet counteroffensive of the winter. The battalion lands in Krassnogwardeisk and is transported by land to Ljuban and then to Wyriza. They receive eight weeks of combat training and then are forwarded to the Police Rifle Regiment where along with the 291 Infantry Division they go into action on May 3, 1942 in the Krassnaja Gorka sector. They take heavy losses and the battalion is dissolved with the survivors being absorbed into the SS Police Division.[1]

Police Battalion 85 (Reserve)

This battalion was formed with personnel from the Kattowitz area.

Field Post Number(s): 12047

Commanding Officer: Major Oppenberg

On May 5, 1941 the battalion was issued eight Model 1908 machine guns.[1]

In October 1941 the 1st company is sent to Lvov to help form Police Battalion 310.

The battalion formed the II/Police Regiment 13 in 1942 in Belorussia. The battalion was the II/Police Regiment Center from May to June 1942.

Einsatzgruppen/Atrocity Activity

January 28, 1943: The regiment is assigned to Operation "*Erntefest* II" carried out west of the Minsk to Slutsk highway between January 28 and February 9, 1943. According to a German report, 2,400 partisans were killed and 2,300 partisan sympathizers executed.

Regiment /Battalion Locations & Actions
May 1942: In Smolensk, Poland.

July 1942: In Kattowitz.

August 1-5, 1942: Participating in Operation "Nordpol III" (North Pole). The battalion along with the III swept a thickly forested area near Demidov. The operation is said to have mostly taken place at night.

August 17-29, 1942: The entire regiment is participating in Operation "Grief" along with the Police Regiment 14. See Police Battalion 6 for more details.

September 1-7, 1942: This regiment and Police Regiment 14 participates in Operation "Breslau." Total German casualties are five dead and ten wounded.[2]

November 1942 to January 1943: The battalion was in Smolensk.

February 8-26, 1943: This battalion formed *Kampfgruppe* "West" which included three other *kampfgruppes* that were used for Operation "Hornung." *Kampfgrupppe* "West" also included Police Battalion 6 and *Schuma* Battalion 18. For more details see Police Battalion 13.

March 25, 1943: In Smolevichi.

April 17-24, 1943: The battalion along with I/13 participate in Operation Zauberflöte (Magic Flute). Other units included the SS Police Regiment 2, I/SS Police Regiment 23, SS *Sonder* Battalion Dirlewanger, Druzhina SS Battalion, elements of 390 *Feldausbildungs* Division, elements of the141 Reserve Infantry Division, Alarm (emergency) units from the Minsk garrison, SD detachments and a special company carried out a cleansing operation in the city of Minsk, which had become infested with partisans.

The city was cordoned off and thoroughly combed with 76,000 people checked to see if they had the correct papers. Of these 52,000 were taken to collection points to be further investigated. Five hundred and fifty people were shipped to Germany to contribute as forced laborers while 712 were held for local labor projects. Two people were shot on the spot for unknown infractions.[3]

July-August: 1943: The regiment belonged to a force of 4 SS Police Regiments plus other units that were brought up to attack the partisan "Kovpak Brigade" that was rampaging through northwestern Ukraine and Galicia as part of Opereration "Wehrwolf." The Germans considered the"Kovpak Brigade" an elite force because it had Russian paratroopers as part of its troops. Kovpak himself was a member of the Communist Party and a veteran of the Russian civil war. The brigade order of battle consisted of five battalions of infantry each equipped with twenty machine guns. The brigade had an attached artillery company armed with nine field guns (76mm and 45mm). They also had a signals company and a calvary company to provide for scouting and screening of the route.

While Kovpak had his successes in the field with the primary one being able to operate for almost a year in German territory. He did not inflict any strategic level damage on the Germans. He did almost destroy a company (6th) of SS Police Regiment 4 in an engagement on July 18, 1943. In the end his troops were caught in the open by the Luftwaffe and suffered heavy casualties and they ended up retreating back into Soviet controlled territory.

September 1943: In Lublin.

December 30, 1943 to January 20, 1944: The entire regiment with a strength of 2,239 is on the front line between Polotsk and Nevel under SS and Police *Kampfgruppe* "von Gottberg" (Total strength 8,132).

April 1944: Transferred from Belorussia to Klagenfurt, Austria and Oberkrain in Slovenia to reinforce the anti-partisan units under HSSPF in Wehrkreis XVIII. Most sources state that the regiment was stationed in Austria just across the border from Slovenia and returned to these garrisons after each anti-partisan operation in Slovenia concluded.

April 29, 1944: Elements of SS Police Regiment 13 and 14 engaged the Partisan 15th Division which was attacking garrisons in the Trebnje and Lumemberk area to the southeast of Ljubljana.

May 14-25 1944: SS Police Regiment 14 and 25, *Landesschützen* Regiment 18, *Gebirgsjäger* Regiment 134, *Ersatz* Artillery Regiment 112 and a large number of Steirischen *Wehrmannschaft* (indigenous German militia from Styria) carried out anti-partisan Operation "Anton I." Assembling in Kamnik, Celje, Sostanj, Crna and Slovenjgradec, the surrounding German forces attacked the four brigades of the Partisan 4th Operations Zone in their mountain redoubt. According to postwar Yugoslav accounts, the partisans were able to evade their attackers and there were few casualties on either side.

September 25, 1944: The battalion skirmished with a partisan band around Moravce.

December 11, 1944: After the regiment assembled in Crna and SS Police Regiment 28 and Lehr Regiment Brandenburg in Kamnik, the combined force advanced on the Gornja Savinja Valley to destroy elements of the Partisan 14th Division that had been occupying the villages of Luce, Ljubno as well as other communities along the valley. Several days after the operation began a column from SS Police Regiment 25 and strong elements from *Landesschützen* Regiment 18 moved forward from the east and south, driving the partisans from most of the valley. Casualty figures are not known.

March 20, 1945: Stationed in their permanent garrisons. The battalion staff is in Ferlach, Austria.[4]

April 14, 1945: The regiment is southwest of Mönichwald operating with the remains of the III Panzer Corp as they withdraw through Austria on their way to surrender to the Americans.

Police Battalion 91 (Reserve)

The battalion was formed with personnel from the Offenbach area in 1939. The 1st company was formed with personnel from the Kassel area. The 2nd company with men from Frankfurt. The 3rd company was formed with men from Weimar.
Field Post Number(s): 33747, 13683

Guard Detachment in Warsaw.

Commanding Officer(s): Major Faust
Other Officers: The 1st company commander was 1st Lt. Erwin Lins (1939 to 1943). The 4th Company Commander was Captain Hans Hoffman. He was replaced in 1941 by Captain Wilhelm Ahrens.
In Poland in 1939 as the IV/Police Battalion 6, Police Group 6, AOK 4. From October 1939 to February 1940 they were attached to Police Regiment Warsaw.

The battalion formed the I/Police Regiment 8 in 1942.

Einsatzgruppen/Atrocity Actions
November 1939: In Ostrow, Poland where they killed at least 360 Jews for allegedly starting a fire.

October 1940: Elements of the battalion are in Chotimsk providing security troops for the ghetto there.

October or November 1941: The 1st company is in the Grodno ghetto providing security.

Right: Three members of the battalion in Belvedere Park across from Hans Franks residence in Warsaw. Below: Members of the battalion in their barracks.

February-March 1942: The 4th company was executing Jews in actions in Wolkowysk and the surrounding towns.

April 1942: In Krynki where the 3rd company was reported to have killed all old and sick Jews in the hospital there.

July 12, to May 8, 1942: The battalion and *Einsatzkommando* 8 are in Chotimsk where they are assisting in the liquidation of the Jewish ghetto.[1]

This battalion is responsible for the deaths of 907 people.[2]

Regiment/Battalion Locations & Activities
October 1939 to February 1940: In Lublin.

February 1940: The battalion returned to Germany.

April 1940: The battalion arrives in Norway where it assigned to patrol the Norwegian/Swedish border.

July 1940: In Narvik.

October 1940: The battalion is in Grodno. The 2nd company is stationed in Augustowo and the 3rd company is in Wolkowysk.

May 1942: In Brjansk.

July 1942: In Chotimsk where they were operating with Army Security Division 221.

1st Lieutenant Fredrich and 2nd Lieutenant Dustehues in Kassel Germany.

September 1942: The battalion is fighting partisans near Rasrytoje with the 1st company taking heavy casualties. They lost one officer and twenty two men. The 3rd company had 25-30 Ukrainian auxiliaries attached to it.

August 1942: In Gomel.

November 2, 1942: The battalion is back in Grodno.

The battalion ready for inspection in Poland.

January 1943: The regiment is destroyed in combat. The surviving remnants of the battalion were transferred to Police Rifle Regiment 36.

October 29, to November 18, 1944: The regiment is North of Paks on the Danube helping defend Budapest from the approaching Soviet army. The regiment may have been rebuilt using large numbers of Hungarian auxiliaries. They were assisting in the defense of the Solt bridgehead where the regiment along with other units with Hungarian auxillaries were deemed so unreliable that machine guns were setup behind them to discourage movement to the rear.[3]

January 1945: Remnants of the battalion may have been used to form SS Police Regiment 50 that fought on the Oder front and were annihilated.

Police Battalion 92 (Reserve)
This battalion was formed using personnel from the Kassel area.
Field Post Number(s): 00869+
Active in Poland as the I/Police Regiment 1, Police Group 1, AOK 14. Later they were assigned to Police Regiment Cracow.

Police Battalion 93 (Reserve)
The battalion was formed with personnel from the Kassel area in Frankfurt in August, 1939.
Field Post Number(s): Unknown
Commanding Officer(s): Major Erich Klein (September 1941 to ?), Major Hutter, Major Wilhelm Kissel.
Other Officer(s): The 1st company commander was Captain Janicke. Later Lieutenant Westermann.
The battalion formed the III/Police Regiment 24 in Lvov in July, 1942.
January-February 1943: The battalion is transferred from Slovenia to France and reassigned to SS Police Regiment Griese. Later the battalion became the I/Police Rifle Regiment 35.

Einsatzgruppen/Atrocity Activity
Below is a report that is quoted in its entirety from Christopher Browning's book. It is an excellent example of what one of the duties of the police consisted of, and the experience was probably similar for many of the battalions:[1]

7./Police24
Lemberg (Lwow), 14 September 1942
To: Commander of the Order Police in the district of Galicia, Lemberg
Subject: Jewish Resettlement

After carrying out Jewish Resettlement actions on 3 and 5 September in Skole, Stryj and Chodorow, for which Captain of the SchutzPolice Kröpelin was in charge of the Order Police involved and which has already been reported in detail, the 7th Company of the 24th Police Regiment arrived as ordered in Kolomyja on the evening of 6 September. I immediately contacted *Kriminalkommissar* and SS *Obersturmführer* Leitmeritz, head of the branch office of the Security Police in Kolomyja, and First Lieutenant Hertel of the SchutzPolice station in Kolomyja.

Contrary to the experience in Stryj, the action planned for 7 September in Kolomyja was well prepared and made easy for all units involved. The Jews had been informed by the above mentioned agencies and the Labor office to gather at the collection point of the Labor Office for registration on 7 September at 5:30 a.m. Some 5,300 Jews were actually assembled there at the appointed time. With all the manpower of my company, I sealed the Jewish quarter and searched thoroughly, whereby some 600 additional Jews were hunted down.

The loading of the transport train was completed about 7:00 p.m. After the Security Police released some 1,000 from the total rounded up, 4,769 Jews were resettled. Each car of the transport was loaded with 100 Jews. The great heat prevailing that day made the entire action very difficult and greatly impeded the transport.

After the regular nailing up and sealing of all cars, the transport train got underway to Belzec about 9:00 p.m. with a guard of one officer and nine men. With the coming of deep darkness in the night, many Jews escaped by squeezing through air holes after removing the barbed wire. While the guard was able to shoot many of them immediately, most of the escaping Jews were eliminated that night or the next day by the railroad guard or other police units.

This transport was delivered in Belzec without noteworthy incident, although given the length of the train and the deep darkness, the guard had proved to be too weak, as the commander of the transport guard from 6th Company of Police Regiment 24, who returned directly to Stanislau (Stanislawow), was able to report to me in person on 11 September.

On 8 September, some 300 Jews old and weak, ill, frail, and no longer transportable were executed. According to the order of 4 September, of which I was first informed on 6 September, concerning use of ammunition, 90% of those executed were shot with carbines and rifles. Only in exceptional cases were pistols used.

On 8 and 10 September, actions in Kuty, Kosow, Horodenka, Zaplatow, and Sniatyn (?) were carried out. Some 1,500 Jews had to be driven on foot marches 50 kms from Kuty or 35 kms from Kosow to Kolomyja, where they were kept overnight in the courtyard of the Security Police prison with other Jews brought together from the region. Other than the Jews rounded up in Horodenka and Sniatyn, who had already been loaded onto ten cars at each location by the Security Police, another 30 cars were loaded in Kolomyja. The total number sent to Belzec on the Resettlement train of 10 September amounted to 8,205.

In the actions in the area around Kolomyja on 8 and 10 September, some 400 Jews had to be eliminated by shooting for the well known reasons. In the great roundup of Jews to be resettled by 10 September in Kolomyja, the Security Police loaded all Jews into the 30 available train cars despite the objections I expressed. Given the great heat prevailing on those days and the strain on the Jews from the long foot marches or from waiting for days without being given any provisions worth noting, the excessively great overloading of most of the cars with 180 to 200 Jews was catastrophic in a way that had tremendously adverse effects on the transport.

How densely the ten cars each in Horodenka and Sniatyn were loaded with Jews by the Security Police is beyond my knowledge. In any case, both transports arrived in Kolomyja with completely inadequate guard, so that the barbed wire closing the air holes was almost entirely removed. As quickly as possible I had this train moved out of the train station in Kolomyja and coupled with the 30 cars standing on a side track far from the station. The Jewish Police (*Ordnungsdienst*) and members of the train station construction crew from Kolomyja were employed until the onset of darkness to close up all the insufficiently sealed cars in the usual regulation manner. A commando of one officer and fifteen men under the leadership of Captain Witzmann was assigned to guard the parked resettlement train of 50 cars until departure and to prevent any escape attempt. Given the already described strains on the Jews, the negative effect of the heat, and the great overloading of most of the cars, the Jews attempted time and again to break out of the parked train cars, as darkness had already set in toward 7:30 p.m. At 7:50 p.m. the guard commando of the resettlement train, with nine men under Corporal Jäcklein, arrived at the side track. Breakout attempts from the parked train could not be prevented in the darkness, nor could escaping Jews be shot in flight. In all train cars the Jews had completely undressed because of the heat.

As the train left Kolomyja on schedule at 8:50 p.m., the guard took up their stations. The guard commando, as initially stipulated by me, was divided into five men in a passenger car at the front and five men in a passenger car at the end of the train. On account of the length of the train and its total load of 8,205 Jews, this distribution proved to be unsuitable. Next time Corporal Jäcklein will arrange a distribution of guards along the entire train.

Throughout the entire trip the policemen had to remain in the cabooses, in order to be able to counter the escape attempts of the Jews. Shortly into the journey the Jews attempted to break through the sides and even through the ceilings of certain train cars. They were partially successful in perpetrating this scheme, so that already five stations before Stanislau, Corporal Jäcklein had to ask the stationmaster in Stanislau by telephone to lay out nails and boards in order to seal the damaged cars as required by orders and to request the station guard to watch the train. As the train entered Stanislau, the train station workers and the station guards were present to carry out the necessary repairs and in addition take over guarding the train.

The work took one and one half hours. When the train subsequently resumed its journey, it was discovered at the next stop some stations later that once again large holes had been broken by the Jews in some of the train cars and that for the most part the barbed wire fastened on the outside of the ventilation windows had been torn off. In one train car the Jews had even been working with hammer and saw. Upon interrogation they explained that the Security Police had left these tools with them, because they could make good use of them at their next work place. Corporal Jäcklein made the Jews hand over the tools. During the further journey, at every station stop, help was needed to nail up the train, because otherwise the rest of the trip would not have been at all possible. At 11:15 a.m. the train reached Lemberg.

Because no relief for the escort commando arrived, the escort commando J. (Jäcklein) had to continue guarding the train until Belzec. After a brief halt at the Lemberg train station, the train continued to the suburban station of Kleparow, where nine train cars marked with the letter "L" and destined for the labor camp, were turned over to SS-*Obersturmführer* Schulze and unloaded. SS-*Obersturmführer* Schulze then had some additional 1,000 Jews loaded. About 1:30 p.m. the transport departed for Belzec.

With the change of engine in Lemberg, such an old engine was hooked up that further travel was possible only with continuous interruptions. The slow journey was time and again used by the strongest Jews to press themselves through the holes they had forced open and to seek their safety in flight, because in jumping from the slow moving train they were scarcely injured. Despite the repeated requests to the engineer to go faster, this was not possible, so that the frequent stops on open stretches became increasingly unpleasant.

Shortly beyond Lemberg the commando had already shot off the ammunition they had with them and also used up a further 200 rounds that they had received from army soldiers, so that for the rest of the journey they had to resort to stones while the train was moving and to fixed bayonets when the train was stopped.

The ever greater panic spreading among the Jews due to the great heat, overloading of the train cars, and stink of dead bodies when unloading the train cars some 2,000 (200 ? *) Jews were found dead in the train made the transport almost unworkable. At 6:45 p.m. the transport arrived in Belzec, and around 7.30 p.m. was turned over by Corporal Jäcklein to the SS-*Obersturmführer* and head of the camp there. Until the unloading of the transport around 10:00 p.m., J. had to remain in the camp, while the escort commando was used to guard the train cars parked outside the camp. Because of the special circumstances described, the number of Jews who escaped from this transport cannot be specified. Nonetheless, it can be assumed that at least two thirds of the escaping Jews were shot or rendered harmless in some other way.

In the actions themselves for the period of 7 10 September 1942, no special incidents occurred. The cooperation between the Security Police and the Order Police units involved was good and without friction.

(signed)
Westermann
Reserve Lieutenant of the Schutz Police
And Company Commander

* A retyped version of Westermann's report shows the number "200" instead. SchutzPolice *Zugwachtmeister* Josef Jäcklein's report of 14.9.1942 confirms that the real number is 2000.

Regiment/Battalion Locations & Activities
June to November 26, 1940: In the Nederlands.[2]

November 27, 1940 to September 28, 1941: The battalion returns to Germany.

April 1941: In Hannover, Germany.

September 29, 1941: Transferred from Germany to Radovljica in Oberkrain.

December 1941: The battalion claimed forty-eight partisans killed in operations in the Veldes area plus 141 more executed as partisan suspects or while attempting to escape. Attempting to escape was a German euphemism for executed.

December 1941 to January 12, 1942: Together with Police Battalions 44, 171, 181, 325 and Landesschützen Battalion 322 and 857, they took part in the first large anti-partisan operation in Slovenia. It occurred in the mountains and wooded terrain between Ljubljana and Kranj and was aimed at destroying the Gorenjski Partisan Battalion which had been recruiting in the area and raiding the German garrison towns. The partisans avoided direct contact with the superior force while claiming they killed 200 Germans over the course of the operation. The actual casualties are not known.

April 1942: The regiment moved out of its garrison and deployed along the border between Oberkrain and the Italian zone of occupation in Slovenia.

July 1942: In Oberkrain and designated as the III/Police Regiment 24.

August 1 1942: The battalion is in Domschale. The battalion commander is staying at 13 Taborg Street. The communications platoon is at 6 Bahnhof Street. The rest of the battalion is at the Volkschool.[3]

August-September 1942: The battalion moved to the Horjul area west of Ljubljana in early August to take part in the final phase of anti-partisan Operation "Enzian" that began on July 13, 1942. There was little action because the few partisans in that area had already dispersed.

September 29, 1942: The battalion is operating in the area east of Kamnik.

November 11, 1942: The battalion participated in a sweep of the Vransko area.

January-February 1943: The battalion is transferred from Slovenia to France and reassigned to SS Police Regiment "Griese." It later became I/Police Rifle Regiment 35. It was immediately replaced in SS Police Regiment "Griese" by redesignating I/SS Police Regiment 23 as III/SS Police Regiment 24.

March 29 1944: In Hungary with the II/SS Police Regiment 12

April 1944: Destroyed in combat.

Police Battalion 101 (Reserve)

For the definite study of this battalion read the Christopher Browning book, *Ordinary Men: the Men of Police Battalion 101 and the Final Solution in Poland.*

This battalion was formed using personnel from the Hamburg area.

Field Post Number(s): 20462

Active in Poland in 1939 as the I/Police Regiment 2.

Formed the III/Police Regiment 25 in Lublin in July 1942.

Einsatzgruppen/Atrocity Activity

"Beginning in mid July 1942 with the roundup of Jews in the town of Jozefow near Bilgoraj, members of Police Battalion 101 were utilized for the mass shooting of Jewish civilians in towns throughout the Lublin district. These included (in addition to Jozefow) Lomazy (August 1942), Miedzyrzec (August 1942), Serokomla (September 1942), Kock (September 1942), Parczew (October 1942), Konskowola (October 1942), Miedzyrzec (a second action in October 1942) and Lukow (November 1942).

Police Battalion 101's participation in the Final Solution culminated in the *Erntefest* [Harvest Festival] massacre of November 3-4, 1943. In the course of this killing action, perhaps the largest directed against Jews of the entire war, an estimated 42,000 Jewish prisoners at the Lublin district concentration camps of Majdanek, Trawniki and Poniatowa were wiped out. It is estimated that during the period between July 1942 and November 1943, Police Battalion 101 was alone responsible for the shooting deaths of more than 38,000 Jews and the deportation of 45,000 others."[1]

Total killed by this battalion is 38,000 with an additional 45,200 people deported to the death camps.[2]

Regiment/Battalion Locations & Activities

The battalion entered Poland as a part of Police Group 2 under Army High Command (AOK) 10.

It assembled on September 1st, 1939 and was transported to Breslau, Germany and then to Tschenstochau, Poland by Hamburg City buses. The battalion was then split up and stationed in Kielce, Tomaszow, and Konskie, Poland.

September to December 1939: Active in the Kielce, Poland area.

May 1940: Posen, Poland.

July 1940: Lodz, Poland.

May 1941: Returned to Hamburg and most of the men were dispersed.

June 1942: The battalion returned for a second tour in Poland.

February 1943: In the Zamosc area.

April 1943: Ostrov & Lubelski areas.

May 1943: In Miedzyrzec.

June 1943: In the Parczew area.

April 1944: In the Chelmno area.

August 1944: I/25 was transferred to Cilli and Ljubjana and in 1945 in area of Krajina. II/25 and battalion operated in Western Poland until 1945.

Police Battalion 102 (Reserve)
The battalion was formed with personnel from the Hamburg area using active duty volunteers and reservists in September 1939 at the Victoria Kaserene.
Field Post Number(s): 27065, 46749
Commanding Officer(s): Major Herman Ziehe (1939 to 1940)
Other Officer(s): 1st Lieutenant Bock was the 1st company commander.
Active in Poland in 1939 as the II/Police Battalion 2 and attached to Police Group 2, AOK 10.

In December 1939 it was attached to Police Regiment Lublin.[1]

The battalion formed the II/Police Regiment 16 in July 1942 until 1943.

Regiment Locations & Actions
September 1939: The battalion is on the Polish/German border near Malapane. They passed through Tschenstochau, Belchatow and Tomaszow on their way to Lublin where the 1st company was stationed.

1939: The battalion was stationed in Lubartow and Krasnick, Poland. In October 1939 all Jewish offices and homes in Lubartow were plundered. In November 1939 all of the Jews in Lubartow, except those employed by the Germans were ordered to move to Parczew and Ostrow, Poland.[2]

January 1940: The battalion was back in Hamburg.[3]

February 1942 to January 1943: The battalion was in the Leningrad area.

October 25, to November 15, 1943: Participated in Operation "Heinrich" in the swampy, heavily wooded lake district between Nevel and the Latvian border.

April 1944: The battalion was in Vilna on ghetto duty.

1945: Last reported in the Courland Pocket.

Riga 1943 The regiment buries its commander, Colonel Kemper in Riga at the Waldfriedhof.

Riga 1943 The regiment buries its commander, Colonel Kemper, as a procession follows the coffin.

Police Battalion 103 (Reserve)
The battalion was formed with personnel from the Hamburg area in September 1939.
Field Post Number(s): 30225+
Commanding Officer(s): Major Heinrich Schultz
In Poland in 1939 as the III/Police Battalion 2 and attached to Police Group 2, AOK 10.

The battalion formed the I/ Police Regiment 12 in July 1942. The battalion also provided cadre for Police Schützen Regiment 31 in 1943.[1]

Regiment/Battalion Locations & Activities
October 1939: Stationed in Posen where they were quartered in a seminary.

May 1940 to 1943: Returned to and stationed in Hamburg. It is unclear to me what this battalion's role in the regiment was. The other two battalions (104, 105) were active in Italy and Hungary. The battalion itself is no longer listed after 1944. In all probability it was gutted for cadre for the new rifle regiment and the remainder used to replace men lost in battle in the regiment.

Above: German Police Headquarters in Hamburg 1933. This is the entrance to Police headquarters in Hamburg.

Opposite
Top: German Police in Hamburg 1932.

Bottom: German Police in Hamburg 1934. Note that they have already begun using the National Socialist Heil Hitler salute.

Police Battalion 104 (Reserve)

The battalion was formed using personnel from the Hamburg area beginning in September 1939 and was ready for deployment in January 1940.

Field Post Number: Unknown

Commanding Officer(s): Major Paul Gustav Giebe, Major Julius Gloe

The battalion formed the II/Police Regiment 12 in July 1942 in Hamburg. In August 1944 the battalion became the I/SS Police Regiment 1 or it was operating under the operational command of that regiment.[1]

Einsatzgruppe/Atrocity Activity

Summer 1940: In Zamosc, Poland. The battalion was stationed in Lublin in January 1940, and later it was transferred to Zamosc were it was involved in executions of Polish civilians and POWs.[2] Zamosc at this time was the center for the mass expulsions of Poles to make room for German and *Volksdeutche* settlers. The expelled Poles were then conscripted for forced labor either in Poland or in Germany.

Regiment/Battalion Location and Activities

January 1940: Stationed in Lublin, Poland and doing Jewish deportations in the area around Lublin. The battalion staff and the 2nd company were stationed in Lublin. The 1st company was in Lubartow. The 3rd company was in Krasnich. See Police Battalion 103 for more details.

Summer 1940: In Zamosc.

December 1940 to July 1942: Back in Hamburg.

1943: In Italy.

April 1944: Transferred to Hungary.

May 1944: In Northern Italy.

April 1945: In Italy, in the western Adriatic sector.

Police Battalion 105 (Reserve)

Battalion formed with personnel from the Bremen area on September 20, 1939. The officers and NCOs were active duty regulars with the rest of the ranks filled in by reserves. This battalion was assigned directly to Heinrich Himmler.

Field Post Number(s): 38739

Commanding Officer: Major Helwes (1941 to 1942).

The battalion formed the III/Police Regiment 12 in July 1942.

In March 1943 the battalion was transferred to III/SS Police Regiment 3.

Einsatzgruppen/Atrocity Activity

May 1942: In Westerbork, Holland where they were assisting in the transport of Jews to Auschwitz. Of the ninety-eight transports of Jews from the Netherlands ninety-three came from Westerbork and for each one the battalion would provide a thirty-man escort.

Regiment/Battalion Location and Activities

May 1940: In Rügen, Germany.

June 1940 to 1941: In Oslo, Norway.

February 1941: The battalion returned to Bremen.

May 1941 to February 1942: Active in Army Group North area where they were operating with the 207 Security Division. The battalion staff and the 2nd company was in Kempolowo; the 1st company was in Wolosow; the 3rd company in Klopizy. Kempolowo was the site of a large Russian POW camp.[1]

February 1942: The battalion was attached to *Kampfgruppe* "Böhme" and assigned to stop elements of the Soviet 2nd Shock Army who were counterattacking the entire width of Army Group North's front. The *kampfgruppe* was originally *Kampfgruppe* "Köppel" but the Police Colonel it was named after disobeyed orders to hold his positions at Mostki and Ljubino and decided to lead his troops in an fast advance to the rear. He was relieved of command upon his safe arrival in the rear. The battalion ended the month with a strength of five officers, twenty-six NCOs, and sixty-one enlisted.

May 1942: The battalion is transferred to Holland.

October 1943: In Italy.

December 1944: In Verona, and later Campiglia where they were operating with or as a part of SS Police Regiment 15.[2]

Police Battalion 111 (Reserve)
The battalion was formed with personnel from the Dessau and/or Hannover area.
Field Post Number(s): 10742
The battalion was in Poland and assigned to Police Regiment Radom in 1939. In June they had one armored car platoon.[1] In January 1942 they were attached to Police Regiment Cracow.
The battalion formed the II/Police Regiment 8 in May 1942.

Regiment/Battalion Location and Activities
December 1939 to October 1940: In Kielce, Poland.

October 1940 to January 1942: The battalion is in Hallendorf, Germany with the battalion staff in Hannover.

January 1942: In Rzeszow, Poland.

July 1942: The battalion is detached and operating with Army Security Division 286.

September 8, 1942: The battalion is in Mogilev.

January 1943: The regiment was destroyed in the Army Group South area of operations. See Police Battalion 51 for more details.[3]

October 29 to November 18, 1944: The regiment is north of Paks on the Danube helping defend Budapest from the approaching Soviet army. The regiment may have been rebuilt using Hungarians auxiliaries. They were assisting in the defense of the Solt bridgehead where the regiment along with other units with a large percentage of Hungarian auxiliaries were deemed so unreliable that machine guns were setup to the rear of them to discourage movement to the rear.[4]

June 1944: The regiment is disbanded in Koblenz, Germany. Remnants may have gone to SS Police Regiment 50 which was destroyed in 1945 defending the approaches to Berlin.

Police Battalion 112 (Reserve)
This battalion was formed with personnel from Magdeburg.
Field Post Number(s): 04097
Commanding Officer(s) Major Kurt Güdler (1945).[1]
In July 1942 the battalion became the II/Police Regiment 9 and each battalion was split off to assist an Army Security Division.

Regiment Locations & Activities
October 1941: The Hague.

The Jewish Market in Kielce

Goering salutes the battalion in Hannover in the 1930s.

July 1942: They were operating with the 207 Security Division around Mustvee, Estonia.

February 24 to March 20, 1943: The battalion participated in Operation "Winterzauber" (Winter Magic) on the Latvian/ Russian border. The operation had two *Einsatzgruppen* operating under SSPF Schröder and KdO Knecht. The units involved were; a company from the 10 *Gendarmerie* (Motorized) with two officers and twenty-nine men; The 20 *Gendarmerie* (Motorized); SS and Police Company z.b.V.; Police Communications Company 33. The enemy casualties were seventy-seven killed in action, 931 executed, and forty prisoners.[2]

October 25 to November 15, 1943: Participated in Operation "Heinrich" in the swampy, heavily wooded Lake District between Nevel and the Latvian border.

The regiment was assigned to Army Group North and destroyed in Russia in July 1944. This fits the timeframe when Army Group North was crushed by the Soviet Army with their offensive that began on June 22, 1944. Various available police regiments were pulled together to form *Kampfgruppe* "Jecklin" near Vydziai where they filled a gap between the 215th Infantry Division and the 3rd Panzer Army. They were in action there on July 4th, 1944 and destroyed. A second and short-lived SS Police Regiment 9 was formed in January 1945.

Police Battalion 121

The battalion was formed with personnel from the Koblenz area.
Field Post Number(s): 24126
Commanding Officer(s): Major Herbert Furck
The battalion formed the III and then the IV/Police Regiment 16 in November 1942.[1]

Regiment Locations & Activities

April 1941: In Diedenhofen, Germany & Luxemburg.

June 1941: Attached to Police Grenze (Border Police) West.

January 1942: Attached to BdO Saarbrücken.

July 1942: Transferred to Russia and working in Army Group North's operational area.

February to August 1942: The battalion was part of *Kampfgruppe* "Jeckeln." The troops were airlifted to the Leningrad area to stop the Russian counter offensive from breaking through German lines. This battalion and Police Battalion 206 were assigned to 212th Infantry division sector.

August 12, 1942: The battalion is patrolling near the mouth of the Tossna River near Iwanoskoje. At this point they have less than 200 men left in the battalion.

January 1943: Destroyed in combat and the remnants became the new I/SS Police Regiment 16 in Holland.[2]

Police Battalion 122 (Reserve)
This battalion was formed with personnel from the Mannheim area.
Field Post Number(s): 11136
Commanding Officer(s): Major(s) Paul Landwehr, Wilhelm Schumacher, Egon Ludovici, Hans Claus.[1] Major Paul Landwehr was killed in action on April 28, 1945 in eastern Germany. His awards were: Knight's Cross that was awarded March 17, 1945. The 1939 wound badge in black; and the Infantry Assault badge. In July 1942 the battalion formed the II/Police Regiment 14. Much of the regiments paperwork, including its war diary were lost either when the regiment was destroyed or later when the remaining records were stored in a basement that was flooded after a bombing raid. Himmler ordered the reconstruction of the regiment's history in 1944. A new Police Regiment 14 was created after the destruction of the first one. This battalion was not present at the destruction of the regiment at Kharkov in January 1943. It was used to form the cadre for the new SS Police Regiment 14. For more details of the destruction of the regiment see Police Battalion 51.

Regiment/Battalion Location and Activities
November 1939 to June 1940: The battalion was assembling in Metz, Germany.

June 1942: The battalion is in the Army Group Center operational area.

September 1-7, 1942: This regiment and Police Regiment 13 participates in Operation "Breslau." Total German casualties are five dead and ten wounded.[2]

September 1942: The battalion is transferred to Holland.

Police Battalion 123 (Reserve)
The Battalion was formed with personnel from the Rhein/Wiesbaden area.
Field Post Number(s): Unknown
Commanding Officer(s):
Other Officers: 1st Lieutenant Hans Lincke, 1st Lieutenant Nikolaus Hornig (1940).[1]
The battalion was issued 18 light machine guns on May 5 1941.[2]

The battalion formed the III/Police Regiment 7 in July 1942.

Regiment/Battalion Location and Activities
The 3rd company was assigned to HSSPF Wiesbaden briefly in 1939, and then again for an unknown period of time from 1940 to 1941.[3]

June 1941: On the Polish border.

January 1941: The entire battalion is in Luxemburg.

Summer 1941: The battalion with the exception of the 3rd company is transferred to Yugoslavia and stationed in Celje.

November 1941: The battalion is stationed in Krsko.

July 1942: The battalion has returned to Hallendorf.

Police Battalion 131 (Reserve)
The battalion was formed with personnel from the Wurzburg area in October 1939 in Zirndorf.
Field Post Number(s): 38064
Commanding Officer: Major Hans Otto Orth.[1]
Other Officers(s): 1st Company commander was Captain Otto Metzner. The 3rd company commander was 1st Lieutenant and SS-*Obersturmführer* Richard Keddi. The battalion Doctor was Dr. Rotlauf.

The battalion companies were each sent to separate existing police regiments to form tank companies. The regiments were; North, Center, South, and z.b.V. The battalion was dissolved on June 20, 1942.

Einsatzgruppen/Atrocity Activity
This battalion worked with *Sonderkommando* 7a.[2]

July 1941: Operating in the Army Group Center area of operation. The 1st company was in Grodno. The 2nd company is in Hoelzel. The 3rd company is in Kalvarija and Vilna, Lithuania. Kalvarija fell to the Germans on June 22, 1941. Sometime in early July approximately ninety people were shot about a mile outside of town. The people shot were a mix of Jews and Lithuanian communists. In late August 1941 the entire Jewish population was transported to the banks of the river Sheshupe on the pretext that they were being transported to a ghetto and on September 1, 1941 they were all shot.

September 1941: The 3rd company and Wehrmacht troops assisted the SD with a Jewish action in Rudnja. Here 850 Jews of both sexes were shot. The 3rd company was assisting *Sonderkommando* 7a during this time period.

Regiment/Battalion Location and Activities
Winter 1939: In Eichstädt, Germany.

Early 1940: In Norway.

Late 1940: The battalion returns to Germany and is in Nürnberg.

June 25, 1941: The 2nd company is in Lida as is *Einsatzkommando* 9. The battalion headquarters and the 3rd company are in Kavarija.[3]

July 1941: The 1st and 3rd companies are split between Vilna, Lida, and Grodno with the battalion headquarters and 3rd company in Wilejka at the end of the month.

August 1941: The battalion is assigned to the 403 Security Division in the Panzer Group III area of operations and are conducting anti-partisan operations near Smolensk.

September 1941: The battalion headquarters is in Newel. The 2nd company was patrolling the Polozsk to Newel road. Later during this month the headquarters and 2nd company moved to Welikije/Luki where they provided men for actions being conducted by *Einsatzkommando* 7a.

December 1941: The battalion staff and the 1st company are in Witebsk and the 3rd company is in Boguschewsk where they were doing highway patrols.

January 1942: The battalion is fighting on the front line and assisting with the recapturing of Kaluga along with the 290 Infantry Division. By the middle of January the battalion was down to 220 men from the 550 it had begun the month with. The battalion crumbled completely in combat. This may be partially explained by the actions of the battalion commander who demonstrated his leadership ability by taking the battalion medical vehicle, loading it with all the battalions medical supplies including the battalion doctor, and departing in the general direction of Germany.[4]

June 20, 1942: The remainder of the battalion is dissolved with the men being reclassified as anti tank troops and split among the three existing regiments in the East.

Police Battalion 132 (Reserve)
The battalion was formed with personnel from the Nürnberg area in April 1941.
Field Post Number(s): 14121
In October 1943 the battalion became the III/Police Regiment 9. The battalion was destroyed in combat on the Russian front in July 1944. See Police Battalion 61 for more details. A second short-lived SS Police Regiment 9 was formed in 1945.

Regiment/Battalion Location and Activities
1941: In Posen, Poland.

September 1942: The battalion was stationed in Mogilev.

October 1943: In Lodz, Poland.

October 25 to November 15, 1943: Participated in Operation "Heinrich" in the swampy, heavily wooded lake district between Nevel and the Latvian border.

The regiment was assigned to Army Group North and destroyed in Russia in July 1944. This fits the timeframe when

A police company poses for a group photo picture in Lodz. They were in refresher training there and the photo is dated October to November 1942.

Army Group North was crushed by the Soviet Army with the beginning of their offensive on June 22, 1944. Various available Police Regiments were pulled together to form *Kampfgruppe* "Jecklin," named after the SS-*Obergruppenführer* near Vydziai. They were to fill a gap between the 215th Infantry Division and the III Panzer Army and were destroyed in action on July 4, 1944.

Police Battalion 133 (Reserve)
The battalion was formed with personnel from the Nürnberg area.
Field Post Number(s): Unknown
Commanding Officer(s): Major Gustav Englisch, he joined NSDAP in 1933 and the SS (November 26, 1943) with an SS rank of *Sturmbannführer*.
Other Officer(s): Captain Ernest Lederer, 1st Company Commander. Captain Rehbein 3rd Company Commander.
Assigned as the II/Police Regiment 24 in July 1942.

Einsatzgruppen/Atrocity Activity
October 6, 1941: In Nadvornaya, Ukraine where the battalion killed 2,000 people. Until September 1941 Nadvornaya was occupied by the Hungarians after which the Germans took control of the town. The first Action took place October 6, 1941 when 2,000 Jews were ordered to assemble in the town square. The Jews were transported by truck to the killing site in Bukowinka Forest where ditches had already been prepared. There they were all shot with one source stating that some of them were buried alive. The battalion was assisted in this action by Ukrainian auxiliaries and *gendarmerie*.[1]

September 1941: The 1st company is in Kolomea assisting in the transfer from the ghetto to Belzec concentration camp of 8,700 Jews. Kolomea was being used as a staging area for deportations to the camps and as Jews were shipped out they were quickly replaced with ones being brought in from neighboring villages.

October, 1941: The 1st and 2nd companies are stationed in Stanislawow. At least one of the companies assisted in the killing of 12,000 Jews in one day. Police members marched the Jews from their neighborhood in columns to the large Jewish graveyard outside of town that was fenced off with a high stone wall. Inside the Jews found two large pits had been dug. In small groups they had to march out above the pits on a wooden walkway where they were shot. Security Police and members of this battalion along with a handful of railroad police did the actual shooting. The companies continued doing roundups for deportation and smaller scale killing in Stanislawow until at least March 1942. The ghetto in Stanislawow was where Jews from the small villages in the area were transported to and held for further transportation to Belzec or execution there.[2]

October 16, 1941: The 3rd company is in Delatyn where they assisted in the killing of approximately 2,000 Jews. The victims were buried in three mass graves in the Wilchowets Forest.

November 1942: Stationed in Rawa Ruska which is approximately ten miles from the Belzec death camp and on the railroad line that was used to transport people to Belzec. This camp was finished being built in November 1942 and dismantled in June 1943. The transport trains had a problem with jumpers who escaped out of the boxcars. This happened especially when the train had to wait until the rail yard at Belzec was cleared of previous trains.

July-December 12, 1942: The 1st Company is in the Kolomyia area working with the SD. One of their assignments was a round up on September 7, 1942 of the Jews in Kolomyia ghetto for transportation to Belzec concentration camp for extermination. The Jews of the ghetto were ordered to report for registration for "Resettlement." After a detail had combed the ghetto for stragglers another group was added to those that waited it brought the total to 5,900 Jews awaiting transport. The old and sick were culled from this group and shot. The remainder were marched to the train and packed into the empty cars where upon they were transported to Belzec.

Regiment/Battalion Location and Activities
October 1941: The battalion staff was in Stanislau and the 1st company was in Drohobycz, Poland.

July 1942: The battalion was in Lvov.

October 1942: Stanislawow, Ukraine.

September 1942: Lvov, Poland.

February 1943: The battalion is in Galicia and has been for a number of months.

November 1944: The battalion is in the Kattowitz and Hindenburg area.

Police Battalion 134
The battalion was formed with personnel from the Wurzburg area.
Field Post Number(s): 14268
The battalion formed the III/ Police Regiment 8 in 1942.

Regiment/Battalion Location and Activities
April 1942: In Brünn.

July 1942: The battalion was in Lvov.

April 1943: In Orsha, Belorussia where they were assigned to the 286 Security Division.

January 1943: Most of the regiment was destroyed in Army Group South area. See Police Battalion 51 for the events of the destruction.

March 1945: The remains of the regiment took part in the battle for Berlin as part of SS Police Regiment 50.

Police Battalion 171 (Reserve)
The battalion was formed with personnel from the Vienna, Austria area in Poland in September 1939. On formation the battalion had a company of armored cars (believed to be 12 Steyr armored cars) attached. In 1942 they have a PAK platoon listed.[1]
Field Post Number(s): 11307
Commanding Officer(s): Major Hertlein
Other Officer(s): The 1st company commander was Captain Leo Degeler. The 3rd company commander was Lieutenant Prochiner. Later in 1942 Captain Bräunlich was the 3rd company commander. A 3rd company platoon leader in 1941 was Roman Schwitenburg who by 1944 was the the 3rd company commander. He was replaced as platoon leader by 1st Lieutenant Lohr.

Active in Poland in 1939 as the III/Police Regiment 1. The battalion in December, 1939 was attached to Police Regiment Radom.[2]

The battalion was issued 8 Model 1908 machine guns on May 5, 1941.[3]

The battalion formed the II/Police Regiment 19 in July, 1942 in Veldes.

Einsatzgruppen/Atrocity Activity
Unknown Date: The 3rd company was providing security for transports to Auschwitz.

Regiment/Battalion Locations & Activities
February 1941: In Karlsbad, Sudetenland.

August 1941: Transferred from the Reich (probably Karlsbad) to Kamnik, Slovenia to take part in the first German operation against partisans in Slovenia with a sweep in the mountains southwest of Radovljica.

August 8, 1941: The 3rd company was in Stein and billeted in the local VolkSchool which was located at Adolf Hitler Square.The company was hunting communists and executed any they found. They were especially interested in finding the communist leader Andreas Preschern.

October 1941: The battalion is patrolling the Italian/Slovakian border.

December 1941: The battalion is now in Radovljica. The 3rd company is in Rann.

December 27, 1941 to January 12, 1942: Together with Police Battalions 44, 93, 181, 325 and *Landesschützen* Battalion 322 and 857, they took part in the first large anti-partisan operation in Slovenia. It occurred in the mountains and wooded terrain between Ljubljana and Kranj and was aimed at destroying the Gorenjski Partisan Battalion which had been recruiting in the area and raiding the German garrison towns. The partisans avoided direct contact with the superior force while claiming they killed 200 Germans over the course of the operation. Actual casualties are not known.

June 30, 1942: Elements of the battalion were supporting an Italian anti-partisan operation in the Horjul area near Ljubljana. The 3rd company was in Kranj.

July 1942: In Veldes and redesignated the II/Police Regiment 19.

July 13, to August 1942: The battalion participated in Operation "Enzian" that was carried out to sweep and clear nascent partisan bands from the mountains and forests west of Ljubljana centered on the Horjul area. For the most part, the partisans evaded the sweep.

December 24, 1942: The battalion is operating in the Kamnik area that was at the head of a local rail line. To the north and east of the town was a sparsely populated mountain and forest inhabited by partisan bands.

January 1943: The entire regiment took part in a sweep of the mountains around Kropa. During this time they had the 14 Police Panzer company assigned to them.

June 1944: Transferred to Grenoble, France to reinforce security operations against French partisans.

July 1944: The battalion was encircled by the French partisans in Limoges. One source has the local German garrison commander, General Gleiniger who attempted to surrender Limoges, but it was not accepted by the 19th SS Police Regiment so the regiment assassinated Gleiniger and escaped towards Guéret and Creuse leaving his body in a rubbish pile in the local cemetery. Another possibility is that he committed suicide after surrendering.

October 15, 1944: The 9th company as well as other elements of the regiment was in the Colmar area in Alsace and in combat with the U.S. 442nd Regimental Combat Team. Only a shadow of its former self, the regiment was attached to the 16 *Volksgrenadier* Division.

December 1944: Released from its attachment to the 16 *Volksgrenadier* Division, the regiment began returning to Slovenia during the second half of December.

March 1945: The entire regiment was now using Celje as its permanent garrison, although the battalions and companies were deployed in the field on operations.

April 23, 1945: The battalion is operating in the Kamnik area.[4]

Police Battalion 181 (Reserve)

This battalion was formed with personnel from the Salzburg, Austria area in the fall of 1939.

Field Post Number(s): 24921(?)

Commanding Officer(s): Major Kärnbach (1942).[1]

Other Officer(s): Captain Kaufmann was the communications platoon commander. The 1st company commander was Captain Oremba. Later the 1st company commander was Captain Wilhelm Engelbrecht who won the Knight's Cross for his actions in combat southwest of Grenoble during the Fall of 1944. The 2nd company commander was 1st Lieutenant Garoia. The 3rd company commander was 1st Lieutenant Hartung.

In December 1939 the battalion was attached to Police Regiment Radom.

The battalion was issued eighteen light machine guns on May 5, 1941.[2]

They formed the III/ Police Regiment 19 in July, 1942 in Radom for employment in Southern Austria and Northern Slovenia.

Regiment/Battalion Locations & Activities

April 1941: Transferred to Oberkrain during the second half of April a week or two after the Germans had occupied Yugoslavia with garrisons in Kamnik, Begunje and St. Vid (a suburb of Ljubljana). Their initial task in Slovenia was the maintenance of order and the deportation of Slovenes from what was now part of the Reich.

August 8-9, 1941: Took part in the first German operations against partisans in Slovenia with a sweep in the mountains southwest of Radovljica.

December 12, 1941: The Partisan Cankarev Battalion reportedly ambushed and "destroyed" a fifty-two man patrol from Police Battalion 181 near Skofja Loka, claiming forty-five killed and seven wounded.

December 27, 1941 to January 12, 1942: The battalion together with Police Battalions 44, 93, 171, 325 and *Landesschützen* Battalion 322 and 857, took part in the first large anti-partisan operation in Slovenia. It occurred in the mountains and wooded terrain between Ljubljana and Kranj and was aimed at destroying the Gorenjski Partisan Battalion which had been recruiting in the area and raiding the German garrison towns. The partisans avoided direct contact with the superior force while claiming they killed 200 Germans over the course of the operation. Actual casualties are not known.

December 31, 1941: The battalion is now stationed in Kamnik.

June 30, 1942: Elements of the battalion were supporting an Italian anti-partisan operation in the Horjul area.

August 1, 1942: The battalion is in Crainburg. The commanding officer and Captain Kaufmann communications platoon leader are staying at Adolf Hitler Platz Nr.2.[3]

January 1943: The entire regiment took part in a sweep of the mountains around Kropa.

February 25, 1943: The I/19 and this battalion carried out a limited sweep of the Marija Reka area to the north of Trbovlje.

October 15, 1943: The regiment has been sent into the field to find and destroy a large "bandit" force numbering over 4,000. The II battalion was assigned as a blocking force in St. Georg while the other two battalions were to drive them into the trap. It did not work out as planned. The regiment was outgunned and outnumbered and began calling for air support and backup. For seven days one of the battalions was trapped in Rudolfswerth and had to be resupplied by air. The battalion was rescued by elements of the 9 SS Panzer and 16 SS Panzer Grenadier Divisions.[4]

June 1944: Transferred to Grenoble, France to reinforce security operations against French partisans.

September 1944: The regiment is about thirty-two miles north of Dijon.

October 15, 1944: The 9th company as well as other elements of the regiment was near Colmar in Alsace in combat with the U.S. 442nd Regimental Combat Team. Only a shadow of its former self, the regiment was attached to the 16 *Volksgrenadier* Division.

December 1944: Released from its attachment to the 16 *Volksgrenadier* Division, the Regiment began returning to Slovenia during the second half of December.

February 13, 1945: The battalion is defending the valley and rail line between Kocevje and nearby Ribnica.

March 20, 1945: The entire regiment was now using Celje as its permanent garrison, although the battalions and companies were deployed in the field on operations.[4]

Police Battalion 251

This battalion was formed from the Stuttgart area. Police Battalions 251 to 256 were originally planned for Norway and were formed using younger recruits than what were found in the reserve battalions.

Field Post Number(s): 40059

Commanding Officer(s): Major Richter, Major Carl Rehdanz.

Other Officer(s): The Battalion Adjutant was 1st Lieutenant Helmut Holzbecher.

The 1st company commander was 1st Lieutenant Johann Paehler.

The platoon leader was Walter Moebus.

The 2nd company commander was Captain Herman Kiefer.

The platoon leaders were 1st Lieutenant Wilhelm Lemke and Lieutenant Alois Haker.

The 3rd company commander was 1st Lieutenant Johannes Mennekes.

The platoon leaders were 1st Lieutenant(s) Franz Schaefer, Walter Bobel, Johann Knoll,

The 4th company commander was Lieutenant Franz Pechlaner.

The battalion formed the I/Police Regiment 26 on July 1942 in Drontheim, Norway.

Einsatzgruppen/Atrocity Activity
August 16-20, 1943: In Bialystok where the battalion helped kill 2,000 Jews and deported another 10,000 to Treblinka concentration camp. This was the beginning of the final liquidation of the Bialystok ghetto.[1]

Regiment/Battalion Locations & Activities
August 4 to November 1940: in Deggingen/Württemburg.

October 1940 to April 1942: In Drontheim, Norway. In November 1942 they were conducting ski patrols on the Swedish and Norwegian border.

May 29, 1943: The battalion is in Schneidemühl where it receives 200 recruits from Police *Ausbildung* Battalion Dortmund/Wellinghofen.

September 1943: In Zamosc, Poland. They were sent to fight partisans that were being led by General Kolpak. The General had 3,000 men in his brigade some of whom were Russian paratroopers. They were operating in the Carpathian Mountains.[2]

October 25, to November 15, 1943: Participated in Operation "Heinrich" in the swampy, heavily wooded lake district between Nevel and the Latvian border. This battalion belonged to Section "Wieder" along with Police Battalion 313 and 316 (Estonian); a Police Panzer company; a SD *Einsatzkommando*; three Flak troops; a Police communications company, and two PAK troops.[3]

July 1944: Destroyed in combat with the Russians. See Police Battalion 61 for more details.

Police Battalion 252
This battalion was formed with personnel from Munich.
Field Post Number(s): 42144
In Norway as part of Police Regiment Norway North until 1942.
The battalion formed the I/Police Regiment 28 on July 1942 in Drontheim, Norway. Later the battalion became the I/Police Schützen Regiment 32 in 1943.

Regiment/Battalion Locations & Activities
Summer 1941 to July 1942: In Norway.

July 1943: Assigned to and active with HSSPF White Russia.

Summer 1943: In Baranowice.

October 1943: In Kiev.

July 1944: The regiment was destroyed in Russia. See Police Battalion 61 for more details.

Police Battalion 253
This battalion was formed with personnel from the Munich area.
Field Post Number(s): 44077
Commanding Officer(s): SS-*Sturmbannführer* and Major Heinrich Richter (1941-1942).
Major Richter was a member of NSDAP (May 1, 1937) and the SS from March 1, 1939 SS Number 314 217. After 1942, he was the commanding officer of the II/Police Rifle Regiment 31 (1943-1944). His decorations; Friedrich August Medal in Bronze. The Iron Cross 2nd and 1st Class (1918). The KVK II with Swords (1941). His fitness reports in 1928 twice mentioned a problem with nerves as a result of injuries in World War I. It also mentioned he was a nationalist who shared Adolf Hitler's worldview. His fitness report in February 1943 stated he was "too mild and unsuited for command." The report also mentioned a problem with alcohol. Later his record

states that he spent April to September 1944 hospitalized in Dresden for an unstated illness.

The battalion is in Norway as part of Police Regiment Norway South until 1942.[1]

The battalion formed the II/Police Regiment 28 in July 1942. It later became the new I/SS Police Regiment 15 in February 1943.[2]

Regiment/Battalion Locations & Activities
1940: In Furstenfeldbruck, Germany.

1941 to July 1942: In Southern Norway.

Police Battalion 254
This battalion was formed using personnel from the Königsberg area.
Field Post Number(s): 46931
Commanding Officer(s): Major Kurt Bendzko.
It was transferred to SS Police Division 4 in September 1941.

Regiment/Battalion Locations & Activities
September 1941: In Norway.

Police Battalion 255
This battalion was formed with personnel from the Brüx area.
Field Post Number(s): 44334
Commanding Officer(s): Major Phillip Rehbein
The battalion is in Norway until 1942
They formed the II/Police Regiment 26 sometime in July 1942 in Drontheim

Einsatzgruppen/Atrocity Activity
August 16-20, 1943: In Bialystok where the battalion assisted in killing 25,000 to 30,000 Jews.[1]

August 1943: Assisted in a ghetto liquidation action in Gleboki where they assisted in the deaths of 3,000 Jews. See Police Battalion 13 for more details.[2]

Regiment/Battalion Locations & Activities
July 1942: Drontheim, Norway.

February 1942: Back in Germany.

May 29, 1943: The battalion is in Adlershorst and receives 262 recurits from Dortmund.

June 1943: Now stationed in Zamosc and conducting anti-partisan operations. They were assigned to destroy General Kolpak's partisan band that was operating in the Carpathian Mountains.

October 25 to November 15, 1943: Participated in Operation "Heinrich" in the swampy, heavily wooded lake district between Nevel and the Latvian border. See Police Battalion 251 for details.

July 1944: Destroyed in combat with the Russians. See Police Battalion 61 for more details.

Police Battalion 256
This battalion was formed with personnel from Vienna, Austria.
Field Post Number(s): 40562
Commanding Officer: Major Olsen, Major Ernest August Falk.
The battalion formed the III/ Police Regiment 36 in July 1942 in Drontheim, Norway.[1]

Einsatzgruppen/Atrocity Activity
August 16-20, 1943: In Bialystok where the battalion assisted in killing 25,000-30,000 people.[2]

Regiment/Battalion Locations & Activities
Summer 1941 to July 1942: In Drontheim.

February 1943: Returned to Germany.

June 1943: In Zamosc, Poland conducting anti-partisan operations in the Carpathians with the rest of the regiment where they were trying to find and destroy General Kolpak and his partisan band.

October 25 to November 15, 1943: Participated in Operation "Heinrich" in the swampy, heavily wooded lake district between Nevel and the Latvian border. See Police Battalion 251 for details.

July 1944: Destroyed in combat with the Russians. See Police Battalion 61 for more details.

Police Battalion 301 (Reserve)
The battalion was formed with personnel from the Bochum area. The 301 to 325 series of police battalions were created using younger recruits than the men who formed the reserve battalions. This series was formed for duty in the *Generalgouvernement* and the *Protectorate*.
Field Post Number(s): 09159
Commanding Officer(s): Lt.Col. Erich Klein (? To 1942), Major Herman Dam (1942 to ?).
Other Officer(s): Lt. Willi Thomas, Adjutant.

1st Company Commander: Captain Walter Wilken.

2nd Company Commander: Erich Fredrich (rank unknown).

3rd Company Commander: Karl Leineweber (rank unknown).

4th Company Commander: Edmund Berke (rank unknown).

This battalion had a horse-mounted company. In 1940 the battalion had 2 HMG platoons and an armored car platoon.[1]

In 1941 the battalion was the I/Police Regiment Warsaw.

In July 1942 became the III/Police Regiment 13 in Warsaw. It had been part of Police Regiment Center. Police Regiment Center provided the regimental staff.

Regiment/Battalion Locations & Activities
September 15, 1940: The battalion is in Ostrow Maczowicki.

October 1940 to the end of 1941: The battalion was in Warsaw as a part of Police Regiment Warsaw. They were primarily active outside Warsaw guarding Polish POW camps. During this time they were also executing POWs. These camps were open to the elements and no provision was made to feed these men and as a result cannibalism was not uncommon.[2]

April 1942: In Konstantin.

May 1942: In Koydymowo. In May they were also operating briefly as the III/Police Regiment Center.

August 1-5, 1942: Participating in Operation "Nordpol III" (North Pole). The battalion along with the II swept a thickly forested area near Demidov. The operation is said to have mostly taken place at night.

August 17-29, 1942: The entire regiment is participating in Operation "Grief" along with the Police Regiment 14. See Police Battalion 6.

September 1-7, 1942: This regiment and Police Regiment 14 participates in Operation "Breslau." Total German casualties are five dead and ten wounded.[3]

November 1, 1942: The entire regiment operated in the AOK 9 sector northeast of Smolensk.

January 28, 1943: The regiment is assigned to Operation "*Erntefest* II" (Harvest Festival) which was carried out west of the Minsk and Slutsk highway from January 28, to February 9, 1943. According to a reliable German report, 2,400 partisans were killed and 2,300 partisan helpers or sympathizers executed.

March 31 to April 7 1943: The regiment is divided between SS and Police *Kampfgruppe* "Schimana" and "Kuntze" in Belorussia for Operation "*Lenz Süd*"against several thousand partisans in the Sloboda area. Part of Police Regiment 2, the 12 Police Panzer Company, and SS Special Battalion "Dirlewanger" also participated.

April 1943: The battalion is in Chausy under SSPF Mogilew.

July/August: 1943: The regiment belonged to a force of 4 SS Police regiments plus other units that were brought up to attack the partisan "Kovpak Brigade" that was active in western Ukraine and Galicia. See Police Battalion 85.

September 1943: In Lublin.

October 25, to November 15, 1943: Active in Operation "Heinrich". The SS Police Regiment 13 (less the II battalion which is in Smolensk) plus twenty-eight battalions of police, *Schuma*, security (*Sicherungs*) troops, police tank companies and support units surrounded and attacked a huge concentration of partisans (estimated by the Germans at more than 16,000) in the swampy, heavily wooded lake district between Nevel and the Latvian border. Before the operation made any progress, Soviet breakthroughs in the vicinity forced the troops to end "Heinrich" and switch over to a defensive role against the oncoming regular units of the Red Army. Heavy losses were sustained over the next several weeks.

December 30, 1943 to January 20, 1944: The entire regiment (2,239 men) is in the front line between Polotsk and Nevel under SS and Police *Kampfgruppe* "von Gottberg" (total strength 8,132).

March 1, 1944: The battalion along with the I/13 is attached to SS and Police *Kampfgruppe* "von Gottberg."

April 1944: Transferred from Belorussia to Klagenfurt, Austria and Oberkrain in Slovenia to reinforce the anti-partisan units under the HSSPF in Wehrkreis XVIII. Most sources state that the regiment was stationed in Austria just across the border from Slovenia and returned to these garrisons after each anti-partisan operation in Slovenia concluded.

May 14-25, 1944: SS Police Regiment 14 and 25, *Landesschützen* Regiment 18, *Gebirgsjäger* Regiment 134, Ersatz Artillery Regiment 112, and a large number of Steirischen *Wehrmannschaft* (indigenous German militia from Styria) carried out anti-partisan Operation "Anton I." Assembling in Kamnik, Celje, Sostanj, Crna and Slovenjgradec, the surrounding German forces attacked the four brigades of the Partisan 4th Operations Zone in their mountain redoubt. According to postwar Yugoslav accounts, the partisans were able to evade their attackers and there were few casualties on either side.

June-July 1944: Conducting offensive sweeps and patrols in the area between Bleiburg and Solčava.

August 19-24, 1944: Operating from Crna, the regiment and other forces carried out a sweep of the Logarska valley near Solcava where the Partisan 4th Operations Zone had established a large dump for supplies being dropped by Allied aircraft based in Italy; but unfortunately for the Germans, the partisans succeeded in evacuating the dump before the enemy columns arrived.

December 11, 1944: After the regiment assembled in Črna and the with the SS Police Regiment 28 and Lehr Regiment Brandenburg in Kamnik, the combined force advanced on the Gornja Savinja Valley to destroy elements of the Partisan 14th Division that had been occupying the villages of Luce, Ljubno as well as other communities along the valley. Several days after the operation began a column from SS Police Regiment 25 and strong elements from Reserve *Gebirgsjäger* Regiment 18 and *Landesschützen* Regiment 18 moved forward from the east and south, driving the partisans from most of the valley. Casualty figures are not known.

March 25, 1945: The battalion is in Eisenkappel.[4]

Police Battalion 302

The battalion was formed with personnel from the Munich area.

Field Post Number(s): 46393, 09159

The battalion formed the I/Police Mountain Regiment 18 in May 23, 1942 in Garmisch Partenkirchen, Bavaria. This was a four company battalion.

The battalion was equipped with three 75mm artillery batteries.

The regiment may have had a tank company made up of captured Italian tanks.[1]

Regiment/Battalion Locations & Activities

September 1940: In Norway.

July 26, 1942: Transferred to Oberkrain, Slovenia.

August 1, 1942: The battalion is St. Voit.[2]

August-October 1942: Patrolled the mountains and forests around Horjul to seek out and destroy partisan bands as part of Operation "Enzian" that was already underway. This activity had as much to do with training the battalion as it did with the ongoing operation.

October 12, 1942: The last elements of the regiment departed Slovenia for Garmisch Partenkirchen.

November 1942: Refitting in preparation for transfer.

December 1942: Moved by train to Danzig and then by ship to Oulu, Finland for assignment to the XVIII *Gebirgskorps*/20 *Gebirgs* Army (*General* Dietl) in northern Finland.

July 10 to August 18, 1943: Departed Finland and transferred via Oulu and Danzig to Amfissa in Greece.

September 1943 to September 1944: Now operational as an anti-partisan unit in Greece; over the next nine months the regiment's battalions changed location frequently in Greece as the tactical situation dictated. It is referred to almost daily in the records of Heersgruppe E, usually in connection with minor skirmishes against partisans and reprisal actions against villages and their inhabitants. The anti-partisan war in Greece was brutal and no quarter was given by either side.

June 6-21, 1944: The regiment, together with a *Kampfgruppe* from 117 *Jäger* Division and Greek police battalions conducted Operation "Natter" against Greek partisans in south central Peloponnesus.

August 5-26, 1944: Along with elements of 104 Jäger Division and Greek volunteer and police units, the regiment advanced west and southwest from Amfissa to surround and destroy partisans around the village of Karoutia.

September 1, 1944: Ordered to accompany the 4 SS Police Divisions north to Vrsac on the Yugoslav and Romanian border to block the westward movement of Soviet forces.

September 1944: Withdrew north from Greece to the Belgrade and Vrsac area; along the way the III battalion was ambushed by partisans in the vicinity of Topola and decimated.

September 12, 1944: Most of the regiment is now in Pozarevac.

October 2, 1944: Regimental staff is in Straza and under the tactical command of Panzer Grenadier Division Brandenburg that came under *Generalkommando* Müller/Army HQ. Serbian.

October 11-23, 1944: Took part in the defense of Belgrade along with many other units, but forced to withdraw in the face of numerically superior Soviet and Yugoslav Partisan forces and by October 24, the remnants of the regiment were engaged around Irig.

November 1944: Fought in defensive positions around Erdevik, Syrmia as part of *Kampfgruppe* Lindenblatt to November 11, 1944 and then transferred to the Osijek to Valpovo area where it took up defensive positions along the Danube under *Kampfgruppe* "Nitsche" until the end of January 1945.

December 31, 1944: The regimental staff is in Valpovo and tactically under XXXIV Army Corps/Heers Group E.

February 1945: The regiment moved twenty-four miles to the WNW and took up positions along the Drava in the vicinity of Sopje and Podravska Slatina and remained there until the end of March.

April 1, 1945: The regiment moved northwest again to the Koprivnica to Varasdin area where it was assigned to *Kampfgruppe* "Fischer" and fighting alongside elements of the XV Cossack Cavalry Corps.

May 5, 1945: Began withdrawing toward Maribor near the Slovene and Austrian border, eventually surrendering there on May 13, 1945. Of the initial complement of 4,800 men, the regiment is said to have lost a total of 3,080 killed, wounded and missing.

Police Battalion 303

This battalion was formed with personnel from the Bremen area in 1939. This was a four company battalion with three of them equipped with bicycles.

Field Post Number(s): 38101

Commanding Officer(s): Major Heinrich Hannibal (1941-1942),[1] Major Hassenpusch (1943 to ?).

Other Officer(s): 1st Company Commander was Captain Oswald Altendorf. 2nd Company Commander was Captain Heinrich Ebeling, 1st Lieutenant Gerhard Schulze. 3rd Company Commander was Captain Franz Falter.

The battalion was active with Police Regiment South from 1941-1942. Police Regiment South was assigned to HSSPF South and was used primarily to kill large numbers of civilians. This battalion began the invasion of the Soviet Union with three bicycle powered companies.

The battalion formed the II/Police Regiment 10 in July 1942.

Einsatzgruppen/Atrocity Activity

September 19, 1941: The battalion was in Zhitomir where 18,000 Jews were killed.[2]

The quote below is from the Operational Situation Report USSR No. 106 (October 7, 1941):

> "On September 19, 1941, from 4 o'clock [a.m.], the Jewish quarter was emptied after having been surrounded and closed the previous evening by 60 members of the Ukrainian militia. The transport [deportation] was accomplished in 12 trucks, part of which had been supplied by military headquarters and part by the city administration of Zhitomir. After the transport had been carried out and the necessary preparations made with the help of 150 prisoners, 3,145 Jews were registered and shot.

> After 25 to 30 tons of linen, clothing, shoes, dishes, etc. that had been confiscated in the course of the action were handed over to the officials of the NSV in Zhitomir for distribution. Valuables and money were conveyed to the *Sonderkommando* 4a."

September 29 to October 5, 1941: The battalion is in Babi Yar where they assisted in killing 33,771 people. Also present was Police Battalion 45. The executions were supervised by the HSSPF, SS-*Obergruppenführer* Friedrich Jeckeln. Also present were an unknown number of Ukrainian auxiliaries, SD, Security Police, and local Gestapo representatives. In other actions Jeckeln supervised he used the SS personnel attached to his staff as shooters. He was known for his hands on leadership and for making sure that everyone got their hands bloody. The police battalions were primarily used for crowd control, transportation and rounding up the victims. Given the methods that they used to perform these duties it is highly likely that a number of deaths can be attributed to them. Also given the number of people killed and his propensity for making sure everyone took part it is probable that the Jeckeln's shooters were relieved by members of the battalions. In the next two years another 60,000 people were killed at Babi Yar.

This battalion is responsible for the deaths of 41,599 people.[3]

Regiment Locations & Activities
1941: In Jaslow.

Winter 1941-1942: In the Ukraine, South Russia and attached to *Kampfgruppe* "Prützmann."

1943: In Kupjansk, Ukraine that was liberated by the Soviets in February 1943.

April 1943: The 3rd company and possibly the battalion were in Berezno on April 25, 1943.

February 8, 1943: Attached to SS and Police *Kampfgruppe* "von dem Bach" an active in Operation "Hornung." This battalion, the III/10 (Police Battalion 314), and *Schuma* Battalion 103 formed *Kampfgruppe* "South" which together with three other *Kampfgruppes* were used for Operation "Hornung." For more information on Operation Hornung see Police Battalion 13.

1944: In Rowno.

January-February 1944: Located near Kustyn, Ukraine.

March 15, 1944: Brody, Ukraine.

April 1944: In Kostopol, Ukraine.

May 1944: In Stanislawczik, Poland.

August 1944: Sent to Slovenia.

March 1945: In Idrija, Slovenia.[4]

Police Battalion 304
This battalion formed four companies with personnel from Chemnitz in September 1940.
Field Post Number(s): 46177
Commanding Officer(s): Major Willi Nickel, Major Kurt Deckert (1941-1942), Major Detlef Ohrt,[1] Major George Gewehr.[2]
Other Officer(s): 2nd Company Commander was 1st Lieutenant Franz Xavier Lochbrunner. He was a member of the Hitler Youth from 1933-1938. A member of the SA from 1938-1940. He joined the SS in 1940 and was assigned to the 4 SS Police Division. He served briefly with them until wounded and after a period of time in the hospital joined this battalion.

Effective November 1940 the battalion was the II/Police Battalion Warsaw.

In the fall of 1941 the battalion was used to create Police Regiment z.b.V.

The battalion formed the I/Police Regiment 11 in July 1942 in Southern Russia.

Einsatzgruppen/Atrocity Activity
March 1941: The battalion is under the operational command of HSSPF South that was commanded by SS-*Obergruppenführer* Jecklen. He was one of Himmler's most proliferate murderers and the battalion was probably operating as part of *Einsatzgruppe* 5.

August 25, 1941: Police Battalion 304 reported capturing and executing eight Soviet paratroopers. They were still operating out of Warsaw at this time.

September 5, 1941: Took part in a massacre in Vinnitsa. Vinnitsa was not far from Hitler's command post "Wehrwolf" and the area was rendered "Jew free" rather quickly. The death toll for this action was 2,200 and it started at 0800 in the town market square where the town Jews had been told to assemble. The battalion then did a house-to-house search of the Jewish quarter. The Jews were shot using relays of ten men armed with the model 1898 rifle. It is highly probable they were operating with *Einsatzgruppe* D.

September 16, 1941: Took part in a massacre in Gaisin. Here the battalion shot 100 Jewish men in the town marketplace and then transported 3,000 men and women to a killing site where they were shot. Gaisin and the area around it (Bukovinia) had a number of massacres starting in July of 1941. The Jewish ghetto in Gaisin was not established until October 1941.

September 20, 1941: In Kirowograd. The actions taken in this town, Vinnitsa, and Gaisin are described in the records of the trial of Manfred Pöhlig. In Kirowograd 4,000 Jews were assembled in the town square and transported to the killing site. The record states that he, "participated in the shooting of a total number of at least 5,300 Jews in the course of three execution operations, by herding together the victims, by leading them to the execution sites and by securing these sites, as well as in one instance by single handed shooting of a victim." He received a life sentence. Manfred Pöhlig received an Iron Cross 2nd class for his heroic actions.[3]

September 22-23, 1941: In Uman where 1,412 Jews were killed. I have found different numbers for the total of how many people died there. What is probable is that the Jews were summoned using the pretext of being counted as part of a census and led a short distance away and shot. The Vinnitsa area eventually had over 20,000 Jews killed.

March 28, 1942: They are ordered north from the Ukraine to Belorussia and participated in Operation "Bamberg," a large anti-partisan operation in the Bobruisk area that ran until April 4, 1942. Of the 3,423 killed during the operation by German count, 1,085 are said to have been burned alive after being locked into building by the forces under German command.

Regiment/Battalion Locations & Activities

March 10, 1941: The battalion came under the operational command of HQ *Reichsführer*-SS on this date and possibly with effect from this date.

June 22, 1941: Assigned to advance into the Ukraine with Army Group South on the commencement of hostilities against Russia.

September to October 1941: Assigned to the newly formed Police Regiment z.b.V. in Kiev. The battalion commander at this time was Major Deckert.

January 1942: The 3rd company was on the front line and attached to the 1 SS Division.

November 1942: Conducting anti-partisan operations in the Pripet Marsh area.

Summer 1942: The battalion is operating south and west of Kiev.

June 25 to July 27, 1943: The entire regiment, Police Battalion 307, 8 *Gendarmerie* (Platoon), and the SS Calvary Division participated in Operation "Seydlitz" in the Owrutsch/Mosyr area. They liberated 12,407 cattle, 288 horses, 7,246 sheep, and 124 pigs. Enemy casualties were in the thousands.

December 1944: The battalion, located in Biedlow, was still a four company battalion which included a pioneer platoon. The entire battalion had nine officers and 1,035 men at this time.

April 1944: In Lvov, Poland.

December 1944: In Chelmno where it was destroyed in combat, while the other two battalions were destroyed on the frontline with the LVI Panzer Corp in November.

The 3rd company men and officers.

The 3rd company in Brezeno on April 25, 1943.

Somewhere in Russia.

Men of the 3rd company in Limunowa prior to the invasion of Russia.

The men of 3rd company after getting haircuts give the local boys a trim.

May 1941 Somewhere near Cracow. They are standing on the edge of a large ditch.

The graves of the men of Police Regiment 11.

The men of the 3rd company. The photo was probably taken prior to or just after the invasion of Russia because of the lack of decorations.

The NCOs of 3rd company gather while behind them the companies march.

The 3rd company gathers to enjoy a beer in Poland on May 30, 1941.

The 3rd company on the march on December 29, 1941 to the front line to stop the Soviet counteroffensive.

Men of the 3rd company pose in front of a van in Kiev. This may be a gas van.

Ukranians and the men of 3rd company.

Police Battalion 305
The battalion was formed using personnel from the Hamburg area in April 1940 in Itzehoe.
Field Post Number(s): 20080
Commanding Officer(s): Major Otto Giesecke (1940-1941), Major Georg Robert Wessig (1941-1945).[1]
The battalion for a brief time was the I/Police Regiment 15.

The battalion formed the III/Police Regiment 16 in October 1942.

Einsatzgruppen/Atrocity Activity
Fall 1941: Part of the battalion was in Radom where they assisted the SD in the shooting of sixteen Polish women. They were also assiting in deportations from Kielce and Radom to Auschwitz.

Regiment/Battalion Locations & Activities
October 1940: The battalion was stationed in Kielce, Poland. Kielce had a large ghetto. When it was locked down in 1941 there were 28,000 Jews inside.

Date Unknown: In Kamienna, Poland. A company from this battalion provided guards for an SD.

February-August 1942: The battalion fought outside Leningrad with the 121 Infantry Division along with the 222 Infantry Division, 4 SS Police Division, and Latvian volunteer units in the area of Krasnoje Selo.[2]

Interrogation camp. In 1940 a number of Poles were executed here. Later in 1942 it became a slave labor camp.

April-June 1942: In Ladogasse.

January-April 1943: Stationed in Puschkino with the 2 SS Infantry Brigade (Motorized).

May 1943: In Tilsit.

September 1943 to January 1944: Operating from Tesno.

October 25 to November 15, 1943: Active in Operation "Heinrich."

April 1944: In Wilna.

May 1944: The battalion staff and 2nd company are in Aischisk and the 3rd company is in Rudniki.

July and August 1944: Fighting at the front and with the 132 Infantry Division in Dünaberg.

August 1944: The battalion is with *Kampfgruppe* "Werther" near Riga.

1945: Trapped in Courland pocket until the end of the war.

Above: 1940 Kielce Poland. Men of the 1st company of the battalion pose with their heavy machine gun and mascot.

Below: 1941 Poland. Men of the 1st company of the battalion pose with two heavy machine guns and puppies.

Left: 1941 Kielce, Poland. A member of the 1st company of the battalion stands his guard post.

Above: 1941 Kielce, Poland. The heavy weapons platoon at inspection.

Right: The Jewish Ghetto Police for Radom.

Police Battalion 306

This battalion was formed using personnel from Frankfurt.
Field Post Number(s): 21241
Commanding Officer(s): Major Paul Landwehr, Major Dreir (1941-1942).
Other Officers and Men
1st Company commander: Captain Heinrich Plantius.
2nd Company commander: Captain Johann Josef Kuhr.
3rd Company commander: Rudolf Eckert.
3rd Company platoon leader: Lieutenant Heinrich Gross.
3rd Company: Gerd Kurze.
4th Company commander: Günter Waltz.
Beginning in October 1940 until February 18, 1942 the battalion is stationed in Lublin as part of Police Regiment Lublin.

The battalion formed the II/Police Regiment 15 in July 1942. This was the first version of Regiment 15.

Einsatzgruppen/Atrocity Activity
February 1941: In the Biala Podlaska area and Lublin area where one member of the battalion (Günter Waltz, thirteen year sentence) was tried and convicted of assisting in the shooting of six Polish villagers after an unsuccessful mopping up operation. Also the individual shooting of seven Jews for violating the decree concerning residential restrictions in the *Generalgouvernement* and the shooting of two allegedly escaped Russian POW's. The 2nd company of the battalion was active in this area also during this time period.[1]

November 1941: In Zamosc where the battalion executed 780 Russian POWs. Zamosc had a large POW camp with over 50,000 Russian POWs.

September 4, 1942: In Luninets, where 2,800 Jews were killed.

September 9, 1942: In Wysokie, Poland where 1,400 Jews were killed.

September 11, 1942: In Stolin, Belorussia where 6,500 Jews were killed.

September 1942: In Janow Podlaski, Poland, where 2,500 Jews were killed.

September 10, 1942: In David Gorodok where 1,100 Jews were killed. Apparently the Jews were summoned under the pretext that they would be forming labor battalions to fix damaged roads and bridges. They were then shot.

October 1942: In Pinsk where they assisted in killing at least 16,200 Jews. They were assisted in this action by the 1st Company, Police Battalion 310 and a mounted police unit.[2]

This battalion is responsible for the deaths of 24,480 people.[3]

Regiment/Battalion Locations & Activities
October 1940: In Kielce, Poland.

1940 to February 18, 1942: The battalion was stationed in Lublin, Poland.

June 1941 to February 1942: The 2nd company has two platoons (1 and 3) in Biala Podlaka and the 2nd platoon is in Zamosc. Most of 3rd company is Krasnik.

February 1942: The battalion is on the front lines as part of Kampfgroup "Jeckeln" in the AOK 18 area of operations outside Leningrad. They were fighting near Ladogasse with the 223 Infantry Division.

July 1942: Still fighting at the front but now near Ludsen, Lithuania. July to December 1942: Fighting "bandits" in the Rokitno Swamp. From November to December they were hunting partisans along with the 3 Police Panzer Company west of Pinsk.

December 1942: Recalled to frontline duty and destroyed in the fighting for the Don river.

April-August 1943: In Norway where the survivors are being reformed into the new SS Police Regiment 15.

1943-1945: Stationed in Milano, Italy.

Police Battalion 307 (Motorized)

This battalion was formed with personnel from the Duisburg area in Lübeck at the end of January 1940. The enlisted men were taken from the 1909-1912 year group.
Field Post Number(s): 43985 as the III/24 20822

Commanding Officer(s): Major Paul Kärnbach (1939-1941), Lieutenant Colonel Dressler (1941 to April 1941), Major Theodore Stahr (April 1941 to June 1941),[1] Major/Lieutenant Colonel Siegfried Binz (December 1941 to November 1943),[2] Major Gebelein (Gendarmerie Officer) (November 1943 to November 1944).[3]
Other Officer(s): The 1st company commander was Captain Grube who was decorated with the Iron Cross 2nd Class for his actions with *Einsatzkommando* 8. The 1st company, 1st platoon leader was 1st Lt. Friedrich Niehoff.

The 2nd company commander was 1st Lt. Siegfried Klocker.

The 3rd company, 1st platoon leader was Lieutenant Kayser.

The officers and NCOs' were active duty. All officers were members of NSDAP, and five of them were also members of the SS. The three companies were equipped with six light machine guns and four heavy machine guns. All companies were motorized including the signals platoon with exception of the NSKK (support) company.

In February 1940 the battalion was assigned as Police Battalion Lübeck and based there.

On October 3, 1940 the battalion was assigned as the I/ Police Regiment Center.

On July 28, 1942 the battalion became the I/Police Regiment 23 and on March 29, 1943 the III/SS Police Regiment 24. The regiment was based in Cracow until 1944.

Einsatzgruppen/Atrocity Activity
This is not a complete list of their executions; rather it is more of a geographical trail of their movements. Based on the research done for this book this battalion and many of the other battalions were executing people on an almost daily basis in 1941.

July 1941: The battalion was assigned to *Einsatzgruppe* B.

July 18-26, 1941: In Baranowicze, where as a part of *Einsatzkommando* 8 they killed 381 young Jewish men. This was not the entire battalion as less than 200 men were active in *Einsatzkommando* 8. Quite possibly the battalion had detailed a platoon or company to the *kommando*.

July 1941: In Starobin where the same men who were with *Einsatzkommando* 8 helped kill at least 1,000 Jewish men, women, and children. They were assisted in this action by local citizens of the town. One account mentions that it took three days for dirt covered bodies to stop moving.

July 1941: Brest Litovsk, Poland, Where the battalion helped kill 6,000-10,000 Jews.

July to December 1941: In Slutzk.[4]

August 1941: In Starye Dorogi and Bobruisk. The 2nd Company is in Sluzk where they killed 30-50 women and 4-6 young children.

September 1941: In Tschetschewitschi.

October 1941: In Mogilev.

June 1942: In Tarnow, Poland where the battalion helped to kill or deport 16,000 Jews.

August 1942: Neu Sandau, Poland, where the battalion helped to kill or deport 18,000 Jews.

July 22 to August 3, 1942: The 1st Company was active in the Przemysl, Poland ghetto roundup and deportation to Belzec death camp. Approximately 12,000 Jews were deported and 2,500 elderly or sick were shot. They were assisted by Polish and Ukrainian police auxiliaries Gendarmerie troops, SD, and Estonian auxiliaries.[5]

Regiment/Battalion Locations & Activities
February 10, 1940 to October 2, 1940: In Lübeck assembling and fitting out.

October 3, 1940 to June 23, 1941: In Biala Polaska and later in Terespol that marked the border between Germany and the USSR briefly.

August 1941: Providing rail security. They were working with the 252 and 162 Infantry Divisions. Police Regiment Center fighting with the 252 Infantry Division in August stopped the breakthrough of the 12 Russian Infantry Division near Slutsk.[6]

June-December 1941: While assigned to Police Regiment Center they were providing railroad security and fighting partisans. During this time period they were in; Brest

Litowsk, Baranowitsche, Slusk, Bereza Kartuska, Stare Dorogi Bobruisk, Tescheschwitschi, Mogilev, and back to Tscheschewitschi.

October 1941: Some elements of the battalion are in Smolensk. Smolensk was the headquarters of *Einsatzgruppe* B. Other elements of the battalion were in Bobruisk and in Mogilew. During this time period the battalion assisted in stopping a Soviet breakout attempt near Viazma. The Soviets had landed 6,000 paratroopers at the airfield and were using them as assault troops to stop the German attempt at encircling Moscow from the north. Major Binz supposedly had ridden into battle on a tank shouting "Look here you swine, you can't shoot German police." He was recommended for the Knight's Cross for his actions here.

October 15, 1941: Searching for a large band of partisans (100 men) in the forest west of Nowoje Usinki.

December 1941: Assisted in the recapture of Kaluga. Also involved were the 31, 131, and 61 Infantry Divisions.

January 1 to February 27, 1942: Fighting with the IV Army around Kaluga and Juchnow.

April 1942: The battalion was part of a *kampfgruppe* sent to relieve an encircled Wehrmacht unit in Beresina.

April 1942: The headquarters and 1st company were stationed in Rzeszow. The 2nd company was in Przemysel. The 3rd company had one platoon in Tarnow and its other platoon in Neu Sandez.

August 1942: Conducting anti-partisan operations near Gleboki.

August 25 to September 3, 1942: The battalion operating with the entire regiment as task force "Barkholt" along Latvian Rifle Battalions 15, 18, 26, and Estonian Battalion 256 participated in Operation "*Sumpffieber*" (Swamp Fever) in the swamps near Minsk. Also participating was task force "Binz" which was the SS Police Regiment 24 with their attached Lithuanian and Latvia *Schuma* battalions. The 1st SS Infantry (Motorized) and a number of motorized *gendarmerie* platoons also participated. The goal of the operation was to "stop terror actions and plundering by bandits."

The operation had seven named phases:

Swampfever Nord Treuenfeld 1: Beginning at 05:00 8/25/42 to 9/26/42
Swampfever Nord Treuenfeld 2: Illegible to 8/30/42
Swampfever Nord Barkholt: 8/26/42 to 8/31/42
Swampfever Nord Treuenfeld 3: 8/31/42 to 9/1/42
Swampfever West: 9/3/42 to 9/6/42
Swampfever Southwest: 9/8 to 9/20/42
Kurzenicze: 9/12/42
Miciajewicze: 9/2/42 to 9/3/42

The results were; forty-nine bandit camps and bunkers destroyed, 389 bandits killed, and 8,350 Jews executed. They also reported discovering three heavy machine guns, two light machine guns, one radio, various munitions including hand grenades, and they seized sixty-two horses.

November 1942 to August 1943: Participated in the following Operations; "Tannenbaum." This operations objective was to clear partisans from the area along the Una bend between Bosanski Novi and Buzim. The operation was canceled and the troops switched to Operation "Ristow" that began on December 24 1942.

December 31, 1942: Operating in the Pripet swamps by Lusino.

November 1942 to April 1943: They participated in Operations "Hamburg", "Altona", "Nürnberg", "Franz", "Erntefest I and II", "Hornung", 'Föhn I", and "Lenz Süd."

January 5-14, 1943: This battalion, Police Battalion 22, and all of SS Police Regiment 13 participated in Operation "Franz" which was primarily a labor sweep for bodies to be sent back to the Reich for forced labor.

March 1943: In Rowno providing security for the Rowno to Berditschew road.[7]

November 1942 to March 1943: Operating under the control of the IV Army and the III Panzer Corp where they were patrolling around Kostopol and Janowo Dolina.

April 1943: Operating as part of *Kampfgruppe* "Binz" along with SS Police Battalion 31, and a Latvian and Ukrainian battalion.

June 25 to July 27, 1943: The battalion, SS Police Regiment 11, 8 Gendarmerie (Platoon), and the SS Calvary Division participated in Operation "Seydlitz" in the Owrutsch/Mosyr area. They liberated 12,407 cattle, 288 horses, 7,246 sheep, and 124 pigs. Partisan casualties were in the thousands.

September 1943: Participating in Operation "Heinrich" which was canceled due to a Russian offensive in the same area.

March-June 1944: On the front lines in the Polozk and Newel area with the IV Army and the III Panzer AOK.

June 1944: In the Beresina swamps conducting anti-partisan operations where they participated in Operation "Frühlingsfest" near Lepel. After 1944 the battalion has a horse squadron with 400 horses.

June 26, to July 14, 1944: On the front lines with the 4th and 5th Panzer Army around Orscha, Borissow, and Minsk.

July 15, 1944 to January 17, 1945: Refitting in Kattowitz.

January 18, to March 1945: Fighting on the front line in Bendsburg, Sossnowitz, Petrowitz, Hindenburg, and Gleiwitz. The battalion's total strength was thirty-seven men. They retreated to Koniggrätz moving by horseback.

April 27, 1945: The regiment is stricken from the rolls in Kattowitz.

May 5, 1945: The five remaining men reported to BdO Prague.

May 12, 1945: They surrendered to the Americans near Pilsen and were interned at the POW camp in Lüneburg. Almost all of the information above was written at the Lüneburg POW camp in May, 1946 by Captain Bernhard Lühr.[8]

Police Battalion 308

This battalion was formed using personnel from the Duisburg and Düsseldorf areas in January 1940. The 1st company was from Neudorf and the 2nd, 3rd, and 4th companies were from Hamborn.[1]

Field Post Number(s): 26310
Commanding Officer(s): Major Hans Fleckner.
Other Officer(s): Dr. and 1st Leutenant Otto Klapprich. The battalion adjutant was Captain Manfred Ischner. The 1st company commander was 1st Leutenant Karl Schuster who interestingly enough worked in what in America is called Human Relations after the war in Duisburg.

Einsatzgruppen/Atrocity Activity
October-December 1940: The battalion was in Warsaw and assigned to Police Regiment Warsaw. The men were on ghetto watch and assisting in deportations to Buchenwald and Auschwitz. They were billeted at the university in Warsaw. 1st company provided a commando to the SD/SS that traveled to Stalag 324, 316, and 368 executing communists, Polish intelligentsia, and Jews.

August-September 1941: The 4th squad of the 3rd company was involved in a Jewish action in Tscherjegow.

Fall 1941: The battalion is providing squads for security on the trains carrying Jews from Grodno to Auschwitz.[2]

Regiment/Battalion Locations & Activities
1941: In Biala Podlaska.

September 3 to October 1941: The 3rd company is stationed in Dobejanka.

October 1941 to May 1942: The 1st company is in Brjansk.

December 1941: Elements of the battalion are in Smolensk and in the Juchnow/Medyn area.

January 1942: Assigned to Army Group Center and active in front line fighting. The battalion sent 210 men to the front near Juchnow most of whom never returned.

February 26, 1942: The 2nd company is in Spynka where they were operating with two companies from Police Battalion 82.

March 1942: The battalion was dissolved and the remnants went to Police Battalion 307 and 32.

Above: Members of the battalion eat from a field kitchen. The officer is probably a company commander.

Below: Members of the battalion eat from a field kitchen. Notice the company First Sergeant with his World War I Iron Cross 2nd class ribbon.

Police Battalion 309

This battalion was formed using personnel from the Cologne area on September 19, 1940. It was a three company battalion with one heavy machine gun platoon.

Field Post Number(s): 45785

Commanding Officer: Major/LTC. Ernest Weis (1939-1942), Major Bruckner (1942 to ?).[1]

Other Officer(s): 1st Company: Captain Hans Behrens. He was awarded the Iron Cross 2nd class for his actions in Bialystok on July 11, 1941. Captain Behrens was a member of the *Freikorps* (right wing paramilitary) and then the police during the Weimar Republic. After the war he continued being a policeman and in 1951 was an instructor at the police school in Kiel. He retired in 1955 with a full pension.[2]

2nd Company: 1st Lieutenant Johann Hoehl.

3rd Company: 1st Lieutenant Rolf Joachim Buchs. He was awarded the Iron Cross 2nd class for his actions in Bialystok on July 11, 1941. Lieutenant Buchs joined the SS in 1934. He continued working for the police after the war and in the 1950s was chief of police in Solingen. After a trial in 1968 he received a four year sentence for his war crimes.

3rd company, 4th Platoon Leader, Lieutenant Heinrich Schneider was awarded the Iron Cross 2nd class for his actions in Bialystok on July 11, 1941. He received a pension after the war and worked for the firm of Villbrandt & Zander AG in Wuppertal as a work leader. 3rd Company, Top Sergeant was Georg Schwarz. Sergeant Schwarz continued working for the police and in 1967 was a police *Hauptmeister* in Neuss.

The battalion formed the I/Police Regiment 7 in July 1942.

Einsatzgruppen/Atrocity Activity

June 27, 1941: Bialystok, Poland with the 221st Security Division. The 1st and 3rd Company of this battalion helped burn over 700 Jews alive inside a synagogue. They assisted in killing 2,000-2,200 Jews in Bialystok. *Einsatzkommando* 9 was also active in these actions with them.[3]

July 1941: The 1st Company provided security for a Jewish work camp in Hajnowka, Poland.

August 1941: Tykocin Poland. The Jews were loaded into trucks and drove to the Lopuchowo forest. The Jewish men dug the pits for everyone and then members of Police Battalion 309 and 316 then shot 1,400 people. During the month of August this battalion reported killing 3,274 partisans and Jews and 260 irregulars.[4]

October 1, 1941: The 1st Company is in Kletnja where they killed thirteen Jews.

October 6, 1941: Elements of the battalion was in Nadworna, Poland. On this date 2,500 or one half of the towns Jews were taken about a mile away to the town of Bukowinka and shot.

This battalion is responsible for a minimum of 2,040 deaths.[5]

Regiment/Battalion Locations & Actions

September 23, 1940: The battalion left Cologne for Radom.

January 1941: The battalion is in Pionki.

May 1941: In Ostrolenka. They were assigned to the 221 Security Division and working with the 2nd Regiment of that division on the then border of the Soviet Union and Germany.

June 22, 1941: The 1st company is providing security for a railroad bridge over the Narew River and a supply base near Grabowo. The 2nd, machine gun platoon, and the 3rd company are on the front line awaiting the start order for Barbarossa.

July 24, 1941: The battalion is in Slutsk, then Bobruisk.

August 30, 1941: The battalion is in Smolensk.

September 1, 1941: The battalion headquarters are in Shlobin. The battalion companies are patrolling northwest and east of Shlobin with an emphasis on the Shlobin to Gomel road.

September 9, 1941: The battalion has moved its headquarters to Gomel and its companies are patrolling around the Gomel and Rjepki area. The companies have been split off with each patrolling part of the road net in the Gomel area. The 3rd company is stationed in Dobrjanka during this period.

October 1, 1941: The 1st company is transferred to Kletnja where they are working with the 581 *Feldgenderarmerie Abteilung* (Detachment).

February 1942: The 1st company is patrolling the highway in the Wekuljewo and Letoschniki area. The 2nd company is in Shukowka. The 3rd company is in Potschep.

March 3, 1942: The battalion is west of Brjansk participating in Operation "Anton."

March 6, 1942: At least a platoon-sized unit was detached to participate in Operation "Anton I."

March 16, 1942: The 2nd company is fighting near Rshaniza.

March 20, 1942: The battalion is participating in Operation "Jobst."

April 3, 1942: The 2nd and 3rd companies are south of Brjansk and patrolling the road from there to Prolowka.

May 1942: The 1st and 3rd companies are stationed in Luxemburg.

June 1943: The entire battalion returned to Cologne, and then it is sent to Norway where it finished the war.

A labor deportation in Gomel. The man in the leather coat is Burgermeister Sidorenko who was executed by the Germans as a partisan in 1943.

Lining up for deportation as forced labor.

Police Battalion 310

This battalion was formed using personnel from Berlin/Oranienburg in September 1940.

Field Post Number(s): 22625

Commanding Officer(s): Major Bruno Koschmieder, Major Bruno Holling.

Other Officer(s): The 1st company commander was Captain Heinz Kasper.

The 2nd company commander was Helmet Saur.[1]

The 3rd company commander was Captain Werner Pöhls. Captain Pöhls was a member of the SS having joined in 1933, and the NSDAP in March 1935. He attended SS *Junkerschule* in Braunschweig in 1934.

The 1st company had a horse-mounted platoon.

In October 1941 this battalion received the 2nd company of Police Battalion 74, the 3rd company of Police Battalion 83, and the 1st company of Police Battalion 85.

They were part of Police Regiment Radom until July 1942.

The battalion helped form the III/Police Regiment 15 in July 1942.

Einsatzgruppen/Atrocity Activity

September 1942: In Chimieliszcze and Lesnia where the battalion was conducting anti-partisan operations. As part of these operations they burned down the villages, shot the villagers, and stole the cattle and grain.

September 1942: In Zablocie where they burnt down the village and conducted themselves as they did in Chimieliszcze and Lesnia. The 3rd company arrived in Zablocie with members of the SD and divided into three groups. They then shot 289 people, mainly women and children. They also "liberated" 700 cows, 400 pigs, 70 horses, and farm equipment.[2]

September 22, 1942: In Borki where members of the battalion killed at least 700 people.[3]

October 10, 1942: The battalion is participating in the liquidation of the Brest ghetto where they were assisted by police auxiliaries. They began with an early morning sealing of the ghetto and then ordered everyone to assemble. Those that tried to hide were then found in the house-to-house search and usually shot on the spot or beaten They were then marched to the Brest train station and shipped via overloaded livestock cars to the village of Bereza Kartuzka. Upon arrival, they were unloaded and forced to remove their clothes. They were then marched in groups to the killing site where a trench that had already been dug.

September 1-3, 1942: Participated in Operation "Michel" near Bereza Kartuska. This was followed three days later by Operation "Dreick" southwest of Kobryn. During this operation the 1st company killed 203 men, 372 women, and 130 children. The 3rd company killed 289 men, women, and children. The battalion also carried off 455 cattle, 525 sheep, and 258 pigs.

September 22-23, 1942: A platoon from this battalion assisted by the 16 *Gendarmerie* Motorized killed forty-nine men, ninety-seven women, and 23 children in Borysowka.

October 15-16, 1942: The battalion is in Brest Litowsk assisting in the deportation of 16,000 Jews to Treblinka.

October 23, 1942: The 3rd company is in Malorita/Wiowawo where at 07:00 they killed 128 people. These 128 people consisted of twenty-eight men, forty women, and sixty children. They also carried off forty cows, six pigs, and sixty sheep.[4]

September 29 to November 1, 1942: The 2nd company is in Pinsk were they assisted in the killing of 18,000 Jews. Police Battalion 306 was also present.

Regiment/Battalions Locations & Activities

October 1940 to August 1941: The battalion is stationed in Lvov.

August 1941: The battalion staff is in Lvov. The 1st company is in Tschenstochau with the mounted squad. One platoon from the company is detached and sent to Tarnopol and another is sent to Boryslaw. The 2nd company is in Stanislau where in November they are involved in a Jewish action. They are operating from here until February 21, 1942. The 3rd company is still in Lvov.

November 12, 1941: The 2nd company is in Stanislau.

February 21, to July 1942: Leningrad, Russia area. The battalion was assigned to *Kampfgruppe* "Jeckeln" to stop the Russian counter offensive in the Leningrad area. Five police battalions and the V (Berlin Watch Battalion) from 1st SS Division LSSAH were transported by plane. This battalion was assigned to the operational control of 223 Infantry Division. They had twenty-six dead and sixty-nine wounded while they were on the front line.[5]

July 18, 1942: The battalion is in Dünaberg, Latvia.

August 1942: In the Kobrin area conducting anti-partisan operations. They were on patrol in this area for the next three months.

October 1942: In Brest Litowsk providing ghetto security.

November 1942 to January 1943: On the front lines. See Police Battalion 51 for details.

October 1943: In Pinsk.

1943: In Norway.

Fall 1943: In Italy.

March 1945: Located in Trieste, Italy.[7]

Police Battalion 311

The battalion was formed from the Jena area in January 1940.
Field Post Number(s): 14502
Commanding Officers: Major Danz (1940 to January, 1942), Major Krase (1943 to ?).

In 1941 this battalion was the I/Police Regiment Cracow.

This battalion formed the II/Police Regiment 6 in July 1942.

This battalion is responsible for the deaths of 5,186 people (civilians).

Regiment Locations & Actions
October 15, 1940: The battalion arrives in Poland.

June 1941: The battalion is on the Polish/USSR border near the Bessarabien area.

September 1941: The battalion was in Dnjepropetrowsk. On October 11, 1941 at least 11,000 Jews were shot there.

December 1941 to January 1942: The battalion is with the 444 Security Division fighting partisans around Nowomekowsk and Pawlograd.[2]

January 1943: The regiment was destroyed during the fighting near the Don River with remnants making it to Gdynia, Poland in March 1943. See Police Battalion 51 for more details. A second SS Police Regiment was created in 1944 and was commanded by Lt.Col. Maiwald, the former commander of Police Battalion 72.

Police Battalion 312

The battalion is formed with men from Innsbruck.
Field Post Number(s): 44123, 18146
The battalion formed the II/Police Mountain Regiment 18 in May 1942 in Bavaria.

Regiment/Battalion Locations and Activities
September, 1940: In Northern Norway.

April 1941: The battalion was operating in the far north of Norway as a ski battalion.

July 1942: Herzogwald, Germany.

August 1, 1942: The battalion is in St. Walburga.[1]

See Police Battalion 302 for the regimental history.

Police Battalion 313

This battalion was formed from personnel from Stettin. This was a four company battalion.
Field Post Number(s): 20758
Commanding Officer(s): Major Erwin Grimm
In 1941 the battalion was assigned to Police Regiment Lublin.
This battalion formed the III/Police Regiment 28 in October 1942. Later it became the III/Police Regiment 14 in November 1942. As the III/14 it also had one company of Ukrainian auxiliaries.[1]

Regiment/Battalion Locations and Activities
1941: Zamosz, Poland.

January 1942: The battalion was in Cracow, Brest Litowsk, Bobruisk, and then on the front line in Army Group Center.

August 17-29, 1942: The entire regiment is participating in Operation "Grief" along with the Police Regiment 13. See Police Battalion 6 for more details.

September 1-7, 1942: This regiment and Police Regiment 13 participates in Operation "Breslau." Total German casualties are five dead and ten wounded.[2]

April 1943: (Formation orders dated March 29, and April 19, 1943) in Southern France using Stab (HQ Staff)/Police Regiment Griese as its HQ Staff, I and III/SS Police Regiment 1 as its I and III Battalion and the remnants of the former SS Police Regiment 14 as its II Battalion. The regiment's new home garrison was in Berlin.

June 4, 1943: The battalion is stationed in Litija to counter partisan incursions in the Sava Valley and attacks on the rail line that ran along it.

September 1943: The regiment is ordered by III SS Panzer Corps to advance from Zagreb to Karlovac and then to Ogulin to help disarm the Italian units in the area following Italy's capitulation the previous day. The lead elements of the regiment finally reached Ogulin on September 14, 1943.

September 19, 1943: The battalion is in Ogulin.

October 12, 1943: The battalion and elements of the Panzer Grenadier *Versuchs* Regiment (Motorized) 901 attacked units of the Partisan 8th Division NOVJ in the villages of Josipdol and Skradnik and drove them out. This was the opening phase of a much larger operation called "Wolkenbruch III" that was intended to drive the partisans out of an area they had liberated around Delnice and further to the north and east in Slovenia that included elements of the 71 Infantry Division, 1 SS Panzer Division, 11 SS Panzer Grenadier Division, The 162 (Turkish) Infantry Division, the "Hermann Göring" Division, and 1,200 Slovene Domobrans. By the time the operation ended on November 15, the regiment was operating around Kocevje. "Wolkenbruch III" was conducted with great brutality and many civilians were summarily executed on the spot and their homes and villages burned to the ground.

October 20, 1943: The regiment is reassigned from III SS Panzer Corps to II SS Panzer Corps.

May 14-25, 1944: SS Police Regiment 13 and 25, Landesschützen Regiment 18, *Gebirgsjäger* Regiment 134, Eratz Artillery Regiment 112 and a large number of Steirischen *Wehrmannschaft* (Indigenous German militia from Styria) carried out anti-partisan Operation "Anton I" Assembling in Kamnik, Celje, Sostanj, Crna and Slovenjgradec, the surrounding German forces attacked the 4 brigades of the Partisan 4th Operations Zone in their mountain redoubt. According to postwar Yugoslav accounts, the partisans were able to evade their attackers and there were few casualties on either side.

November 18-24, 1944: The battalion participated in an anti-partisan sweep around the Maribor area.

February 2, 1945: The battalion was attacked by partisans in the Frankolovo to Stranice area near Celje.[3]

March 16, 1945: Most of the regiment was redesignated SS and Police Grenadier Regiment 91 of the new 35 SS Division and the remainder were disbanded. The remainder probably being any of the local ethnic volunteers.

March 20, 1945: The entire regiment is with 35 SS Division near Guben on the Oder near Cottbus. The division was destroyed defending Berlin and it is doubtful that many men of the original battalion survived the war.

Police Battalion 314

This battalion was formed with personnel from Vienna, Austria

Field Post Number(s) 37049

Commanding Officer(s): Major Severt (1941-1942).

Other Officers: The 1st company commander was 1st Lieutenant/Captain Oskar Josef Christ. Lieutenant Walter Bertet was awarded the German Cross in Gold on March 30, 1945 while serving with this battalion.

In 1941 the battalion was a part of Police Regiment Cracow.

The battalion helped form the III/Police Regiment 10 in July 1942.

Einsatzgruppen/Atrocity Activity
July-August 1941: In the Kovel area where they killed at least 8,000 Jews.

September 1941: They assisted *Einsatzkommando* 6 in Vinnitsa and Dnepropetrovsk where at least 11,000 Jews died.

November 1941: In Dnepropetrovsk where the battalion shot 1,000 Jews.

January 1942: In Khakov, Ukraine where they assisted in the killing of 10,000 to 20,000 Jews.[1]

July 1942: Attached an operating under HSSPF South.

Regiment/Battalion Locations & Activities
June 1941: Attached to Police Regiment South.

1941: Assigned to Rzeszow. Rzeszow's ghetto was created in December 1941 and contained 12,500 Jews at its beginning. While stationed here they were officially Police Battalion Reichshof (Rzeszow).

July 1942: In Lubomil, Ukraine area.

Winter 1942-1943: On the front line with *Kampfgruppe* "Prützmann."

January-February 1944: In Galicia.[2]

March 15, 1944: In Brody.

April 1944: In Kostopol.

May 1944: In Stanislawczik.

July 1944: Assigned to HSSPF Adriatic with this battalion stationed in Aidussena.

March 1945: In Görz, Italy.[3]

Heinrich Koch as young man in the 1920s.

Heinrich Koch taken during the first years of the war.

Above: Heinrich Koch and comrades in Jaslow in June, 1941. The man wearing the armband is a Jew.

Left: Heinrich Koch escorts a deportation column in Rzesnow, December 1941.

Opposite
Top: Heinrich Koch and the other company First Sergeants in Krsko, Slovenia in 1944.

Bottom left: Heinrich Koch in Novo Mesto in 1944.

Bottom right: Heinrich Koch in 1944.

Police Battalion 315

This battalion was formed using personnel from Halle in June 1940. It was then transferred to Brünn in the Protektorat (Czechoslovakia) toward the end of the year.
Field Post Number(s): 45718
Commanding Officer: Major Klaus (1941-1943), Major Dall (1943 to ?).[1]
Other Officer(s): The 3rd company commander was Captain Dürer. 1st Lieutenant and SS-*Obersturmführer* Adelbert Buttler.

This battalion was used to create Police Regiment z.b.V. in the fall of 1941.

The battalion formed the II/Police Regiment 11 in July 1942 in the Ukraine.

Einsatzgruppen/Atrocity Activity
November 11-12, 1941: The battalion assisted in the killing of thousands of Jews in Rowno.

March 26 to April 6, 1942: Police Battalion 315 accompanied by the reinforced 707 Infantry Division and the Slovakian Infantry Regiment and carried out an anti-partisan operation in the area between Oktjabrski and Kopakevichi in Belorussia where they murdered a number of the inhabitants. During March the battalion was in Kojno where they killed 150 women and children.

November 1942: The battalion assisted in the death of at least 3,000 Jews in the Kobryn ghetto.

April 1942: The battalion is operating in the Pripjet Marshes where they burnt down twenty villages and in Karlowk where they burnt the village down and killed fifty people.

Regiment Locations & Activities
April 1941: Transferred to Slovenia during the second half of April a week or two after the Germans had occupied Yugoslavia.

April 24, 1941: Occupying garrisons in Maribor, Ljutomer, Konjice and Slovenj Gradec.

July-August 1941: In Zamosc, Lvov, and Tarnopol.

October 1941: In the Ukraine an assigned to Police Regiment. z.b.V. in Rowno.

November 1941: In Zhitomir providing city security.

February 26, 1942: The battalion along with the 102 Infantry Regiment (Slovakian) took part in Operation "Bamberg" in the Glusk, Paritschi, Oktjabrski area south of Bobruisk. In Paritschi they killed thirty-six Jews and two partisans.

April 1942: In Bezirk and the Pripet swamps conducting anti-partisan operations.

March 1943: In Gomel and operating with the 7 Police Panzer Company. The panzer company took heavy casualties during this period with sixteen men killed, two missing in action, and forty-four wounded.

June 25, to July 27, 1943: The regiment took part in Operation "Seydlitz" near Mosyr.

January 1944: The regiment is on the defensive and fighting in the Kostopol, Rowno, and Brody area.

April 1944: In Lvov.[3]

Police Battalion 316

This battalion was formed with personnel from the Recklinghausen area in Bottrop in January 1941. The battalion originally was a bicycle battalion with three companies. The battalion staff and communications platoon were partially motorized. The battalion received a number of men from Police Battalion 204 and Police Battalion 61 in 1941.[1] In March 1943 it is listed as being completely motorized.
Field Post Number(s): 44173
Commanding Officer(s): Major Waldow (? to July/August 1941), Major Heinrich Hoecke (1941), Major Fucha (1942), Major von Rosenberg, Major Kurt Gehrman (1943-1944).[2]
Other Officer(s): The 1st company commander was Captain Walter Nord. Captain Nord received the Iron Cross 2nd Class for his work with the *Einsatzkommando* as did five enlisted men in his company. His platoon leader Lieutenant Koneffe also received the award.

Captain Max Ehrle was the 1st company commander after Captain Nord. The 2nd company commander was Captain Herman Kraiker (SS Number 354 185) and his platoon leader was 1st Lt. Eugene Sturm. Captain Kraiker and one enlisted man in his company received the Iron Cross 2nd Class for their work with the *Einsatzkommando*. Later the 2nd company commander was Captain Heinrich Ebeling. The 3rd company platoon leader 1st Lieutenant Schneider and two enlisted men were decorated for their work with the *Einsatzkommando*. Captain Kraiker was still working for the police in Bochum as of 1965.

Until June 1941 the battalion was part of Police Regiment Böhmen. On June 6, 1941 was transported by train to Radom arriving July 4, 1941. In June 1941 it was assigned as the II/ Police Regiment Center along with Police Battalion 307 and 322.

This battalion formed the I/Police Regiment 4 in July 1942 in France.

Einsatzgruppen/Atrocity Activity
June 1941: Operating with *Einsatzgruppe* B, *Einsatzkommando* 8 and killing Jews in the towns of Bialystok, Slonim, Barananowicze, Sluzk, and Bobruisk. The 1st and 2nd company was active in Slonim in the middle of July killing Jews and establishing the ghetto. The 1st company was detailed to *Einsatzkommando* 8 and assisted in the killing of 2,000 Jews. The Jews were summoned to the town marketplace and transported to the killing site where they were shot by an execution squad of 10-12 men using carbines fired in salvos.

July 1941: In Bialystok where they killed 3,000 Jews. The battalion provided one company for this action. The Jews were shot in antitank ditches outside the city after first being stripped of their valuables. Police Battalion 322 also assisted. During July they also participated in an action in Hansewitschi where they assisted in killing eighty-eight Russians and approximately 200 Jews. In Baranowitsche on July 23, 1941 they killed 1,000 Jews. During July they were based out of Baranowitsche and were operating in a thirty-five mile radius of the town conducting executions.

August 1941: In Tykocin where the Jews were loaded into trucks and drove to the Lopuchowo Forest. The Jewish men dug the pits and then members of Police Battalion 309 and 316 shot them.

September 19, 1941: The battalion assisted in killing 3,726 Jews in and around Mogilew where they were assigned to *Einsatzkommando* 8.

November-December 1941: In Bobruisk where they killed 2,000 Jews.[4] *Einsatzkommando* 7 and 8 were also killing Jews here and it is probable they were working together. The *Einsatzkommandos* killed 5,281 Jews. The 3rd company was the primary company operating in this large action and were assisting in the roundups and security for the continuing series of actions afterwards. The word "roundup" sounds benign but in reality it was brutal with the old, slow, and those who tried to hide shot for the inconvenience they caused.

November 17, 1943: The 1st and 3rd company under SD command are in Anapol where they killed about 300 Jews.

Regiment/Battalion Locations & Activities
June-August 1941: Based in Bialystok and in Radom.

June-July 1941: In reserve for *Einsatzkommando* 8. This battalion and the 322 were transferred to Ostrow/Mazowiecka per HSSPF Mitte (Center) orders.

September to the middle of November 1941: The entire battalion is stationed in Mogilew. In November part of the battalion was conducting security patrols on the Wjasma/ Smolensk highway.

Winter 1941-1942: With Police Regiment Center fighting at the front.

May 1942: The battalion has returned to Bottrop to rest and refit.

July 1942: In the middle of July the battalion leaves Bottrop for Oberkrain.

August 1, 1942: The battalion is in St. Georgon by Crainburg. The commanding officer, Major Fucha was living at Parsonage Nr. 18.[2]

November 1942: In Slovenia.[5]

March 1943: In Paris. The battalion headquarters staff is living in a private house at Rue Chemin 13. The three companies are quartered in schools and the communications platoon is living in a private house. The 3rd company is in a girl's school that had excellent kitchen facilities that were used to feed the battalion.

June 1943: Transferred from France to Poland and now in Krasnik/Sandomierz southwest of Lublin.[6]

Fall 1943 to February 1943: The battalion is stationed in Chelm. It is providing guards for *Sonderkommando* 1005 who were busy trying to clean up the mass graves that resulted from earlier *Einsatzgruppe* and Police massacres.

December 1944: Fighting on the frontline near Grodno then operating as part of *Kampfgruppe* "Hannibal" which ended the war in Lyck.

Police Battalion 317

This battalion was formed from the Wuppertal area in June 1940.

Field Post Number(s): 39745

Commanding Officer: Major/Lt. Colonel Gresser (1941-1942).

Originally the battalion was part of Police Regiment Bohmen as Police Battalion Pazdubitz in January 1941.

May 1942: The battalion is assigned to Police Regiment Center.

The battalion formed the II/Police Regiment 7 in July 1942.

Regiment/Battalion Locations & Activities

January 1941: The battalion is in the Protectorate of Böhmen and Mähren.

June 1941: In Brest Litowsk. The battalion arrived in the General government area in April 1941.

July 1941: In Pardubitz.

August 1941: In Bobruisk and working with Army Security Division 286.

October 1941: In Smolensk.

January 1942: The battalion staff is in Krupka with companies in Borikow Drscha. The battalion is assigned to HSSPF Center.

February-March 1942: The 1st company is conducting anti-partisan operations in the forested area near Klinok. Casualties for the company were ten dead and six wounded.

April 1942: The battalion is working with the 286 Security Division in the Propoisk.

July 1942: Back in Wuppertal. The battalion may have transferred to Norway.

Police Battalion 318

This battalion was formed with personnel from the Vienna area.

Field Post Number(s): 37632

Commanding Officer(s): Major Walter Seltz (1941-1942).

In 1941 the battalion was attached to Police Regiment Mähren.

The battalion was assigned as the III/Police Regiment 6 in July 1942.

Regiment/Battalion Locations & Activities

July 1941: Attached to Army Group South.

April-May 7, 1942: Operating with elements of the 612 Infantry Regiment and conducting anti-partisan operations in the forest near Nowoja Bassan.

August 1942 to June 1943: Conducting anti-partisan operations behind Army Group South. They were supporting the 27th Panzer Division. The 27th Panzer Division was destroyed and disbanded in February 1943.[2]

The battalion was destroyed in the fighting near the Don River. See Police Battalion 51. A second SS Police Regiment was created in 1944 and was commanded by Lt.Col. Maiwald, the former commander of Police Battalion 72.

Police Battalion 319

The battalion is formed from the Cologne/Riehl area.

Field Post Number(s): 40493

Commanding Officer(s): Major Geissler (1941-1942), Major Krasemann (1942 to November 1942).

Other Officer(s): The 1st Company Commander was 1st Lieutenant Heinz Werner Kubitsch.

The battalion originally had only one motorized company while the remaining two companies used bicycles.

The battalion became I/Police Regiment Böhmen in June 1941

In July 1942 the battalion became the I/Police Regiment 27.

Regiment/Battalion Locations & Activities
October 1940 to Summer 1941: Stationed in Prague. The 1st and 2nd companies until January 1942 were in Lithuania, Latvia and northern Russia operating with the 207, 281, 181 Security Divisions.

June 1941: Attached to Police Regiment North in Latvia.

July 1941: The 1st and 3rd companies were in Lithuania and Latvia until January 1942. Here they were operating with Security Divisions 207, 281, and 181.

August 1, 1941 to September 10, 1941: The 3rd company was in Luga, Pjussa, Lyadi, and Malaj Saragora working with the 285th Security Division. During this period the company along with this security division was fighting on the front lines as part of *Kampgruppe* "Fechner" near Iswars, Rejepolka, and Szosnown.

January 1942: The battalion is fighting in the Illmensee area with the 81 Infantry Division near Raschutscha.

April 1942: The battalion is near Staraya Russa where they are in combat as part of Police Regiment North and attached to the 18 Infantry Division.

July 1942: Transferred to Oslo, Norway.

1943: In Bergen, Norway.

Police Battalion 320
This battalion was formed with personnel from the Berlin area in February 1941. In July 1941 the battalion received the 1st company of Police Battalion 33. This company was stationed in Rovno where it may have become Police Company "Rovno."
Field Post Number(s): 46591
Commanding Officer(s): Major Kurt Peterson, Major Kurt Dall.[1]
Other Officer(s): The commanding officer of the 1st company "Ostland" was Alfred Weber.

The 2nd company commander was Captain Hans Wiemer. The 3rd company commander was Captain Heinrich Scharwey.

This battalion was originally part of Police Regiment Bohemia and Mähren. Then the battalion was assigned to Police Regiment z.b.V. in the fall of 1941.[2] Later the battalion formed the III/Police Regiment 11 in July 1942 in Kostopol.

Einsatzgruppen/Atrocity Activity
August 20, 1941: In Starokonstantinow with the 1st SS Infantry Brigade where they killed 439 Jewish men and women.

August 27-28, 1941: In Kaments Podolski where they assisted in the death of 23,600 Jews most of whom were Hungarian. Also assisting was thirty SD members, HSSPF Jecklin and his headquarters company, and Hungarian and Ukrainian auxiliaries.[3]

August 31, 1941: In Minwkowzy which is about twenty miles from Kaments Podolski where they assisted in killing 2,200 Jews.

November 7-8, 1941: In Rovno, Ukraine where 10,650 Jews, 15 Communist officials, and 424 hostages were shot. This was the work of *Einsatzkommando* 5 and besides this battalion a number of auxiliary units were used. Also participating was the 1st company of Police Battalion 33, and Police Battalion 315.[4]

July 14, 1942: In Kostopol where 5,000 Jews were shot in a nearby forest. This action was part of the beginning of the liquidation of the Kostopol ghetto. They were assisted by the 1st company of Police Battalion 33 and Ukrainian auxiliaries.

September-October 1942: The 1st and 3rd companies took about 1,000 Jews from the ghetto in Bereza Kartuska and transported them about a half mile out of town and killed them.

October 29, to November 1, 1942: In Pinsk where they along with Police Battalion 306 killed 8,200 Jews to make room for new arrivals from Germany. The entire battalion assisted in this action.

September-October 1942: The 1st and 3rd company assisted in killing 1,000 Jews from the Bereza Kartusk ghetto. They transported them a half mile from town and then shot them in groups.

Regiment/Battalion Locations & Activities
Winter 1940: Transferred from Berlin to Mladá Boleslav in Czechoslovakia.

February 1941: Stationed in Jung/Bunzlau and Kolin.

April 1941: Transferred to Slovenia during the second half of April a week or two after the Germans had occupied Yugoslavia.

April 24, 1941: Occupying garrisons in Celje, Lasko Gornji Grad.

May 1941, 1941: Departed Slovenia at the end of May for employment in the East.

June 26, 1941: The battalion is in Jaslo where they are part of a large contingent of police assigned to accompany the advance into Ukraine.

September 1941: Under BdO Ukraine and in Rowno where the battalion staff and 3rd company are quartered. The 1st company is in Sarny. The 2nd company is in Luzk.

November 1941: In Rovno.

February 24, 1942: Fighting at the front near Taganrog.

March 28, 1942: Attached to Police Regiment z.b.V.[5]

September 1943: The battalion is fighting partisans near Malischewka which is about 100 miles east of Stolin.

January 1944: The battalion is in the area of Brest Litowsk, and Gomel fighting partisans.

July 1944: Destroyed. See Police Battalion 61 for more details.

Police Battalion 321
The Battalion was formed using personnel from Breslau.
Field Post Number(s): 41064
Commanding Officer(s): Major Petersen (1941-1942), Ltc. Stracke (1942).[1]

In 1941 the battalion was the II/Police Regiment Cracow.

Later it was assigned to Police Regiment North.

It became the II/Police Regiment 27 in July 1942.

Regiment/Battalion Locations & Activities
July 1941: Attached to Army Group North.

July 1942: In Norway. This battalion was stationed in Halden.[2]

Police Battalion 322
This battalion was formed with personnel from the Vienna/ Kagran Training Battalion in Vienna, Austria in 1940.[1] This was a three company battalion. On March 21 1941 the battalion received; one officer, six NCOs, and fifty-eight enlisted men from Police Battalion 64. The battalion then had twelve officers, 101 NCOs, and 436 enlisted men.
Field Post Number(s): 44762
Commanding Officer(s): Major Gottlieb Nagel, Major Carstens.
Other Officer(s): Major Nagels adjutant was 1st Lt. Josef Uhl. The 1st company commander was Reinhard Jörke and later it was Herman Lippman. The 2nd company commander was Captain Ulrich. The 3rd company commander was 1st Lt. Gerhard Riebel and later Captain Schäfer.
Other Officers: 1st Lt. Kohlsaal (1941).

This battalion was originally equipped as a bicycle battalion with only the battalion staff and communications platoon partially motorized.

On April 16, 1941 it was transferred to RFSS Himmler for his personal disposal.

The battalion became the III/Police Regiment Center on June 6, 1941 in Warsaw. On September 18, 1942 the Reserve Police Company "*Wien*" (Vienna) is listed as part of the battalion.

Einsatzgruppen/Atrocity Activity
July 1941: In Bialystok were they assisted in killing a minimum of 3,000 Jews and a number of Russian POWs. The battalion worked with the 221st security division. They also liberated "stolen property" from the Jewish quarter that amounted to twenty truckloads. In this action they were assisted by Police Battalions 306 and 316. While in Bialystok they were barracked in a vocational school on Pisudsky Street.[1]

August 6, 1941: In Bodbiala they shot three women and fifty-one men. Elements of the battalion were also guarding and executing Jews at the Bialowieza prison assembly camp.

August 15, 1941: In Kobrin were they shot 282 Jews.[2]

August 1941: Under the command of KdO *Weissruthenien* (White Russia). The battalion carried out roundups and large-scale executions of Jews in Bialowezie and Narowka Mala. At the end of the month they shot 5,000 Jews from the Minsk ghetto. The 2nd company assisted in the Minsk executions.

September 1941: The battalion is working with *Einsatzkommando* 8.

October 2-3, 1941: Working with *Einsatzkommando* 8 elements of the battalion shot 2,208 Jews in Mogilev.

October 3, 1941: In the Mogilev area where they shot 555 Jews and 378 Poles that had been rounded up the previous day.

November 1941: In Minsk were they assisted in killing 19,000 Jews.

March 2, 1942: Members of the battalion shot four Jewish women for leaving the Smolensk ghetto.[3]

May 1942: In Smolensk where the battalion's records indicate it executed at least 11,000 people between July 1941 and May 1942, including 9,000 Jews.

July 1942: In Minsk where the battalion assisted in the shooting of 9,000 Jews.

May 1944: The 3rd company sent a reinforced platoon to transport Jews to the train station in Siklos.

Regiment/Battalion Locations & Activities
June 10, 1941: The battalion leaves Vienna on June 6, 1941 an arrives in Warsaw, Poland.

July 8, 1941: The battalion is visited by Heinrich Himmler at 4:20 in the afternoon.

July 21, 1941: They assist in removing people from Bialowilza Forest to create a hunting reserve for Herman Göring.

July 24 to September 1941: They are operating under HSSPF White Russia.

July 1941: The battalion is in Ostrow. Police Battalion 316 and 322 are also there.

August 14-16, 1941: The 1st company provided security for RFSS Himmler's visit to Minsk.

August 1941: While doing anti-partisan patrols they find a radio in the village of Lawry Nowi. The battalion is operating from Baranowiecse.

October 7 1941 to January 28, 1942: They are attached to Police Regiment Center.

November 1941: The battalion is fighting in vicinity of the railroad line near Rosalawl and Janiwo. They are also patrolling the road between Smolensk and Wittebak.

November 11, 1941: The battalion stops to replenish their munitions at Depot Bialystok.

January 1942: The battalion is in Smolensk.

March-May 1942: The battalion is fighting partisans and patrolling the Smolensk to Orscha, and Smolensk to Witebsk roads. The partisan bands were growing in strength and the battalion companies were engaging partisan bands that increasingly were company strength in size. During this time period the battalion lost one officer, and had four wounded. NCO and enlisted losses were seven men with fourteen wounded. The battalion had twenty officers and 442 men at this point.

June 28, 1942: They are ordered to take part in Operation "Enzian," a large four week anti-partisan sweep carried out in July in Slovenia.

July 1942: Arrived in Belgrade.

August 1, 1942: The battalion is in Höflein by Crainburg. The commanding officer, Major Carstens is staying at the Villa

Slanc. The 1st company is in Castle Majeritach Nr.1, The 2nd company and the communications platoon are staying in a Volkschule. The 3rd company is stationed at Castle Cross.

October 10, 1942: The regiment is now operational after two months of formation and training.

October 23, 1942 to April 1943: The battalion is in Kragujevac south of Belgrade.

April 4, 1943: The battalion is transferred to Cuprija.

April 9, 1943: The battalion is assigned to protect the procurement of grain in the Svilajnac area. After that task was completed around April 20, it swept the area east of Svilajnac for Chetnik bands but by April 26, had not made contact with them.

May 2, 1943: The battalion was brought in to keep a close watch over the Goc and Zeljin mining and industrial area.

May 23, 1943: The battalion was combing the area south and southwest of Trstenik for the Keserovic Chetnik band.

July 13-18, 1943: The 1st company is in the Cacak area. The 3rd company is in the Vrnjacka Banja area.

August 10-18, 1943: The battalion participated in Operation "Stiefelknecht" (BootJack). It was a combing of the Kopacnik and Jastrebac Mountains west of Nis to seek out and destroy the Keserovic Chetnik bands totaling six brigades (2,000 men).

August 19, 1943: SS Police Regiment 5 is ordered to move from Kragujevac to Arandelovac in order to make barracks space available for arriving units.

September 1, 1943: The battalion is in Krusevac.

September 24, 1943: The battalion moves from Krusevac to Topola.

October 3-8, 1943: Operation "Maiskolben (Corn Cob)." An operation against guerrilla organizations in the mountains between Valjevo and Cacak with III and V Hipo Battalion, Bulgarian 24th Division, 9/Regiment 4 Brandenburg, elements of Panzer Company z.b.V. 12, and SFK battalions; the results were disappointing for the Germans with only 100 partisans killed and 500 suspects arrested.

October 10-20, 1943: The regiment swept the area from Cacak through Uzice to Bajina Basta on the Drina together with elements of the Bulgarian 24th Division in an attempt to catch insurgents fleeing toward East Bosnia after "Maiskolben".

October 31, to November 5, 1943: The regiment carried out Operation "Hammelbraten" (Roast Mutton) about twelve miles south of Cacak against Chetniks; the enemy had abandoned their camp in the woods and there was little contact. The regiment was transferred to Kragujevac to rest and refit after the operation.

November 15, 1943: The battalion is transferred from Topola to Vreoci, a rail junction.

December 1, 1943: The battalion is back in Topola.

January 1, 1944: The battalion is in Pozega.

January 29, 1944: SS Police Regiment 5 set out from Celic and over the next several days swept the road past Koraj toward Bijeljina, encountered numerous road blocks and fought several skirmishes with strengthening partisan forces.

February 16 to March 5 1944: The battalion leaves from Topola to join a joint operation with the III/Regiment 4, 3 battalions of SFK, II Battalion of Bulgarian 70th Infantry Regiment in Operation "Treibjagd" (Witch Hunt) against the Simic Chetnik bands in the Arandelovac area between the Kolubara and Morava Rivers twenty miles to the south of Belgrade. A total of 81 Chetniks were claimed killed, 913 captured and many wounded. On conclusion of "Treibjagd" the battalion returned to Topola.

March 1944: The entire regiment departed Serbia for Operation "Cannae" (Occupation of Hungary). The battalion is working with the II/Police Regiment 12 and was assigned to watch the Hungarian southern border by Titel.

April 4, 1944: The 3rd company is fighting Croatian "bandits" near Keresanje.

April 30, 1944: The 3rd company is in Siklós Hungary and assigned to guard Jews there.

May 1944: All through May, an especially towards the end of the month the company had been involved firefights with company sized groups of partisans who were well equipped with SMG's and grenades. By the end of May the company was operating around Jelenak.

June 4, 1944: The 3rd company is attacked by approximately 200 partisans on horseback. The company reported killing thirty partisans.

June 18, 1944: The 3rd company is participating in Operation "Endlich" (Finally) which was a very minor operation that never amounted to more than patrols for the 3rd company.

July 1944: Participated in anti-partisan Operation "Trumpf" (Trump) in the West Morava Valley along with the Bulgarian 27th Division, all five regiments of the Serbian Volunteer Corps (SFK), Chetniks and other German units. The objective was to block the northern movement of four Partisans divisions (21st, 22d, 24th and 25th) that had just been formed in southern Serbia.

July-August 1944: Almost immediately following the conclusion of "Trumpf" at the end of July, the regiment was employed in Operation "Draufgänger (Dare Devil)" aimed at destroying partisan forces in Montenegro to prevent their penetration into Serbia. The enemy formations were delayed but not destroyed.

October 12, 1944: The regiment is now in Obrenovac as part of the defensive ring around the Serbian capital of Belgrade. The city was liberated on October 20, by units of the Soviet 3rd Ukrainian Front and partisan forces. The regiment and other remnants of the German defense retreated across the Sava into Syrmia.

October 1944: The regiment had been part of the forces assigned to "Brückenkopf Obrenovac," part of the defensive ring on the southwest side of Belgrade. The bridgehead was evacuated during the night of October 13/14 and SS Police Regiment 5, *Feldgenderarmerie* Troop 861, *Sturmgeschütz* Company "Gewitter" and a Luftwaffe Alarm Battalion were ordered to Semlin and reassigned to *Kampfkommandant* Belgrade.

October 22, 1944: The regiment is engaged in the Semlin area as part of Division z.b.V. Stephan, which was composed of a mixed collection of miscellaneous units evacuated out of the Belgrade area.

January-April 1945: The regimental staff, I Battalion, and this battalion are in the Vocin area of Croatia as part of Division z.b.V. Geiger (formerly Division z.b.V. Stephan).

April-May 1945: The main body of the regiment withdrew toward Zagreb in the latter part of April and surrendered in the Celje area on May 13, 1945.[4]

Police Battalion 323

This battalion was formed with personnel from Konigsberg in Tilsit.

Field Post Number(s): 43315

Commanding Officer: Major Bernhard Griese, (until May 1942), Major Gustav Zuschneid, (May 1942 to ?).

Other Officer(s): 1st Leutenant Nowak.

The battalion formed the II/Police Regiment 4 in July 1942 in Paris.

Einsatzgruppen/Atrocity Activity

June to Fall 1941: The battalion is assigned to ghetto security duties in Kowno.

July 1942: In Paris and assisting with the deportation of Jews to Auschwitiz concentration camp. They were transporting the Jews to the railroad station at Le Bourget/Drancy. The battalion was barracked in Clignancourt on the northern edge of Paris.

Regiment/Battalion Locations & Activities

Winter 1941: The battalion was in Kovno.

January 13, 1941: The battalion defended a twelve mile wide sector near Orscha against a Soviet Paratrooper regiment or division. The Knight's Cross was won by Major Bernhard Griese there. The battalion by January 22, 1942 had ten dead, fourteen wounded, 118 with injuries caused by the cold, and 102 in the hospital.[1]

September 1941: The battalion relieves Police Battalion 322 in Bialowieza.[2]

January 12, 1942: In Mogilew.

March 1942: The battalion staff is in Kamenez while all the companies are in Jelnja.

June 1943: In Galicia conducting anti-partisan operations and later in the Grodno area on the front lines.

December 1944: In Lvov.[3]

June 1944: The 3rd company is in the East Carpinthians conducting patrols.

1945: At the end of the war the battalion was part of *Kampfgruppe* "Hannibal" in East Prussia.

Police Battalion 324
This battalion was formed with personnel from Stuttgart.
Field Post Number(s):
Commanding Officer(s): Major Kuhlennbeck
The battalion was transferred to the 4 SS Police Division to replace combat losses.

Police Battalion 325
The personnel for this battalion came from Dresden.
Field Post Number(s): 19754
The battalion formed the III/Police Mountain Regiment 18 in May 1942 in Bavaria.

Regiment/Battalion Locations & Activities
Mid-December 1941: Transferred from Germany to Kranj in Oberkrain.

December 27, 1941 to January 12, 1942: Together with Police Battalions 44, 93, 171, 181 and *Landesschützen* Battalion 322 and 857, took part in the first large anti-partisan operation in Slovenia. It occurred in the mountains and wooded terrain between Ljubljana and Kranj and was aimed at destroying the Gorenjski Partisan Battalion which had been recruiting in the area and raiding the German garrison towns. The partisans avoided direct contact with the superior force while claiming they killed 200 Germans over the course of the operation. Actual casualties are not known.[1] See Battalion 302 for the rest of this battalion's history.

Appendix 2
Battalions by Regiment

1

Police Battalion 2

Police Battalion 3

Police Battalion 10

Battalions 2 and 3 were transferred to Police Regiment Griese in 1943 where they became I and III of SS Police Regiment 14.

2

Police Battalion 11

Police Battalion 13

Police Battalion 22

3

Police Battalion 66. Transferred to SS Police Regiment 5 in 1944.

Police Battalion 68

Police Battalion 105. This battalion formed the III/Police Regiment 12 in July 1942. In March 1943 the battalion was transferred to SS Police Regiment 3.

4

Created from Police Regiment Warsaw

Police Battalion 316

Police Battalion 323

Police Battalion 62 (Motorized). The battalion formed the III/Police Regiment 4 in August 1942. Later the battalion formed the I/Police Regiment 28 "Todt" in November 1942.

5

Police Battalion 64. After 1944

Police Battalion 322

Police Battalion 66.

6

Police Battalion 82 (Motorized)

Police Battalion 311

Police Battalion 318

The regiment was rebuilt in October 1944 in Hungary.

7

Police Battalion 309

Police Battalion 317

Police Battalion 123

8

Police Battalion 91

Police Battalion 111

Police Battalion 134

9

Police Battalion 61

Police Battalion 112

Police Battalion 132

In 1944 the regiment was destroyed and the remnants went to SS Police Regiment 16 in the Balkans.

10

Police Battalion 45

Police Battalion 303

Police Battalion 314

11

Police Battalion 304

Police Battalion 315

Police Battalion 320

12

Police Battalion 103. The battalion also provided cadre for Police Schützen Regiment 31

Police Battalion Police Battalion 105

The battalion formed the III/Police Regiment 12 in July 1942. In March 1943 the battalion was transferred to SS Police Regiment 3.

13

Police Battalion 6.

Police Battalion 85

Police Battalion 301

14

1st Version

Police Battalion 51

Police Battalion 63

Police Battalion 122. The battalion was originally the III/14.

2nd Version
Police Battalion 2
Police Battalion 313.

15
1st Version
Police Battalion 305 The battalion for a brief time was the I/Police Regiment 15.
The battalion formed the III/Police Regiment 16 in October 1942
Police Battalion 306
Police Battalion 310

2nd Version
Police Battalion 253

16
Police Battalion 56. The battalion was the I/Police Regiment 16 until 1943.
Police Battalion 102
Police Battalion 121
Police Battalion 305. The battalion for a brief time was the I/Police Regiment 15.
The battalion formed the III/Police Regiment 16 in October 1942.

17
Police Battalion 42
Police Battalion 74
Police Battalion 69
The battalion formed the III/Police Regiment 17 in July 1942 in Riga, Latvia. The battalion contributed one company to the new II/SS Police Regiment "Todt" 28 in 1943. Another source (Curilla) has the battalion forming the II/28 in November 1942 with Police Battalion 62 filling out the rest of the German strength of the regiment.

18
Police Battalion 302
Police Battalion 312
Police Battalion 325

19
Police Battalion 72
Police Battalion 171
Police Battalion 181

20
Created from Police Regiment Böhmen using battalions from Prague, Kolin, and Klattau.

21
Created from Police Regiment Mähren

22
Police Battalion 41
Police Battalion 53

23
Police Battalion 307 (Motorized). In March 1943 the battalion became the III/SS Police Regiment 23.

24
Police Battalion 83
The battalion formed the I/Police Regiment 24 in Lvov in July, 1942. The regimental staff was not formed until April 21, 1943 and may have been the staff of the former Police Regiment Radom.
Police Battalion 133
Police Battalion 93

25
Created from Police Regiment Lublin
Police Battalion 65 "Cholm" (Motorized)
Police Battalion 67
Police Battalion 101

26
Police Battalion 251
Police Battalion 255
Police Battalion 256

27
Police Battalion 319
Police Battalion 44. The battalion formed IV/ Police Regiment 27 in 1942. In June 1943 it became the I/SS Police Regiment 27.
Police Battalion 9
Police Battalion 321

28 "Todt"

Police Battalion 69. The battalion formed the III/Police Regiment 17 in July 1942 in Riga, Latvia. The battalion contributed one company to the new II/SS Police Regiment "Todt" 28 in 1943. Another source (Curilla) has the battalion forming the II/28 in November 1942 with Police Battalion 62 filling out the rest of the German strength of the regiment.
Police Battalion 62

36

Police Battalion 256. The battalion formed the III/ Police Regiment 36 in July 1942 in Drontheim, Norway

Appendix 3
Other Police Battalions, Regiments of Interest

Police Battalion 1. Was used to create Police Shützen (Rifle) Regiment 36 on June 24, 1943 which disbanded in 1944.

Police Battalion 4. Sent to 4 SS Police Division

Police Battalion 5. Stationed in the Warthegau.

Police Battalion 8. April 16, 1942: The battalion is cannabilized for men to make up for losses in the east.

Police Battalion 12. July, 1942: In Minsk, Russia

Police Battalion 32. May 16, 1942: The battalion was dissolved, possibly as a result of its encounter with a Soviet paratroop regiment on January 23, 1942.

Police Battalion 43. December 1939: In Lublin, an assigned to Police Regiment Lublin. August 1940: The battalion is transferred to Warsaw.

Police Battalion 63. The battalion was scheduled to form the II/Police Regiment 14 in November 1942. Instead Police Battalion 122 took its place and this battalion stayed in Wismar.

Police Battalion 71. December 1939: Attached to Police Regiment Radom

Police Battalion 81. 1940 to 1942: Possibly a company each in Beuthen, Olmütz, Brünn. 1942: The battalion was dissolved.

Police Battalion 84. October 1942: Transferred to SS Police Division 4 to make up for their combat losses around Leningrad, Russia.

Police Battalion 92. Active in Poland as the I/Police Regiment 1, Police Group 1, AOK 14. Later they were assigned to Police Regiment Cracow.

Police Battalion 131. The battalion was dissolved on June 20, 1942 and was sent to the following regiments; North, Center, South, and z.b.V.

Police Battalion 254. It was transferred to SS Police Division 4 in September 1941.

Police Battalion 308. In March 1942 the battalion was dissolved and the remnants went to Police Battalion 307 and 32.

Police Battalion 324. The battalion was transferred to the 4 SS Police Division to replace combat losses.

ENDNOTES

Chapter One : The German Police

[1] Browning, Christopher R. 1993. *Ordinary Men: Reserve Police Battalion 101 and the Final Solution in Poland*. Harper Perennial

[2] United States Holocaust Museum. Selected records from the Hauptamt Ordnungspolizei collection [microform], 1921 to1945. RG68.046m, Reel 10.

Chapter Two: Into Poland

[1] Brest-Litovsk was the city where the Russians had signed an armistice on March 3, 1918 and withdrew as combatants from World War I.

[2] Tannenburg was the name of the battle that was the worst defeat of the Russians by the Germans in World War I. It is quite possible in the choice of this operation name that Hitler, Himmler, and Heydrich were already looking ahead to Russia.

[3] Alexander B. Rossino. April 2005. *Hitler Strikes Poland: Blitzkrieg, Ideology, and Atrocity*. University Press of Kansas. pg.12, Dr. Best, Group Size, pg.15, Special List. Also Police Group List.

[4] Heydrichs Memo to the Chiefs of the *Einsatzgruppen*, September 21, 1939

[5] Baldur von Schirach was head of the Hitler Youth in 1939.

[6] Hans Frank, later Governor General of the *Generalgouvernement* for the occupied Polish territories. He was found guilty of war crimes and hung on October 1, 1946.

[7] The Trial of German Major War Criminals Sitting at Nuremberg, Germany. July 16 to July 27, 1946. One Hundred and Eighty Eighth Day: Saturday, 27th July, 1946 (Part 3 of 8). pg.445.

[8] The Avalon Project at Yale Law School: Documents in Law, History and Diplomacy, www.yale.edu/lawweb/avalon/imt/proc/judpolan.htm (Accessed August 17, 2006).

[9] Richard Overy. 2004 *The Dictators: Hitler's Germany, Stalin's Russia*. Norton. pg.577.

Chapter Three: Into Russia

[1] Nazi Conspiracy and Aggression, Vol. III. USGPO, Washington, 1946, pp.409-413.

[2] Order #21 Signed By Keitel Concerning Jurisdiction of Military, SS, and Police Forces During Barbarossa[2] Nazi Conspiracy and Aggression. Vol. II. USGPO, Washington, 1946, pp. 528-546.

[3] Richard Overy. 2004 *The Dictators: Hitler's Germany, Stalin's Russia*. Norton. pg.577.

[4] Membership of a police officer in the SS would count as membership in a criminal organization. Police were issued SS military identity books (*Soldbuch*) after the police became an SS organization in 1943. The SS runes were erased by many police after the war was over.

Chapter Four: The Partisans

[1] A. Fyodoro. *The Underground Committee Carries On*. Moscow. 1952.

[2] Wolfgang Curilla. *Die deutsche Ordnungspolizei und der Holocaust im Baltikum und in Weißrußland 1941 to 1944*. Schöningh. 2005. pg.58.

Appendix 1

Police Battalion 1

[1] Police Rifle Regiments were formed using one German battalion and two battalions created from suitable local personnel.

[2] *Schuma* were volunteers from occupied counties who were formed into battalion-sized units for use as auxiliary police.

[3] Molodechno is forty miles northwest of Minsk. It fell on July 5, 1944. I could not find any information of the whereabouts of Police *Shützen* Regiment 36 after August 30, 1944.

[4] Lieutenant Colonel William M. Connor. *Analysis of Deep Attack Operation: Operation Bagration: Belorussia*. Combat Studies Institute, Fort Leavenworth, Kansas, March 1987.

Police Battalion 2

[1] United States Holocaust Museum. Selected records from the *Hauptamt Ordnungspolizei* collection [microform], 1921 to 1945. RG68.046m, Reel 55, Also May 15, to December 31, 1941 information, Wound Badge date

[2] Stefan Klemp. 2005. *"Nicht ermittelt "Polizeibataillone und die Nachkriegsjustiz*. Klartext Verlag. pg.67.

[3] Antonio Munoz, Dr Oleg V. Romanko. 2003. *Hitler's White Russians: Collaboration, Extermination and Antipartisan Warfare in Byelorussia, 1941 to 1944*. Europa Books. pg.180.

[4] Werner Haupt, 1998. *Army Group South: The Wehrmacht in Russian, 1941 to 1945*. Schiffer Publishing.

[5] H.L. deZeng IV. German Police and Auxiliary Police Units in the Balkans 1941 to 1945. (Unpublished). Almost all Slovenia information.

Police Battalion 3

[1] Captain Siegling was a member of the Nazi party having joined in 1933. He became a member of the SS in 1941. Captain Siegling must of demonstrated outstanding leadership qualities as he was the commanding officer of *Schuma* Battalion 57 and in 1944 he was an SS *Standartenführer* and commander of the 30 Waffen Grenadier Division (Russian 2). *Schuma* Battalion 57 during his command was known for its brutality.

[2] Stefan Klemp. 2005. *"Nicht ermittelt "Polizeibataillone und die Nachkriegsjustiz*. Klartext Verlag. pg.80 for Mogilev, pg.82 for locations, pg.418 for *Shützen* information. pg.447 for company locations.

[3] Antonio Munoz, Dr Oleg V. Romanko. 2003. *Hitler's White Russians: Collaboration, Extermination and Antipartisan Warfare in Byelorussia, 1941 to 1944*. Europa Books. Has it with *Einsatzgruppe* A, pgs.116-130. This is possibly because the companies were split up to work with various SD commanders. pg.180.

[4] United States Holocaust Museum. Selected records from the *Hauptamt Ordnungspolizei* collection [microform], 1921 to 1945. RG68.046m, Reel 10. I also found several letters from men in the 3rd company written in 1943 complaining that they were too old to continue serving as front line soldiers. Their ages were the late forties and early fifties.

[5] Norman Davies. 2003. *Rising 44: The Battle for Warsaw*. Penguin Books. pg.86. Writes that on September 24, 1943 a conversation between the Governor of Warsaw, SA *Gruppenführer* Ludwig Fischer and SS *Brigadeführer* Dr. Walter Bierkamp that Bierkamp stated, "...the security situation in Warsaw as deplorable ... 25,000 former Polish officers and 30,000 Jews were hiding in the city, were not registering for work, were operating against German interests, and ought to be shot."

[6] Roland Pfeiffer. 2003. *Zur Geschichte der Ordnungspolizei*. www.lexikon der wehrmacht.de/Zusatz/SS/Ordnungspolizei R.htm. (Last Accessed August 15, 2006)

[7] Krisztian Ungvary. 2005. *The Siege of Budapest*. Yale University Press. pgs. 78 to 79.

[8] Wolfgang Curilla. 2006. *Die deutsche Ordnungspolizei und der Holocaust im Baltikum und in Weissrussland 1941 to 1944*. Death totals.

Police Battalion 5

[1] The *Warthegau* was a Nazi administrative area that consisted of a large part of western Poland. This area was to be completely Germanized and consequently many Poles were forcibly resettled or imported to the Reich as slave labor.

Police Battalion 6

[1] United States Holocaust Museum. Selected records from the *Hauptamt Ordnungspolizei* collection [microform], 1921 to 1945. RG68.046m, Reel 55.

[2] United States Holocaust Museum. Selected records from the *Hauptamt Ordnungspolizei* collection [microform], 1921 to 1945. RG68.046m, Reel 7. Lothar wrote an article entitled "Radom" that was well received. He was given an autographed photo of Dr. Hans Frank and a copy of *Mein Kampf*.

[3] Stefan Klemp. 2005. *"Nicht ermittelt "Polizeibataillone und die Nachkriegsjustiz*. Klartext Verlag. pgs. 67, 418 as a part of Police Regiment Center, pg.84 Mogilev and Minsk area.

[4] Alexander B. Rossino. April 2005. *Hitler Strikes Poland: Blitzkrieg, Ideology, and Atrocity*. University Press of Kansas. Abid. pgs.62-70.

[5] H.L. deZeng IV. *German Police and Auxiliary Police Units in the Balkans 1941 to 1945*. (Unpublished). Almost all Slovenia information.

Police Battalion 8

[1] Roland Pfeiffer. 2003. *Zur Geschichte der Ordnungspolizei*. www.lexikon der wehrmacht.de/Zusatz/SS/Ordnungspolizei R.htm. (Last Accessed August 15, 2006).

[2] Stefan Klemp. 2005. *"Nicht ermittelt "Polizeibataillone und die Nachkriegsjustiz*. Klartext Verlag. pg.418.

[3] United States Holocaust Museum. Selected records from the *Hauptamt Ordnungspolizei* collection [microform], 1921 to 1945. RG68.046m. Reel 19. All information after July 1940.

Police Battalion 9

[1] Dr. Gantz in 1944 was a *Major* and commanding officer of the 2nd Regiment in *Brigade Siegling*. This brigade was commanded by Hans Siegling who served as a company commander in Police battalion 3. Brigade Siegling later became the 30 Waffen Grenadier Division (Russian).

[2] Daniel J. Goldhagen. 1996. *Hitler's Willing Executioners: Ordinary Germans and the Holocaust*. Knopf. pgs. 151, 152.

[3] Roland Pfeiffer. 2003. *Zur Geschichte der Ordnungspolizei*. www.lexikon der wehrmacht.de/Zusatz/SS/Ordnungspolizei R.htm. (Last Accessed August 15, 2006).

[4] Wolfgang Curilla. 2006. *Die deutsche Ordnungspolizei und der Holocaust im Baltikum und in Weissrussland 1941 to 1944*. pgs. 259-293 abrid. Almost all Einsatzgruppe info. pgs. 447-449. Company info.

Police Battalion 10

[1] *Major* Stahr later was the commanding officer of Police Battalion 307.

[2] Stefan Klemp. 2005. *"Nicht ermittelt" Polizeibataillone und die Nachkriegsjustiz*. Klartext Verlag. pgs. 67, 419, 448.

[3] H.L. deZeng IV. *German Police and Auxiliary Police Units in the Balkans 1941 to 1945*. (Unpublished). 1942 Slovenia information.

[4] United States Holocaust Museum. RG18.002M*90, *Befehlshaber der Ordungpolizei das Ostland*, USHM, R83, Reel 10. Battalion Commanders.

[5] United States Holocaust Museum. RG 48.004M Military Institute of Prague 1941 to 1944 Reel 2. August 1942 Information.

Police Battalion 11

[1] He was also commander of the Police *Shützen* Regiment 32. Later he was commander of a regiment in the 14 Waffen-SS Grenadier Division der SS (Ukrainian 1).

[2] USA v. KAZYS CIURINSKAS. This opinion is available on the Internet through findlaw.com. All of the above 1941 actions including the totals and dates came from this court document.

[3] Stefan Klemp. 2005. *"Nicht ermittelt "Polizeibataillone und die Nachkriegsjustiz*. Klartext Verlag. pg.24, pg.419 for Poland in 1939.

[4] United States Holocaust Museum. Selected records from the *Hauptamt Ordnungspolizei* collection [microform], 1921 to 1945. RG 68.046m. Reel 26.

[5] Munoz, Antonio and Oleg Romanko. 2003. *Hitler's White Russians: Collaboration, Extermination and Antipartisan Warfare in Byelorussia, 1941 to 1944*, Bayside, NY: Europa Books, pg.106 for notes on auxiliaries, pg.154 for the GFP information.

[6] Christopher R. Browning. *Ordinary Men: Reserve Police Battalion 101 and the Final Solution in Poland* (Harper Perennial). pg.18.

[7] United States Holocaust Museum. *Befehlshaber der Ordungpolizei das Ostland*, R83, Reel 10, July 1941 locations, Operations Hornung, Cottbus, November 1939 Ostrow, Minsk info, Company information.

[8] Schimana, Walter. *SS-Gruppenführer* and *Generalleutnant* the Waffen-SS and *Polizei*. NSDAP Number 49 042, joined December 7, 1926. SS Number 337 753, joined August 15, 1939. He committed suicide while awaiting trial in Salzburg, Austria on September 12, 1948.

[9] Wolfgang Curilla. 2006. *Die deutsche Ordnungspolizei und der Holocaust im Baltikum und in Weissrussland 1941 to 1944*. pg.150-175 abrid, pg.738 Operation "Herman".

[10] From http://www.shtetlinks.jewishgen.org/Pilviskiai/pilviskiai3.html (Accessed November 17, 2006.) For the quoted material on the actual events.

Police Battalion 13

[1] Stefan Klemp. 2005. *"Nicht ermittelt "Polizeibataillone und die Nachkriegsjustiz*. Klartext Verlag. pg.113-115 for guard duty and locations, Minsk pg.419.

[2] Daniel J. Goldhagen. 1996. *Hitler's Willing Executioners: Ordinary Germans and the Holocaust*. Knopf. pg.271.

[3] Roland Pfeiffer. 2003. *Zur Geschichte der Ordnungspolizei*. www.lexikon der wehrmacht.de/Zusatz/SS/Ordnungspolizei R.htm. (Last Accessed August 15, 2006).

[4] United States Holocaust Museum. Latvian Central State Historical Archive (Riga) records [microform], 1941 to 1945. Reel 4.

Police Battalion 22

[1] United States Holocaust Museum. *Befehlshaber der Ordungpolizei das Ostland*, RG 18.002M*90, R 83, Reel 10, For company locations in 1941 and 1942 also.

[2] French L. Maclean. 1999. *The Field Men: The SS Officers Who Led the Einsatzkommandos: The Nazi Mobile Killing Units*. Schiffer Military History. pg.18.

[3] *Holocaust Chronicle*. John Roth. Publications International, Ltd.

[4] Wolfgang Curilla. 2006. *Die deutsche Ordnungspolizei und der Holocaust im Baltikum und in Weissrussland 1941 to 1944*. Death totals. Pg.728 Operation "Föhn I and II".

Police Battalion 32

[1] *Major* Binz was also the commanding officer of the Police Battalion 307. In 1943 he was promoted to commander of a regiment in the 14 Waffen-SS Grenadier Division der SS (Ukrainian 1) the Galizische SS Freiwilligen (Volunteer) Regiment 4. Major Leo von Braunschweig was the commander of the second version of SS Police Regiment 15.

[2] French L. Maclean. 1999. *The Field Men: The SS Officers Who Led the Einsatzkommandos: The Nazi Mobile Killing Units* Schiffer Military History. pg.19.

[3] Phillip W. Blood. 2006. *Hitler's Bandit Hunters: The SS and the Nazi Occupation of Europe*. pg.60.

Police Battalion 33

[1] Munoz, Antonio and Oleg Romanko, *Hitler's White Russians: Collaboration, Extermination and Antipartisan Warfare in Byelorussia, 1941 to 1944*, Bayside, NY: Europa Books, 2003, pgs. 105, 117, 198. *Major* Dall has also is recorded as being the commanding officer of Police Battalion 320 and 315.

[2] Stefan Klemp. 2005. *"Nicht ermittelt "Polizeibataillone und die Nachkriegsjustiz*. Klartext Verlag. pgs. 121, 122 Baltic auxiliary's pg.454.

[3] Wolfgang Curilla. 2006. *Die deutsche Ordnungspolizei und der Holocaust im Baltikum und in Weissrussland 1941 to 1944*. Death totals.

Police Battalion 41

[1] Roland Pfeiffer. 2003. *Zur Geschichte der Ordnungspolizei*. www.lexikon der wehrmacht.de/Zusatz/SS/Ordnungspolizei R.htm. (Last Accessed August 15, 2006).

[2] Case Nr.1005, Court: LG/BG Karl Marx Stadt 860320, Ob. Gericht der DDR 860710; LG/BG Dresden 940225. Much of the locations and atrocities came from the two German cases.

[3] Alexander B. Rossino. 2005. *Hitler Strikes Poland: Blitzkrieg, Ideology and Atrocity*. University Press of Kansas. pg.96.

[4] Stefan Klemp. 2005. *"Nicht ermittelt "Polizeibataillone und die Nachkriegsjustiz*. Klartext Verlag. pg.122. pg.377 for Majdanek. pg.454 for the battalion's destruction.

[5] United States Holocaust Museum. http://www.ushmm.org/wlc/article.php?lang=en&Moduleld=10005222. (Accessed August 18, 2006).

[6] Werner Regenberg. 2002. *Armored Vehicles and Units of the German Order Police*. Schiffer Books.

[7] Case Nr.1004, Court: LG/BG Karl Marx Stadt 870514, Ob. Gericht der DDR 870909.

[8] Two members of the battalion were convicted and given life sentences for their participation in various actions from 1939-1944. Kurt Brückner, who was a platoon leader and Eberhard Täschner. The court documents were a source for a number of locations.

Police Battalion 42

[1] Alexander B. Rossino. 2005. *Hitler Strikes Poland: Blitzkrieg, Ideology and Atrocity*. University Press of Kansas.

[2] H.L. deZeng IV. *German Police and Auxiliary Police Units in the Balkans 1941 to 1945*. (Unpublished). For all 1944 to 1945 information.

Police Battalion 44

[1] United States Holocaust Museum. Selected records from the *Hauptamt Ordnungspolizei* collection [microform], 1921 to 1945. RG68.046m. Reel 26.

[2] Case Nr.1074, Court: LG/BG Leipzig 620814, Ob. Gericht der DDR 621017.

[3] H.L. deZeng IV. *German Police and Auxiliary Police Units in the Balkans 1941 to 1945*. (Unpublished).

Police Battalion 45

[1] Stefan Klemp. 2005. *"Nicht ermittelt "Polizeibataillone und die Nachkriegsjustiz*. Klartext Verlag. pg.125.

[2] Christopher R. Browning. *Ordinary Men: Reserve Police Battalion 101 and the Final Solution in Poland* (Harper Perennial). For Slawuta and Sudylow information.

[3] Vasily Grossman and Anthony Beevor. 2006. *A Writer at War: Vasily Grossman with the Red Army 1941 to 1945*. The Harvill Press. Abrid. pgs. 258 to 259.

[4] French L. Maclean. 1999. *The Field Men: The SS Officers Who Led the Einsatzkommandos: The Nazi Mobile Killing Units* Schiffer Military History. pgs. 19, 110.

[5] Wolfgang Curilla. 2006. *Die deutsche Ordnungspolizei und der Holocaust im Baltikum und in Weissrussland 1941 to 1944*. pg.833 Death total, pgs. 732, 733 Operation "Weichsel I and II".

[6] United States Holocaust Museum. Military Historical Institute (Prague) Records, 1941 to 1944 RG 48.004M. Reel 1.

Police Battalion 51

[1] Werner Regenberg. 2002. *Armored Vehicles and Units of the German Order Police*. Schiffer Books.

[2] Wolfgang Curilla. 2006. *Die deutsche Ordnungspolizei und der Holocaust im Baltikum und in Weissrussland 1941 to 1944*. pg.457. Belynitschi Golowtschin, pg.716 Karlsbad.

[3] Phillip W. Blood. 2006. *Hitler's Bandit Hunters: The SS and the Nazi Occupation of Europe*. pg.146. Includes the details on the poor performance of the regiment in combat.

[4] United States Holocaust Museum. 1956. *Chef der Bandenkampfverbände Truppen u. Schulen der Ordnungspolizei*. R20. The 14th Regiment history had huge gaps as most of it was lost outside of Kharkov. The remaining records were stored in a basement which was flooded after a bombing raid. On September 9, 1944 Himmler ordered the reconstruction of the regiment's history. The Bundesarchiv began a further reconstruction in 1953 which formed the report that the above information was taken from.

Police Battalion 53

[1] Wolfgang Curilla. 2006. *Die deutsche Ordnungspolizei und der Holocaust im Baltikum und in Weissrussland 1941 to 1944*. Deportations. pg.264 Pleskau, company locations

[2] Stefan Klemp. 2005. *"Nicht ermittelt" Polizeibataillone und die Nachkriegsjustiz*. Klartext Verlag. pg.126 for Czechoslovakia, pg.423 Grodzisk, Police Regiment North.

[3] United States Holocaust Museum. Selected records from the *Hauptamt Ordnungspolizei* collection [microform], 1921 to 1945. RG68.046m. Reel 31. See PB 65 for more details.

Police Battalion 56

[1] A section was a smaller grouping inside a *Kampfgruppe*. Large operations like this would often have four or five sections. They operated independently within the *Kampfgruppe* yet had to meet the operation parameters. They had surprisingly rigid march schedules with preprogrammed destinations that they were expected to meet.

[2] United States Holocaust Museum. *BdO der Ordnungspolizei das Ostland*. RG 18.002M*90. Folder 38, Reel 8.

Police Battalion 61

[1] Stefan Klemp. 2005. *"Nicht ermittelt" Polizeibataillone und die Nachkriegsjustiz*. Klartext Verlag. pg.424 the Balkans. pgs. 129 to 133. Company commanders and the bar in Warsaw.

[2] Wolfgang Curilla. 2006. *Die deutsche Ordnungspolizei und der Holocaust im Baltikum und in Weissrussland 1941 to 1944*. pg.716. Kalisch, Poland.

[3] Daniel Jonah Goldhagen. *Hitler's Willing Executioners: Ordinary Germans and the Holocaust* (Vintage).

[4] United States Holocaust Museum. *BdO der Ordungpolizei das Ostland*, RG 18.002M*90, Reel 8 Estonian Police and destruction of regiment.

Police Battalion 62

[1] Stefan Klemp. 2005. *"Nicht ermittelt "Polizeibataillone und die Nachkriegsjustiz*. Klartext Verlag. pg.67, 137, 138, Cracow, commanders, France.

[2] Munoz, Antonio and Oleg Romanko. 2003, *Hitler's White Russians: Collaboration, Extermination and Antipartisan Warfare in Byelorussia, 1941 to 1944*. Europa Books, 2003 pg.181.

[3] H.L. deZeng IV. *German Police and Auxiliary Police Units in the Balkans 1941 to 1945*. Slovenia information.

Police Battalion 63

[1] United States Holocaust Museum. *Chef der Bandenkampfverbände Truppen u. Schulen der Ordnungspolizei*.

[2] H.L. deZeng IV. *German Police and Auxiliary Police Units in the Balkans 1941 to 1945*. Slovenia Information.

Police Battalion 64

[1] United States Holocaust Museum. Selected records from the *Hauptamt Ordnungspolizei* collection [microform], 1921 to 1945. RG68.046m. Reel 26.

[2] H.L. deZeng IV. *German Police and Auxiliary Police Units in the Balkans 1941 to 1945*. Most Slovenia information.

[3] Daniel Jonah Goldhagen. 1996. *Hitler's Willing Executioners: Ordinary Germans and the Holocaust*. pg.272 including Sajmiste, Serbia information.

[4] Order of Commanding General in Serbia, October 4 1941, ordering mass execution of concentration camp inmates for the killing of twenty-one German Soldiers. Trials of War Criminals Before the Nürnberg Military Tribunals, Washington, U.S Govt. Print. Off., 1949 to 953, Vol. XI, p.976:

[5] Stefan Klemp. 2005. *"Nicht ermittelt" Polizeibataillone und die Nachkriegsjustiz*. Klartext Verlag. pgs. 153 to 158.

Police Battalion 65

[1] Stefan Klemp. 2005. *"Nicht ermittelt" Polizeibataillone und die Nachkriegsjustiz*. Klartext Verlag. pg.166 for the NCO an officer names and the Cracow hospital shooting. Shootings of Jews.

[2] Major Weis was also the commanding officer of Police Battalion 309.

[3] Wolfgang Curilla. 2006. *Die deutsche Ordnungspolizei und der Holocaust im Baltikum und in Weissrussland 1941 to 1944*. Death Totals.

[4] United States Holocaust Museum. Selected records from the *Hauptamt Ordnungspolizei* collection [microform], 1921 to 1945. RG68.046m. Reel 31

[5] H.L. deZeng IV. *German Police and Auxiliary Police Units in the Balkans 1941 to 1945*. Most of the Slovenian information.

Police Battalion 66

[1] Stefan Klemp. 2005. *"Nicht ermittelt" Polizeibataillone und die Nachkriegsjustiz*. Klartext Verlag. pg.177 for 1940 information.

[2] H.L. deZeng IV. *German Police and Auxiliary Police Units in the Balkans 1941 to 1945*.

Police Battalion 67

[1] Stefan Klemp. 2005. *"Nicht ermittelt" Polizeibataillone und die Nachkriegsjustiz*. Klartext Verlag. pg.179 for 3rd company in Bilgoraj, pg.179 for commanders.

[2] French L. Maclean. 1999. *The Field Men: The SS Officers Who Led the Einsatzkommandos: The Nazi Mobile Killing Units*. Schiffer Military History. pg.19.

[3] http://holocaust info.dk/belzec/belzec_deportations.htm (last accessed August 22, 2006).

[4] Stefan Klemp. 2005. *"Nicht ermittelt" Polizeibataillone und die Nachkriegsjustiz*. Klartext Verlag.

[5] Hitler's willing Zamosc and Bilgoraj totals pg.272 Luga information pg.191, refitting pg.198, Willing has them in Copenhagen in May 1943.

[6] This quote came from http://www.jewishgen.org who list the source for the translation as from: Pinkas Hakehillot: *Encyclopedia of Jewish Communities, Poland*, Volume VII, pages 93 to 97, published by Yad Vashem, Jerusalem.

[7] United States Holocaust Memorial Museum. "The Holocaust." *Holocaust Encyclopedia*. http://www.ushmm.org/wlc/article.php?lang=en&ModuleI d=10005222 (accessed June 21, 2006).

[8] United States Holocaust Museum. Selected records from the *Hauptamt Ordnungspolizei* collection [microform], 1921 to 1945. RG68.046m.

Police Battalion 69

[1] Major Sonnenberg was also the commanding officer of Police Battalion 12.

[2] Stefan Klemp. 2005. *"Nicht ermittelt" Polizeibataillone und die Nachkriegsjustiz*. Klartext Verlag. pgs. 184 to 187, pg.426, for company locations and death totals.

[3] Wolfgang Curilla. 2006. *Die deutsche Ordnungspolizei und der Holocaust im Baltikum und in Weissrussland 1941 to 1944*.

Police Battalion 72

1 Stefan Klemp. 2005. *"Nicht ermittelt" Polizeibataillone und die Nachkriegsjustiz*. Klartext Verlag. pg.200, pg.426, for 3rd company plundering.

[2] H.L. deZeng IV. *German Police and Auxiliary Police Units in the Balkans 1941 to 1945*. Slovenia information.

[3] The 442 was a Japanese-American infantry unit and was the most decorated unit in U.S. military history.

Police Battalion 81

[1] Alexander B. Rossino. 2005. *Hitler Strikes Poland: Blitzkrieg, Ideology and Atrocity*. University Press of Kansas.

Police Battalion 82

[1] Antonio Munoz, Dr Oleg V. Romanko. 2003. *Hitler's White Russians: Collaboration, Extermination and Antipartisan Warfare in Byelorussia, 1941 to 1944*. Europa Books. pg.180.

[2] Case Nr.1013, Lfd. Nr. 1013 Court: BG Neubrandenburg 810620, LG Neubrandenburg 408/92. OLG Rostock II WsRh 10/94. Johannes Piehl was the 1st company commander and the battalion adjutant. Chrzanow was about ten miles from the Auschwitz concentration camp. Chrzanow was a town with a significant percentage of Jews and a ghetto that was liquidated in late 1942. Much of the information on the battalion locations came from the court case.

Police Battalion 83

[1] Daniel J.Goldhagen. 1996. *Hitler's Willing Executioners: Ordinary Germans and the Holocaust*. Knopf. pg.183.

[2] United States Holocaust Museum. Selected records from the *Hauptamt Ordnungspolizei* collection [microform], 1921 to 1945. RG68.046m. Reel 11.

[3] Wolfgang Curilla. 2006. *Die deutsche Ordnungspolizei und der Holocaust im Baltikum und in Weissrussland 1941 to 1944*. pg.400 Latvian 26 Schuma Battalion.

[4] Antonio Munoz, Dr Oleg V. Romanko. 2003. *Hitler's White Russians: Collaboration, Extermination and Antipartisan Warfare in Byelorussia, 1941 to 1944*. Europa Books.

White Russians. pg.210 to 214 for EG Anhalt information, Bryansk, pg.293, *Kampfgruppes* pgs. 294 and 392.

Police Battalion 84

[1] Friedrich Husemann. 2002, *In Good Faith: The History of the 4th SS Polizei Panzer Grenadier Division*, Vol. 1: 1939 to 1943. J.J. Fedorowicz Publishing Inc. pg.270 to 290 abrid.

Police Battalion 85

[1] United States Holocaust Museum. Selected records from the *Hauptamt Ordnungspolizei* collection [microform], 1921 to 1945. RG 68.046m. Reel 26.

[2] Wolfgang Curilla. 2006. *Die deutsche Ordnungspolizei und der Holocaust im Baltikum und in Weissrussland 1941 to 1944*. pg.713. Operation "Breslau."

[3] Phillip W. Blood. 2006. *Hitler's Bandit Hunters: The SS and the Nazi Occupation of Europe*. pg.186 to 196. For most of the details on the Kovpak Brigade.

[4] H.L. deZeng IV. *German Police and Auxiliary Police Units in the Balkans 1941 to 1945*.

Police Battalion 91

[1] Stefan Klemp. 2005. *"Nicht ermittelt" Polizeibataillone und die Nachkriegsjustiz*. Klartext Verlag. pg.428 for all 1942 information.

[2] Wolfgang Curilla. 2006. *Die deutsche Ordnungspolizei und der Holocaust im Baltikum und in Weissrussland 1941 to 1944*. pg.813 Death totals pg.648.Chotimsk.

[3] Krisztian Ungvary and John Lukacs. 2005. *The Siege of Budapest: One Hundred Days in World War II*. Yale University Press. pg.75.

Police Battalion 93

[1] Christopher Browning. Reprint edition (March 17, 1993). *Ordinary Men: Reserve Police Battalion 101 and the Final Solution in Poland*. Harper Perennial.

[2] Stefan Klemp. 2005. *"Nicht ermittelt" Polizeibataillone und die Nachkriegsjustiz*. Klartext Verlag. pg, 429

[3] United States Holocaust Museum. Military Institute of Prague 1941 to 1944. RG 48.004M Reel 2.

[4] H.L. deZeng IV. *German Police and Auxiliary Police Units in the Balkans 1941 to 1945*. Slovenia information.

Police Battalion 101

[1] http://www.jewishvirtuallibrary.org/jsource/Holocaust/battalion101.html (Last accessed August 22, 2006).

[2] Wolfgang Curilla. 2006. *Die deutsche Ordnungspolizei und der Holocaust im Baltikum und in Weissrussland 1941 to 1944*. pg.829 Death totals.

Police Battalion 102

[1] Stefan Klemp. 2005. *"Nicht ermittelt "Polizeibataillone und die Nachkriegsjustiz*. Klartext Verlag. pg.67, 216 for active duty volunteers, locations 1942 to 1944.

[2] http://www.deathcamps.org/occupation/lubartow ghetto.html. (Last accessed August 22, 2006).

[3] Roland Pfeiffer. 2003. *Zur Geschichte der Ordnungspolizei*. www.lexikon der wehrmacht.de/Zusatz/SS/OrdnungspolizeiR.htm. (Last Accessed August 15, 2006).

Police Battalion 103
[1] Stefan Klemp. 2005. *"Nicht ermittelt" Polizeibataillone und die Nachkriegsjustiz*. Klartext Verlag. pg.218 for Police Schützen Regiment 31, Seminary.

Police Battalion 104
[1] Stefan Klemp. 2005. *"Nicht ermittelt "Polizeibataillone und die Nachkriegsjustiz*. Klartext Verlag. pg.219 for company locations. Also of interest in Klemps book is that the postwar *Stasi* (East German State Security) were very interested in the members of this battalion and had pulled a number of individuals' records. pg.451 for becoming the I/1.
[2] http://www1.uni hamburg.de/rz3a035//police101.html. (Last accessed August 22, 2006).

Police Battalion 105
[1] Munoz, Antonio and Oleg Romanko. 2003 *Hitler's White Russians: Collaboration, Extermination and Antipartisan Warfare in Byelorussia, 1941 to 1944*. Europa Books. pg.103.
[2] Stefan Klemp. 2005. *"Nicht ermittelt" Polizeibataillone und die Nachkriegsjustiz*. Klartext Verlag. pg.220 company locations, pg.451 for Italy.

Police Battalion 111
[1] Werner Regenberg. 2002. *Armored Vehicles and Units of the German Order Police. 1936 to 1945*. Schiffer Publishing.
[2] Stefan Klemp. 2005. *"Nicht ermittelt" Polizeibataillone und die Nachkriegsjustiz*. Klartext Verlag. pgs. 67, 430, 449.
[3] Munoz, Antonio and Oleg Romanko. *2003 Hitler's White Russians: Collaboration, Extermination and Antipartisan Warfare in Byelorussia, 1941 to 1944*. Europa Books. pg.219 Mogilew, pg.180. Army Group South.
[4] Krisztian Ungvary and John Lukacs. 2005. *The Siege of Budapest: One Hundred Days in World War II*. Yale University Press.

Police Battalion 112
[1] United States Holocaust Museum. Selected records from the *Hauptamt Ordnungspolizei* collection [microform], 1921 to1945. RG68.046m. Reel 55.
[2] Wolfgang Curilla. 2006. *Die deutsche Ordnungspolizei und der Holocaust im Baltikum und in Weissrussland 1941 to 1944*. pg.727 "Winterzauber".

Police Battalion 121
[1] Munoz, Antonio and Oleg Romanko, *Hitler's White Russians: Collaboration, Extermination and Antipartisan Warfare in Byelorussia, 1941 to 1944*, Bayside, NY: Europa Books, 2003.
[2] Stefan Klemp. 2005. *"Nicht ermittelt "Polizeibataillone und die Nachkriegsjustiz*. Klartext Verlag. pg.431 for Officers, Luxemburg, and destruction.

Police Battalion 122
[1] Major Landwehr was also the commanding officer of Police Battalion 306. He was awarded the Knights Cross on March 17, 1945.
[2] Wolfgang Curilla. 2006. *Die deutsche Ordnungspolizei und der Holocaust im Baltikum und in Weissrussland 1941 to 1944*. pg.713 Operation "Breslau."

Police Battalion 123
[1] 1st Lieutenant Nikolaus Hornig was later transferred to Police Battalion 306 and 181.
[2] United States Holocaust Museum. Selected records from the *Hauptamt Ordnungspolizei* collection [microform], 1921to1945. RG 68.046m. Reel 26.
[3] Stefan Klemp. 2005. *"Nicht ermittelt" Polizeibataillone und die Nachkriegsjustiz*. Klartext Verlag. pg.224, HSSPF assignment, Luxemburg.

Police Battalion 131
[1] Major Ohrt was also the commander of Police Battalion 304.
[2] Stefan Klemp. 2005. *"Nicht ermittelt" Polizeibataillone und die Nachkriegsjustiz*. Klartext Verlag. pg.226 Officer names, and locations, Sonderkommando info, pg.431 for 1939/1940 info.
[3] Wolfgang Curilla. 2006. *Die deutsche Ordnungspolizei und der Holocaust im Baltikum und in Weissrussland 1941 to 1944*. pg.606. *Einsatzkommando* 9.
[4] Phillip W. Blood. 2006. *Hitler's Bandit Hunters: The SS and the Nazi Occupation of Europe*. pg.60.

Police Battalion 133
[1] Daniel J. Goldhagen.1996. *Hitler's Willing Executioners: Ordinary Germans and the Holocaust*. Knopf. pg.272 for totals for Nadvornaya and Stanislawow, pg.196 Kolomyia area information.
[2] *Hans Krueger and the Murder of the Jews in Stanislawow Region (Galicia)* Dieter Pohl. Published by the Shoah Resource Center. Yad Vashem. The International School for Holocaust Studies.
[3] Wolfgang Curilla. 2006. *Die deutsche Ordnungspolizei und der Holocaust im Baltikum und in Weissrussland 1941 to 1944*. pg.833. Death totals.

Police Battalion 171
[1] United States Holocaust Museum. Military Institute of Prague 1941 to 1944. RG 48.004M Reel 2.
[2] Stefan Klemp. 2005. *"Nicht ermittelt "Polizeibataillone und die Nachkriegsjustiz*. Klartext Verlag. pg.67 Radom, pg.229 and 432 for 1941 information and Dachau.
[3] United States Holocaust Museum. Selected records from the *Hauptamt Ordnungspolizei* collection [microform], 1921 to 1945. RG 68.046m. Reel 26.
[4] Stefan Klemp. 2005. *"Nicht ermittelt" Polizeibataillone und die Nachkriegsjustiz*. Klartext Verlag.

Police Battalion 181
[1] In August 1943 *Major* Kärnbach was the commanding officer of the Galician SS Volunteer Formation Battalion (*Galician SS Freiwilligen Eratz Battalion Heidenheim*).
[2] United States Holocaust Museum. Selected records from the *Hauptamt Ordnungspolizei* collection [microform], 1921to1945. RG68.046m. Reel 26.
[3] United States Holocaust Museum. Military Institute of Prague 1941 to 1944. RG48.004M Reel 2.
[4] Phillip W. Blood. 2006. *Hitler's Bandit Hunters: The SS and the Nazi Occupation of Europe*. pg.254 to 255.
[5] H.L. deZeng IV. *German Police and Auxiliary Police Units in the Balkans 1941 to 1945*.

Police Battalion 251
[1] Stefan Klemp. 2005. *"Nicht ermittelt" Polizeibataillone und die Nachkriegsjustiz*. Klartext Verlag. pg.455.
[2] United States Holocaust Museum. Selected records from the *Hauptamt Ordnungspolizei* collection [microform], 1921 to 1945. RG68.046m. Reel 26.
[3] United States Holocaust Museum. Military Historical Institute Prague 1941 to1944. RG48.004M. Reel 2.

Police Battalion 253
[1] United States Holocaust Museum. Selected records from the *Hauptamt Ordnungspolizei* collection [microform], 1921 to 1945. RG68.046m. Reel 55.
[2] Stefan Klemp. 2005. *"Nicht ermittelt" Polizeibataillone und die Nachkriegsjustiz*. Klartext Verlag. pg.450. Regiment information.

Police Battalion 255
[1] *With the Partisans and In the Red Army*, Dov Katzovitch, Petach Tikva. http://www.jewishgen.org/yizkor/Dokshitsy/dok274.html (Accessed August 23, 2006).
[2] Stefan Klemp. 2005. *"Nicht ermittelt "Polizeibataillone und die Nachkriegsjustiz*. Klartext Verlag. pg.434, there were two major operations in Gleboki. The first took place in June 1942 when at least 3,000 Jews were shot in the woods outside of town. From Mr. Katzovitch's account they were SS/SD men and Ukrainian auxiliaries. The second and final action was in August 1943 when German Police and auxiliaries attempted to liquidate the ghetto and were met with resistance. Some accounts mention house to house battles, others like Mr. Katzovitch state that when the Germans encountered resistance they withdrew an encircled the ghetto.

Then they set it on fire and killed whoever tried to escape. He states that the encirclement was rather sloppily executed so many Jews escaped to join partisan groups.

Police Battalion 256

[1] Roland Pfeiffer. 2003. *Zur Geschichte der Ordnungspolizei*. www.lexikon der wehrmacht.de/Zusatz/SS/Ordnungspolizei R.htm. (Last Accessed August 15, 2006).

[2] Daniel J. Goldhagen. 1996. *Hitler's Willing Executioners: Ordinary Germans and the Holocaust*. Knopf. pg.272.

Police Battalion 301

[1] Werner Regenberg. 2002. *Armored Vehicles and Units of the German Order Police*. Schiffer Books.

[2] Stefan Klemp. 2005. *"Nicht ermittelt" Polizeibataillone und die Nachkriegsjustiz*. Klartext Verlag. pg.435 for the officers and 1942 locations.

[3] Wolfgang Curilla. 2006. *Die deutsche Ordnungspolizei und der Holocaust im Baltikum und in Weissrussland 1941 to 1944*. pg.713 "Operation "Breslau."

[4] H.L. deZeng IV. *German Police and Auxiliary Police Units in the Balkans 1941 to 1945*. (Unpublished) Slovenia information.

Police Battalion 302

[1] Munoz, Antonio and Oleg Romanko. 2003. *Hitler's White Russians: Collaboration, Extermination and Antipartisan Warfare in Byelorussia 1941 to 1944*. Europa Books. pg.180.

[2] United States Holocaust Museum. Military Institute of Prague 1941 to 1944. RG48.004M. Reel 2.

[3] H.L. deZeng IV. *German Police and Auxiliary Police Units in the Balkans 1941 to 1945*. (Unpublished). Slovenia information.

Police Battalion 303

[1] Major Hannibal ended the war as a SS *Brigadeführer* and Major General of the Police.

[2] Daniel J. Goldhagen. 1996. *Hitler's Willing Executioners: Ordinary Germans and the Holocaust*. Knopf. pg.272.

[3] Wolfgang Curilla. 2006. *Die deutsche Ordnungspolizei und der Holocaust im Baltikum und in Weissrussland 1941 to 1944*. pg.833 Death totals.

[4] United States Holocaust Museum. Selected records from the *Hauptamt Ordnungspolizei* collection [microform], 1921 to 1945. RG68.046m. Reel 33.

Police Battalion 304

[1] Major Ohrt was also commander of Police Battalion 131. Major Willi Nickel, later became the commander of SS Police Regiment 14 in 1944.

[2] Major Gewehr later became the regiment commander.

[3] DDR. Case Nr.1002, Courts:LG/BG Halle 880711, Ob. Gericht der DDR 881017, LG/BG Magdeburg 920603 Also sentenced to life imprisonment for similar actions from this battalion was Karl Jäger. The court states the death toll for this battalion in 5 separate actions in the Ukraine as 16,000 Jews and others.

Police Battalion 305

[1] Major Georg Robert Wessig was executed by the Soviets in 1946 for war crimes.

[2] Stefan Klemp. 2005. *"Nicht ermittelt" Polizeibataillone und die Nachkriegsjustiz*. Klartext Verlag. pg.246

Police Battalion 306

[1] Case Nr.589, Court: LG Augsburg 650402

[2] Daniel J. Goldhagen. 1996. *Hitler's Willing Executioners: Ordinary Germans and the Holocaust*. Knopf. pg.272 all totals and places from except David Gorodok. Klemp pg.247 co's and Lublin, pg.436 for 2nd company activity.

[3] Wolfgang Curilla. 2006. *Die deutsche Ordnungspolizei und der Holocaust im Baltikum und in Weissrussland 1941 to 1944*. Death total. pg.624 June 1941 to February 1942 pg.629 February and July 1942 info.

Police Battalion 307

[1] Major Stahr was also the commanding officer of Police Battalion 10.

[2] Major Binz also served as the commanding officer of Police Battalion 32.

[3] United States Holocaust Museum. Selected records from the *Hauptamt Ordnungspolizei* collection [microform], 1921 to1945. RG68.046m. Reel 11. KG Binz and CO dates almost all movement and location info after 1942. The documents list the battalions as Regiments "Barkholt" and "Binz."

[4] Stefan Klemp. 2005. *"Nicht ermittelt" Polizeibataillone und die Nachkriegsjustiz*. Klartext Verlag. pg.249, 436 CO's and SS/NSDAP, EK assignment, most 1941 locations, regiment.

[5] Daniel J. Goldhagen. 1996. *Hitler's Willing Executioners: Ordinary Germans and the Holocaust*. Knopf. pg.272.

[6] Phillip W. Blood. 2006. *Hitler's Bandit Hunters: The SS and the Nazi Occupation of Europe*. pg.60. Includes Binz's quote.

[7] Wolfgang Curilla. 2006. *Die deutsche Ordnungspolizei und der Holocaust im Baltikum und in Weissrussland 1941 to 1944*. pg.736.

[8] United States Holocaust Museum. Military Historical Institute Prague 1941 to 1942. RG48.004m. Reel 2.

Police Battalion 308

[1] Stefan Klemp. 2005. *"Nicht ermittelt" Polizeibataillone und die Nachkriegsjustiz*. Klartext Verlag. pg.32, pg.437.

[2] Wolfgang Curilla. 2006. *Die deutsche Ordnungspolizei und der Holocaust im Baltikum und in Weissrussland 1941 to 1944*. Grodno to Auschwitz. Juchnow.

Police Battalion 309

[1] *Major* Bruckner was also the commanding officer of Police Battalion 41. *Major* Weiss was also the commanding officer of Police Battalion 65.

[2] Heiner Lichtenstein, *Himmlers grüne Helfer. Die Schutz- und Ordnungspolizei im "Dritten Reich"*, Köln 1990, Neuauflage 2003. For post war. pg.70 to 86.

[3] Christopher R. Browning. *Ordinary Men: Reserve Police Battalion 101 and the Final Solution in Poland* (Harper Perennial) pgs. 11, 12. "When several Jewish leaders appeared at the headquarters of 221st Security Division. They approached *General* Pffugbeil and knelt at his feet, begging for army protection, one member of this battalion unzipped his fly and urinated on them while the General turned his back."

[4] Richard Rhodes. 2002. *Masters of Death: The SS Einsatzgruppen*. Knopf. pgs. 309 to 316 Abid.

[5] Phillip W. Blood. 2006. *Hitler's Bandit Hunters: The SS and the Nazi Occupation of Europe*. Potomac Books. Pgs. 45 to 60 Abid.

[6] Wolfgang Curilla. 2006. *Die deutsche Ordnungspolizei und der Holocaust im Baltikum und in Weissrussland 1941 to 1944*. pg.831 Death totals pgs. 511 to 525. June 22, 1941 info, Jobst, Anton.

Police Battalion 310

[1] Captain Saur was also listed as 3rd company commander in Police Battalion 306.

[2] Case Nr.1036, 1005; Heinrich Frohn and Otto Balke received life sentences. Court: LG/BG Suhl 740715 Ob. Gericht der DDR 740820, Participation in the shooting of Polish hostages, Soviet civilians (predominantly within the context of 'antipartisan warfare') as well as of Jews (during the liquidation of the Brest ghetto), as members of the execution party or through the shutting off of villages, the guarding of execution sites or the transportation of the victims. Crime Location: Brest, Chmieliszcze, Tschenstochau, Oltusz Lesnia, Zablocie

[3] Dennis Showalter, Edward B. Westermann. *Hitler's Police Battalions: Enforcing Racial War in the East* (University Press of Kansas) pg.14, 216, 220

[4] Lfd Nr. 1036. BG Suhl von 15.02.1974. OG von 20.08.1974

[5] Stefan Klemp. 2005. *"Nicht ermittelt" Polizeibataillone und die Nachkriegsjustiz*. Klartext Verlag. pg.268 1942 most information.

[6] Wolfgang Curilla. 2006. *Die deutsche Ordnungspolizei und der Holocaust im Baltikum und in Weissrussland 1941 to 1944*. pg.831. Death totals.

[7] United States Holocaust Museum. Selected records from the *Hauptamt Ordnungspolizei* collection [microform], 1921 to 1945. RG68.046m. Reel 31.

Police Battalion 311

[1] Wolfgang Curilla. 2006. *Die deutsche Ordnungspolizei und der Holocaust im Baltikum und in Weissrussland 1941 to 1944*. pg.833 Death totals.

[2] Stefan Klemp. 2005. *"Nicht ermittelt" Polizeibataillone und die Nachkriegsjustiz*. Klartext Verlag. pg.438.

Police Battalion 312

[1] United States Holocaust Museum. Military Institute of Prague 1941 to 1944. RG48.004M Reel 2.

Police Battalion 313

[1] United States Holocaust Museum. 1956. *Chef der Bandenkampfverbände Truppen u. Schulen der Ordnungspolizei*. R20.

[2] Wolfgang Curilla. 2006. *Die deutsche Ordnungspolizei und der Holocaust im Baltikum und in Weissrussland 1941 to 1944*. pg.713. Operation "Breslau."

[3] H.L. deZeng IV. *German Police and Auxiliary Police Units in the Balkans 1941 to 1945*. (Unpublished) Slovenia information.

Police Battalion 314

[1] Dennis Showalter, Edward B. Westermann . *Hitler's Police Battalions: Enforcing Racial War In The East* (University Press of Kansas) pgs. 183, 203.

[2] Stefan Klemp. 2005. *"Nicht ermittelt" Polizeibataillone und die Nachkriegsjustiz*. Klartext Verlag.pg.450 Locations.

[3] United States Holocaust Museum. Selected records from the *Hauptamt Ordnungspolizei* collection [microform], 1921 to 1945. RG68.046m. Reel 33.

Police Battalion 315

[1] *Major* Dall was also commanding officer of Police Battalion 33 and 320. Police Battalion 33 transferred its 1st company to this battalion in 1942.

[2] Wolfgang Curilla. 2006. *Die deutsche Ordnungspolizei und der Holocaust im Baltikum und in Weissrussland 1941 to 1944*. pg.650 to 652. Gomel activity. Operation Bamberg

[3] United States Holocaust Museum. Selected records from the *Hauptamt Ordnungspolizei* collection [microform], 1921 to 1945. RG68.046m Reel 10

Police Battalion 316

[1] Stefan Klemp. 2005. *"Nicht ermittelt" Polizeibataillone und die Nachkriegsjustiz*. Klartext Verlag. pg.280 for company and EK info. pg.204 replacements.

[2] United States Holocaust Museum. Military Institute of Prague 1941 to 1944. Reel 2.

[3] Richard Rhodes. 2002. *Masters of Death: The SS Einsatzgruppen and the Invention of the Holocaust Masters of Death*. Knopf. pgs. 309 to 316 abid.

[4] Daniel J. Goldhagen. 1996. *Hitler's Willing Executioners: Ordinary Germans and the Holocaust*. Knopf. pg.273.

[5] H.L. deZeng IV. *German Police and Auxiliary Police Units in the Balkans 1941 to 1945*. (Unpublished) Slovenia information.

[6] Wolfgang Curilla. 2006. *Die deutsche Ordnungspolizei und der Holocaust im Baltikum und in Weissrussland 1941 to 1944*. pgs. 435 to 458 Abid. Baranowitschi, Einsatzkommando 8. Companies involved, Death total.

Police Battalion 317

[1] Wolfgang Curilla. 2006. *Die deutsche Ordnungspolizei und der Holocaust im Baltikum und in Weissrussland 1941 to 1944*. pg.697 Police Battalion Pazdubitz.

Police Battalion 318

[1] Wolfgang Curilla. 2006. *Die deutsche Ordnungspolizei und der Holocaust im Baltikum und in Weissrussland 1941 to 1944*. pg.709 612 Infantry Regiment.

[2] United States Holocaust Museum. Selected records from the *Hauptamt Ordnungspolizei* collection [microform], 1921 to 1945. RG68.046m. Reel 31.

Police Battalion 320

[1] *Major* Dall was also recorded as the commanding officer of Police Battalion 33 and 315.

[2] Stefan Klemp. 2005. *"Nicht ermittelt" Polizeibataillone und die Nachkriegsjustiz*. Klartext Verlag. pg.284 commanding officers, 1941 information

[3] Richard Rhodes. *Masters of Death: The SS Einsatzgruppen and the Invention of the Holocaust* (Knopf) Has the staff of HSSPPF (Jeckeln) doing most of the shooting while this battalion provided cordon security. pg.128, 130. On the Jews of Kaments Podolski he quotes the historian Randolph Braham, "...the indigenous Jews of Kaments Podolski were compelled to march about 10 miles to a series of craters created by bombings. They were ordered to undress and brought into the crossfire of machineguns. Many of them were actually buried alive." This is only partially correct as they were not were not "indigenous Jews". They were Hungarian Jews who had been expelled from Hungary. United States Holocaust Museum. Military Historical Institute (Prague) records [microform], 1941 to 1944. RG 48.004M Reel 1.

[4] Wolfgang Curilla. 2006. *Die deutsche Ordnungspolizei und der Holocaust im Baltikum und in Weissrussland 1941 to 1944*. pg.619 Einsatzkommando info, Kostopol ghetto pg.622. September 1943.

[5] H.L. deZeng IV. *German Police and Auxiliary Police Units in the Balkans 1941 to 1945*. (Unpublished) Slovenia information.

Police Battalion 321

[1] Roland Pfeiffer. 2003. *Zur Geschichte der Ordnungspolizei*. www.lexikon der wehrmacht.de/Zusatz/SS/Ordnungspolizei R.htm. (Last Accessed August 15, 2006).

[2] Stefan Klemp. 2005. *"Nicht ermittelt "Polizeibataillone und die Nachkriegsjustiz*. Klartext Verlag. pg.455.

Police Battalion 322

[1] E. Klee, W. Dressen, V. Riess. *The Good Old Days*, The Free Press, NY, 1988. pgs. 8 to 21, abrid.

[2] Richard Rhodes. 2002. *Masters of Death: The SS Einsatzgruppen and the Invention of the Holocaust*. Knopf. pg.48, also of interest from this page is mention that Himmler arrival in Bialystok in July 8, 1941.

[3] Munoz, Antonio and Oleg Romanko. 2003. *Hitler's White Russians: Collaboration, Extermination and Antipartisan Warfare in Byelorussia, 1941 to 1944*. Europa Books. pg.273.

[4] United States Holocaust Museum. Military Historical Institute (Prague) records [microform], 1941 to 1944. RG 48.004m. Reel 2.

[5] United States Holocaust Museum. Selected records from the *Hauptamt Ordnungspolizei* collection [microform], 1921 to 1945. RG68.046m. Reel 10. For the executions they kept a ledger that along the top had a column for the date, location, and whether the people they executed were Russian soldiers, civilians, Jews, or women. The women's column was divided into Russians and Jews. Surprisingly there was no column for kids.

[6] H.L. deZeng IV. *German Police and Auxiliary Police Units in the Balkans 1941 to 1945*. (Unpublished) Slovenia information.

[6] Wolfgang Curilla. 2006. *Die deutsche Ordnungspolizei und der Holocaust im Baltikum und in Weissrussland 1941 to 1944*. Death totals. pg.546 to 547. June 10, 1941 and July 8, 1941 info. pg.568. March to May 1942. *Einsatzkommando* info.

Police Battalion 323

[1] Wolfgang Curilla. 2006. *Die deutsche Ordnungspolizei und der Holocaust im Baltikum und in Weissrussland 1941 to 1944*. pg.697.

[2] E. Klee, W. Dressen, V. Riess. *The Good Old Days*. The Free Press, NY,1988.

[3] Stefan Klemp. 2005. *"Nicht ermittelt" Polizeibataillone und die Nachkriegsjustiz*. Klartext Verlag. pg.32, and 294.

Police Battalion 325

[1] H.L. deZeng IV. *German Police and Auxiliary Police Units in the Balkans 1941 to 1945*. (Unpublished). Slovenia information.

BIBLIOGRAPHY

Angolia, John R., and Taylor, Hugh Page, *Uniforms, Organizations & History of the German Police*, Volume 1, Bender Books, 2005.

Beevor, Anthony, *The Fall of Berlin 1945*, Viking, 2002.

Browning, Christopher R., *Ordinary Men: Reserve Police Battalion 101 and the Final Solution in Poland*, Harper Perennial, 1993.

Carrell, Paul, *Scorched Earth: The Russian German War 1943-1944*, Schiffer Military History, 1994.

Connor, Lieutenant Colonel William M., *Analysis of Deep Attack Operation: Operation Bagration*.

Conot, Robert E., *Justice at Nuremburg*, Carroll & Graf Publishers, 1984.

Duffy, Christopher. *Red Storm on the Reich: The Soviet March on Germany 1945*, Da Capo Press, Reprint edition, April 1993.

Fyodorvich, Alexi, *The Underground Committee Carries On*, Moscow: Foreign Languages Publishing House, 1952.

Goldhagen. Daniel Jonah, *Hitler's Willing Executioners: Ordinary Germans and the Holocaust*, Vintage, Reprint Edition, January 28, 1997.

Hastings, Max, *Armageddon: The Battle for Germany 1944 to 1945*, Knopf, 2004.

Haupt, Werner, *Army Group South: The Wehrmacht in Russia, 1941-1945*, Schiffer Military History, 1998.

Haupt, Werner, *Army Group North: The Wehrmacht in Russia, 1941-1945*, Schiffer Military History, 1997.

Klemp, Stefan, *"Nicht ermittelt". Polizeibataillone und die Nachkriegsjustiz, Ein Handbuch*, Klartext Verlag, 2005.

Maclean, French L., *The Field Men: The SS Officers Who Led the Einsatzkommandos. The Nazi Mobile Killing Units*, Schiffer Military History, 1999.

Munoz, Antonio J., *The German Police*, Axis Europa Inc., 1991.

Munoz, Antonio and Oleg Romanko, *Hitler's White Russians: Collaboration, Extermination and Antipartisan Warfare in Byelorussia, 1941 to 1944*, Europa Books, 2003.

Overy, Richard, *Interrogations: The Nazi Elite in Allied Hands, 1945*, Penguin, Reprint edition, 2002.

Padfield, Peter, *Himmler: Reichsführer-SS*, Cassell, 2002.

INDEX